OPEC's Investments
and the
International Financial
System

OPEC's Investments and the International Financial System

RICHARD P. MATTIONE

THE BROOKINGS INSTITUTION
Washington, D.C.

Copyright © 1985 by
THE BROOKINGS INSTITUTION
1775 Massachusetts Avenue, N. W.

Library of Congress Cataloging in Publication data:

Mattione, Richard P.
  OPEC's Investments and the international financial
system.
  Bibliography: p.
  Includes index.
  1. Investments, Foreign.   2. Investments, Arab.
3. Petroleum industry and trade—Finance.   4. International finance.   5. Organization of Petroleum Exporting
Countries.   I. Title.   II. O.P.E.C.'s investments and
the international financial system.
HG4538.M38   1985   332.6'7314   84-23242

ISBN 0-8157-5510-4
ISBN 0-8157-5509-0 (pbk.)

1 2 3 4 5 6 7 8 9

SE

THE BROOKINGS INSTITUTION is an independent organization devoted to nonpartisan research, education, and publication in economics, government, foreign policy, and the social sciences generally. Its principal purposes are to aid in the development of sound public policies and to promote public understanding of issues of national importance.

The Institution was founded on December 8, 1927, to merge the activities of the Institute for Government Research, founded in 1916, the Institute of Economics, founded in 1922, and the Robert Brookings Graduate School of Economics and Government, founded in 1924.

The Board of Trustees is responsible for the general administration of the Institution, while the immediate direction of the policies, program, and staff is vested in the President, assisted by an advisory committee of the officers and staff. The by-laws of the Institution state: "It is the function of the Trustees to make possible the conduct of scientific research, and publication, under the most favorable conditions, and to safeguard the independence of the research staff in the pursuit of their studies and in the publication of the results of such studies. It is not a part of their function to determine, control, or influence the conduct of particular investigations or the conclusions reached."

The President bears final responsibility for the decision to publish a manuscript as a Brookings book. In reaching his judgment on the competence, accuracy, and objectivity of each study, the President is advised by the director of the appropriate research program and weighs the views of a panel of expert outside readers who report to him in confidence on the quality of the work. Publication of a work signifies that it is deemed a competent treatment worthy of public consideration but does not imply endorsement of conclusions or recommendations.

The Institution maintains its position of neutrality on issues of public policy in order to safeguard the intellectual freedom of the staff. Hence interpretations or conclusions in Brookings publications should be understood to be solely those of the authors and should not be attributed to the Institution, to its trustees, officers, or other staff members, or to the organizations that support its research.

Foreword

During the decade following the quadrupling of oil prices in late 1973, Saudi Arabia, Kuwait, and other OPEC members built up sizable financial holdings that gave them an important role in international financial markets. Perhaps inevitably, the accumulation of such large sums raised widespread fears that the actions of these nations could disrupt world financial markets, that oil markets and energy supplies would become unstable, and that shifts in political power would increase international tensions.

Recent changes in oil market conditions have reduced these fears, but the investment strategies of individual OPEC members continue to be of interest because of the size of the holdings, the interactions between investment strategies and decisions on oil policy, and concerns about OPEC investments in the energy and financial industries.

In this study Richard P. Mattione examines the size and distribution of the investments, their effects on the international financial system, and the motivations behind the investment strategies of individual OPEC members, particularly Saudi Arabia and Kuwait. He argues that investments in the United States and elsewhere have been motivated more by conventional financial considerations than by oil policy, development plans, or political goals.

When he wrote this book, Mattione was a research associate in the Brookings Foreign Policy Studies program. Many individuals in the United States, Great Britain, and the Middle East provided assistance during the course of the research. While observing their requests for anonymity, Mattione remains grateful for their help.

The author thanks J. Andrew Spindler for his assistance throughout the project; John D. Steinbruner, Sharif Ghalib, and an anonymous reviewer for detailed comments on earlier drafts of the manuscript; and his many

former colleagues at Brookings for their helpful comments and suggestions. Bruce Dickson verified the factual content of the manuscript, James
R. Schneider edited it, Nancy Snyder was the proofreader, and Florence
Robinson compiled the index. Finally, he wishes to acknowledge the work
of Virginia Black, who typed the many drafts.

This book enlarges upon work originally conducted under a grant for
research on energy and national security funded by the U.S. Department
of Energy. It was also partially supported by grants from the Ford Foundation, the German Marshall Fund of the United States, and the National
Science Foundation. The Brookings Institution is grateful for this support.

The views expressed in this book are those of the author and should not
be ascribed to the Department of Energy, the Ford Foundation, the German Marshall Fund of the United States, or the National Science Foundation, to those who commented on the manuscript, or to the trustees,
officers, or staff members of the Brookings Institution.

BRUCE K. MACLAURY
President

October 1984
Washington, D.C.

Contents

CHAPTER ONE

Introduction

FEW EVENTS of the past decade have so affected the global economic and political landscape as the sharp changes in the price of oil. The 1973–74 and 1979–80 price increases caused a significant transfer of wealth from industrial countries to members of the Organization of Petroleum Exporting Countries (OPEC); they also created the perception that a significant transfer of political power had occurred.[1] The oil shocks required a period of adjustment in world patterns of consumption and investment during which the OPEC nations built up sizable financial claims on the rest of the world. Thus international financial markets inevitably assumed a crucial role in the adjustment process, and OPEC nations became major investors in those markets.

Several OPEC nations accumulated sizable surpluses after 1973. The foreign holdings of the public sector in Saudi Arabia, for example, were approximately equal to the total assets of Citicorp or Bank of America (the world's largest banks) at the end of 1983. The holdings of the public sectors in Kuwait and the United Arab Emirates were each large enough to rank alongside the ten largest U.S. banks. The net foreign assets of these three countries should remain substantial through several years of soft oil markets.

Such large sums of money have raised fears that actions of the OPEC nations could affect world financial markets, and for that reason the financial decisions of OPEC investors (especially the countries with large surpluses) deserve analysis. Doubts about the intents of OPEC investors plagued the American public in general and certain journalists and con-

1. The thirteen members of OPEC are Algeria, Ecuador, Gabon, Indonesia, Iran, Iraq, Kuwait, Libya, Nigeria, Qatar, Saudi Arabia, the United Arab Emirates, and Venezuela.

gressmen in particular. They worried whether the size of the surpluses would make particular markets, countries, or institutions dependent on OPEC funds. Although the countries with large surpluses have avoided sudden changes in the composition of their investments in the past to avoid disrupting markets, the possibility of intentional or inadvertent disruptions nevertheless remains and must be assessed in light of the size and volatility of the countries' current account imbalances.

OPEC financial decisions also affect energy markets. All OPEC countries rely on oil for most export and government revenues. The performance of these economies would be completely linked to short-term oil market conditions if government spending had to move strictly in line with revenues. Those countries with substantial financial reserves, however, can adjust development expenditures more gradually. This in turn weakens the link from temporary oil price changes to decisions to increase or decrease oil exports.[2] As a result, the financial resources and strategies of the various OPEC countries influence their own oil policies and the current behavior of crude oil markets.

Investment decisions are also likely to influence the longer-run course of crude oil and products markets. The Arabian peninsula producers in particular have made investments in other energy-related activities in order to exploit their own resources more efficiently and to diversify their economies. Kuwait has been actively investing overseas, while the Saudis are building domestic refineries and petrochemical complexes that will produce largely for export. These countries, which already own a major share of the world's oil reserves, will soon be capable of supplying 3 percent to 5 percent of world demand for certain basic petrochemicals. A better understanding of how such investments mesh with the financial and oil policies of the OPEC members is necessary.

This study focuses on three aspects of OPEC's foreign investments since 1973: the size and distribution of the funds, their role in the international system, and the motivations behind the investment strategies of the various nations. These subjects have been neglected in previous studies of the 1970s. Although considerable attention has focused on the role of financial markets in the adjustment process, most analyses have been devoted to the problem of recycling OPEC surpluses, especially to the role of multilateral financial institutions and Western banks in channeling funds to the non-OPEC developing countries.

2. Of course, the OPEC nations still cannot delay adjustments of either oil policy or development spending to permanent shocks for very long.

The first task, of course, is to determine the payments positions of the OPEC nations over the last ten years and to estimate the cumulative surpluses or deficits accrued by individual members. Chapter 2 uses official sources to provide data on OPEC's holdings and on broad trends in the placement of OPEC's investments in international markets.

Before beginning detailed discussions of these investments, it is necessary to place OPEC's surpluses within the broader context of the adjustment problems generated by the increases in oil prices. Many options are available for dealing with payments imbalances, including the option of increasing development spending to reduce the surpluses. This fiscal adjustment played a larger role in the adjustment to oil shocks than was at first thought possible. Still, the size of the shocks made it almost inevitable that financial adjustment would play an important role. In the early 1970s it seemed that the problem of recycling funds from surplus to deficit countries might be insuperable. This perception led to arguments about the need for new mechanisms and institutions under the guidance of the governments of industrial countries and multilateral financial institutions. Eventually, though, the system proved to have the flexibility necessary to handle OPEC's investments. There were also debates about the impact of oil price shocks on the dollar and the currencies of other industrial countries. Chapter 3 discusses these broader issues.

Several related issues have been the focus of discussions on the disruptive potential of OPEC investment decisions: the extent to which such investments give OPEC nations significant control over particular financial markets or sectors of the world economy; the sort of disruptions those investments could cause, either intentionally or inadvertently; and how Western governments and international markets would respond to disruptions. Comparing OPEC investments in a particular market to the size of that market and closely related markets makes it clear that these nations have not had control of financial markets and indeed would find it difficult to attain such control. By analyzing scenarios for the large-scale transfer of OPEC funds it is possible to assess the potential for disruptions and the response of Western governments and international markets to them. Chapter 4 presents these issues and then closes with a brief examination of the relevance of the freeze on Iranian assets to these questions.

So far the investments have been described as "OPEC" investments, but there are significant differences between the investment strategies of individual OPEC members. One must therefore identify the economic, financial, and political factors motivating those strategies. Detailed analyses of the investment strategies of Saudi Arabia and Kuwait are presented in chapters 5 and 6, while chapter 7 reviews the investment strategies of other OPEC members. These analyses show that oil policy and development policy provide the main economic constraints within which financial factors (such as rates of return, diversification, and safety) can influence investment decisions. While it is conceivable that political concerns or a desire to strengthen OPEC's influence in oil markets might have overwhelmed economic and financial considerations, the evidence shows they did not.

There is one category of "investments," foreign aid, in which political explanations seem important. Even OPEC foreign aid, however, has often coincided with Western interests, as chapter 8 shows in reviewing various countries' decisions. The analysis of investment strategies ends in chapter 9 with a look at the involvement of OPEC (more specifically, Arab) commercial banks in international lending and the impact of these banks on global financial flows.

Chapter 10 closes this study with a summary of the results from the earlier chapters and the implications for the financial strategies of OPEC members during the 1980s.

A Note on Data Sources

This study required detailed data on OPEC investments since 1974. Official sources of these data, however, are insufficient. Saudi Arabia, for example, publishes data on the size of the foreign assets of the Saudi Arabian Monetary Agency (SAMA), which controls the bulk of government funds, but many other nations publish data only on the foreign holdings of central banks and commercial banks. For this reason, data on the balance of payments must be used to estimate total private and public-sector holdings of net foreign assets, a process detailed in chapter 2 and the Appendix.

The research also required data on the composition of a country's holdings—short term or long term, bank deposits or government bonds or equities, and so forth. Some data are available on these characteristics, but they are not very detailed. Many Western nations report the holdings in their own country of all OPEC countries aggregated or ot all Middle Eastern countries, but rarely do they report data on individual OPEC members. Some Western nations collect data on the deposits of individual

OPEC nations in banks inside the Western nation's borders, but these data are published only after being lumped together with data on a given country's bank deposits in other Western nations.

Thus it is necessary to supplement official sources with unofficial data on individual investments of the OPEC countries. The occasional public interviews of finance ministers and central bankers with reporters and the author's own off-the-record interviews with bankers and officials handling some of the transactions have supplemented the available data. Most often, though, one must depend on guesses and the slow process of piecing together and reconciling the various data. The relevant chapters discuss the methods of constructing the estimates.[3] Even with those caveats, however, it should be possible for the reader to learn from the story told in the following chapters.

3. The most-cited unofficial sources in this study are the *Middle East Economic Digest*, *Middle East Economic Survey*, *Euromoney*, *Institutional Investor*, the *Financial Times* of London, the *Wall Street Journal*, and the *New York Times*.

CHAPTER TWO

OPEC's Foreign Assets

THE SURPLUSES of the OPEC nations after the first oil shock and the consequent increase in their holdings of foreign assets had no real precedent. This situation thus engendered a great deal of interest and concern about the strategies guiding the investment of those funds and the challenges such investments might pose for the international system. Before such questions are addressed, however, it is appropriate to present the available data on broad trends in the size and distribution of OPEC's foreign assets.

The first step is to estimate the size of the accumulated foreign holdings, because these nations rarely publish statistics on the foreign assets held by their public and private sectors. The standard method uses the balance of payments accounts of individual nations to estimate yearly changes in foreign holdings.

A country's balance of payments can be conveniently broken down into the ten elements shown in table 2-1. Theoretically these ten items will add to zero during any given period of time because any credit is balanced by a corresponding debit.[1] In practice, however, it is necessary to add a last item, called "errors and omissions" in official data, that accounts for the statistical discrepancies that always exist.[2] The sum of items 4, 5, 9, and 10 in a given period provides a direct measure of the change in a country's net holdings of foreign assets during that period. For all nations, however,

1. For example, the import of a $1,000 machine by the United States is balanced by a $1,000 claim on the United States.
2. The statistical discrepancy in the global balance of payments has worsened in recent years. Two important causes of that discrepancy are the underreporting of transportation services earnings by nations that encourage use of flags of convenience and the underreporting of foreign investment income by both industrial nations and OPEC countries. For further details, see Organization for Economic Cooperation and Development, "The World Current Account Discrepancy," *Occasional Studies*, supplement to the *OECD Economic Outlook* (Paris: OECD, June 1982), pp. 46–63. The

Table 2-1. *Elements of the Balance of Payments*

Inflows	Outflows
1. Merchandise imports	6. Merchandise exports
2. Imports of services	7. Exports of services
3. Unilateral transfers to foreigners	8. Unilateral transfers from foreigners
4. Purchases of money and other assets from foreigners	9. Sales of money and other assets to foreigners
5. Official purchases of gold and foreign currencies	10. Official sales of gold and foreign currencies

data on these four items are in general neither as reliable nor as quickly available as data on the other six items. Thus the current account balance, which is the sum of items 1, 2, 3, 6, 7, and 8, is used instead of the more direct measure to estimate the net holdings of foreign assets. This equivalence is straightforward: when the current account shows a surplus, a nation is exporting more goods and services than it is importing and is therefore increasing its net claims on other countries.[3]

The annual current account surpluses have varied considerably over the years, as table 2-2 shows. Although OPEC as a whole ran surpluses from 1974 to 1977 and again from 1979 to 1981, the surpluses have disappeared fairly quickly after the first year of a shock.[4] This disappearance was

---

U.S. current account deficit for 1981–82 totaled $7 billion, while errors and omissions totaled $65.4 billion. The discrepancy in the world accounts, a figure that includes current account deficit or surplus of Western nations with countries that are not International Monetary Fund members, totaled $135.6 billion in the same period. For U.S. data see IMF, *Balance of Payments Statistics*, vol. 35 (May 1984), p. 40; for global data see IMF, *Annual Report 1983* (IMF, 1983), p. 18.

3. Of course, it is often necessary to estimate certain components of the current account, but these estimates are usually easier to make than estimates of changes in the other (capital account) items.

4. An alternative measure, the balance for goods, services, and private transfers, shows that OPEC nations ran a surplus every year from 1974 to 1981. Using this alternative measure, the OPEC Secretariat estimated a balance of $412.9 billion accumulated from 1974 to 1982, and the International Monetary Fund estimated that all developing-country oil exporters had a surplus of $422.1 billion at the end of this period (see table 3-1). The Bank for International Settlements (BIS) estimated a balance on goods, services, and private transfers of $395 billion accumulated over the same period. The measure in table 2-2 provides a better estimate of the increase in net foreign asset holdings than this alternative, however, because it corrects for official unilateral transfers. For the other estimates see OPEC, *Annual Statistical Bulletin, 1982*, table 9; and BIS, *Annual Report* (50th issue, p. 85; 52d issue, p. 94; and 53d issue, pp. 87, 95, 96).

Table 2-2. *Current Account Balances of High Absorbers and Low Absorbers within OPEC, 1974–82*[a]

Billions of dollars

Year	High absorbers [b]	Low absorbers [c]	OPEC total
1974	26.6	39.0	65.6
1975	6.6	24.0	30.6
1976	5.3	27.7	33.0
1977	1.2	21.6	22.8
1978	−11.8	7.5	−4.3
1979	19.1	34.8	53.9
1980	22.9	77.2	100.1
1981	−16.5	66.2	49.8
1982	−25.3	13.1	−12.3
1974–82	28.0	311.1	339.1

Source: Appendix table A-1. Countries are grouped according to definitions in Bank for International Settlements, *Fifty-Second Annual Report* (BIS, 1982), p. 94.

a. Balances on goods, services, and private and official transfers.

b. Algeria, Ecuador, Gabon, Indonesia, Iran, Iraq, Nigeria, Venezuela.

c. Kuwait, Libya, Qatar, Saudi Arabia, United Arab Emirates.

quicker following the second shock; the OPEC current account was near balance in 1982 and showed a large deficit in 1983.[5] Such an aggregated level of data, however, obscures the diverse propensities of the OPEC nations in accumulating foreign assets.

One factor, absorptive capacity, has probably been cited most frequently as a means of differentiating between OPEC members. Absorptive capacity represents an attempt to measure the ability of a nation to adjust spending to changes in income. High absorbers are those nations able to increase spending very quickly in response to larger incomes; low absorbers are those nations unable to respond as quickly. High absorbers would therefore not be expected to run large sustained surpluses, while the low absorbers would. The data in table 2-2 demonstrate this difference. In 1975, a year after the first shock, the current accounts of the high absorbers were already near balance, while the low absorbers ran substantial surpluses until 1978. After the second shock the low absorbers once again accounted for most of the surplus. The high absorbers, already in deficit in 1981, incurred further sizable deficits in 1982.

Absorptive capacity, however, is at best an imperfect measure of the differing propensities among OPEC nations to run sustained surpluses. A

5. The 1983 figure is based on preliminary IMF estimates of the deficit of oil-exporting developing countries shown in table 3-1.

more complete explanation of the size of each nation's surplus relies on three other interrelated factors. The first, of course, is oil policy, because oil accounts for most of the exports of these nations and, in many cases, for most of the GNP and government revenue. The second factor is development strategy: none of these nations has completed its infrastructure (such as ports and highways) or industrial development, and all of them devote a large share of their revenues to such spending. Most made extensive investments in infrastructure following the first oil shock, and they are now much more able to increase their expenditures quickly if oil revenues and development policies allow. The third factor is investment policy or, in the case of high absorbers, the access to foreign aid or loans.

Changing any one of these affects the surplus. As can be seen from the trade data in table 2-3, OPEC members have consciously made different decisions on exports following the second oil shock. Kuwait, a low absorber, consistently had one of the smallest multiples of 1978 export revenues (excluding Iran and Iraq, whose production was curtailed by war), but only because it decided to reduce production sharply. Although Libya and Nigeria had sharp increases in revenues from 1978 to 1980 because of their efforts to keep prices high, the same pricing policy led to sharp falls in revenues from 1980 to 1982. Saudi Arabia experienced the highest rate of revenue growth, but for a very different reason: it increased its already high level of production in an attempt to moderate prices. Other countries with relatively high growth in export revenues were Qatar and the United Arab Emirates (low absorbers) and Algeria (a high absorber). Absorptive capacity alone obviously cannot explain these differences in behavior.

The expenditure side of the balance sheet also provides evidence that absorptive capacity can be a misleading concept. Over this period three high absorbers—Ecuador, Venezuela, and Algeria—consistently had low rates of growth in imports in comparison to other OPEC nations. Iraq and Indonesia consistently had the highest increases in import expenditures compared to 1978, but low absorbers such as Saudi Arabia and the United Arab Emirates also expanded their imports considerably. Libya expanded imports rapidly until 1981 and then cut back when its oil revenues fell sharply. Furthermore, if the ratio of import growth to export growth is used to make comparisons across countries, the high absorbers (excluding Iran and Iraq because of war-related disruptions) are Kuwait and Saudi Arabia, while the low absorbers are Algeria and Venezuela. The reasons for such varied behavior will be pursued in later chapters within the con-

Table 2-3. Changes in the Merchandise Trade Accounts of OPEC Nations, 1980–82

Country	Export revenues as multiple of 1978 revenues[a]			Import expenditures as multiple of 1978 expenditures[b]			Ratio[c]		
	1980	1981	1982	1980	1981	1982	1980	1981	1982
Algeria	2.16	2.24	n.a.	1.28	1.27	1.25	1.69	1.76	n.a.
Ecuador	1.67	1.69	1.42	1.39	1.35	1.22	1.20	1.25	1.16
Gabon	1.96	n.a.	n.a.	1.42	1.56	1.36	1.38	n.a.	n.a.
Indonesia	1.88	1.91	1.45	1.64	2.01	2.55	1.15	0.95	0.57
Iran	0.64	0.46	0.79	0.59	0.57	0.47	1.08	0.81	1.68
Iraq	2.38	0.95	0.89	2.22	3.10	3.13	1.07	0.31	0.28
Kuwait	1.89	1.55	0.94	1.36	1.57	1.59	1.39	0.99	0.59
Libya	2.15	1.53	1.37	1.60	2.48	1.29	1.34	0.62	1.06
Nigeria	2.51	1.81	1.55	1.43	1.59	1.15	1.76	0.70	1.35
Qatar	2.45	2.45	1.83	1.04	1.36	1.68	2.36	1.80	1.09
Saudi Arabia	2.70	2.99	2.01	1.48	1.73	2.00	1.82	1.73	1.01
United Arab Emirates	2.27	2.21	1.84	1.61	1.65	1.53	1.41	1.34	1.20
Venezuela	2.09	2.19	1.79	1.07	1.22	1.20	1.95	1.80	1.49

Source: International Monetary Fund, *International Financial Statistics*, vol. 36 (October 1983).

n.a. Not available.

a. Exports of goods only.

b. Imports of goods only, on an f.o.b. basis.

c. Export revenue multiplier divided by import expenditure multiplier.

Table 2-4. *OPEC Cumulative Current Account Surpluses by Country*
Billions of dollars unless otherwise specified

Country	Cumulative current account surplus[a]			Percent of total OPEC 1974–82 surplus
	1974–78	1979–82	1974–82	
Saudi Arabia	61.6	98.6	160.1	47.2
Kuwait	31.8	48.8	80.6	23.8
United Arab Emirates	11.7	23.9	35.5	10.5
Iran	26.3	4.9	31.2	9.2
Libya	10.2	12.0	22.2	6.5
Iraq	14.6	5.7	20.3	6.0
Qatar	4.6	8.1	12.7	3.7
Venezuela	−0.7	5.6	4.9	1.4
Gabon	0.2	1.7	1.9	0.6
Ecuador	−1.2	−3.6	−4.8	−1.4
Indonesia	−2.9	−4.5	−7.4	−2.2
Nigeria	−0.2	−7.2	−7.4	−2.2
Algeria	−8.2	−2.5	−10.8	−3.2
OPEC total	147.7	191.4	339.1	100.0

Source: Appendix table A-1.
a. Balance on goods, services, and private and official transfers. Figures may not add because of rounding.

text of the oil, development, and investment or borrowing policies mentioned earlier.

While it would appear inexact to use the term "low absorptive capacity" to identify the countries with large surpluses, it is clear that OPEC's surpluses have been concentrated in countries with small populations. The estimates of net changes in holdings of foreign assets on a country-by-country basis show the extent to which a few Middle Eastern nations are responsible for most of the foreign assets OPEC has accumulated (table 2-4). Saudi Arabia dominates the picture, having added $160.1 billion to its net foreign assets from 1974 to 1982.[6] The Saudi surpluses represent 47 percent of total OPEC current account surpluses during this period. Kuwait and the United Arab Emirates are in second and third positions,

6. It bears emphasizing once again that the estimated cumulative surplus of $339.1 billion in tables 2-2 and 2-4 reflects the narrower measure of current account surpluses after official transfers. The measure thus corresponds to the increase in net holdings of foreign assets. For estimates of the broader measure of current account surpluses before official transfers see footnote 4 of this chapter.

Table 2-5. *Estimated Distribution of OPEC Investable Surplus, 1974–83*
Billions of dollars

Distribution	1974	1975	1976	1977	1978	1979	1980	1981	1982	1983	1974-82	1974-83
United States[a]	11.5	7.9	11.1	7.4	0.4	7.0	15.0	14.9	10.1	-8.5	85.5	76.9
Treasury bills and certificates	5.3	0.5	-1.0	-0.9	-0.9	3.3	1.4	-0.5	0.4	-1.1	7.5	6.4
Treasury bonds and notes	0.2	2.0	4.3	4.3	-1.5	-1.2	8.2	10.9	6.9	-5.5	34.0	28.5
Other U.S. bonds	0.9	1.6	1.2	1.7	0.8	0.4	3.5	3.5	-0.8	-1.2	12.8	11.6
U.S. stocks	0.2	1.7	1.8	1.4	0.8	0.7	1.2	1.2	0.4	-0.8	9.3	8.5
Commercial bank liabilities	4.2	0.6	1.9	0.4	0.8	5.1	-1.2	-2.1	4.7	0.7	14.4	15.1
Foreign direct investment	0.1	0.0	0.0	0.0	0.1	0.0	0.3	2.9	0.8	0.7	4.2	4.8
Other	0.6	1.7	3.0	0.4	0.4	-1.3	1.6	-0.9	-2.3	-1.2	3.3	2.0
Other than United States[a]	46.3	29.5	28.0	31.0	14.5	47.7	79.0	42.3	-10.3	-1.5	308.0	306.5
Eurobanking market[b]	22.5	8.0	11.0	12.0	2.5	29.0	32.0	2.7	-25.5	-14.5	94.3	79.7
United Kingdom[b]	7.5	0.3	-1.0	0.7	0.3	2.5	3.5	1.0	0.5	0.0	15.3	15.3
Other developed and nonmarket countries	6.5	9.7	9.3	9.3	5.7	8.3	28.7	21.7	3.7	1.0	103.0	104.0
Less developed countries[c]	6.0	7.3	7.5	8.5	6.5	8.5	10.3	12.7	8.5	7.3	75.7	83.0
International financial institutions, IMF position, SDRs, gold	3.7	4.3	1.3	0.5	-0.5	-0.5	4.5	4.0	2.5	4.7	19.7	24.5
Total identified investments[a]	57.7	37.5	39.0	38.5	15.0	54.7	94.0	57.2	-0.1	-9.9	393.5	383.4

Source: Treasury Department data prepared by the Office of International Banking and Portfolio Investment, dated June 26, 1984.
a. Figures may not add because of rounding.
b. Foreign currency deposits placed in London are included in the Eurobanking market, not in the United Kingdom placements.
c. Includes grants.

with almost 24 percent and 11 percent, respectively. Together these three Arabian peninsula producers account for over 81 percent of OPEC's surpluses since the first oil shock, and their share grew in the early 1980s because they were the last countries to have their balance of payments affected by the oil market glut (see Appendix table A-1). The net foreign assets of most OPEC nations fell in 1983, however, as soft oil market conditions forced them to run current account deficits. Developments in 1983–84 and the likely path for the future are discussed in chapters 5 through 7.

International Deployment of OPEC's Identified Surplus

Most of OPEC's foreign investments from 1974 to 1982 have been identified. These investments total $393.5 billion, including $75.7 billion of grants, concessional loans, and investments in developing countries (table 2-5). The estimated current account surplus during this period is $339.1 billion after official transfers (see table 2-2) and around $395 billion before official transfers.[7] Total funds available for grants and investments were probably between $430 billion and $440 billion, once the timing of oil payments and the borrowings of several less wealthy nations are accounted for.[8] Thus over 89 percent of OPEC's investments during that period have been identified. Because current account deficits forced most OPEC countries to liquidate investments during 1983, identified investments totaled only $383.4 billion for the 1974–83 period.

Five main explanations have been advanced for the unidentified investments.[9] One possibility is that the current account figures understate

7. See footnote 4 of this chapter for details on this second measure.

8. The gross surpluses of the surplus nations exceed aggregate OPEC current surpluses, with the difference equal to the deficits of a few of the nations. U.S. Treasury data indicate that the cumulative investable cash surplus exceeded the cumulative current account surplus by $44.5 billion from 1974 to 1982. Thus $393.5 billion, or at least 89.4 percent, of an investable cash surplus of at most $440 billion has been identified. The Treasury data were prepared by the Office of International Banking and Portfolio Investment and are dated May 31, 1984.

9. Sharif Ghalib, "Assessment of the Magnitude and Current Disposition Patterns of the Aggregate Official Arab Financial Surplus," in Wharton Economic Forecasting Associates, *Proceedings of the Wharton Middle East Economic Outlook Conference* (Washington, D.C.: WEFA, 1982), pp. 90–91.

imports, especially military purchases. If this is true, it means that the current account surpluses and thus the funds available for investment are overstated. Second, the traditional investment data do not include fiduciary accounts with Swiss banks, which amounted to $11.90 billion at the end of 1982 (table 2-10). Third, gold held by both the private and public sectors may be understated. Both the second and third items represent financial assets that can be used as a hedge against such political disruptions as revolution and thus may involve a bias toward underreporting. Fourth, the industrial countries simply do not collect data on some smaller investments outside the banking sector and thus almost surely miss some OPEC investments. Finally, OPEC's joint ventures in developing countries are difficult to track. These sources are listed in approximately declining order of importance. Together they should account for almost all of the discrepancy.

The surpluses from 1974 to 1983 have been invested in both the Eurocurrency markets and many national markets. The largest portion, an estimated $79.7 billion, or 20.8 percent, was held in bank deposits outside the domestic U.S. and U.K. banking systems (table 2-5). When these deposits are combined with the $15.1 billion deposited at bank branches in the United States and any further deposits with domestic banking systems worldwide, at least $94.8 billion or 24.7 percent of OPEC's identified foreign investments from 1974 to 1983 were in bank deposits.

The United States has been the most favored national market for OPEC, having attracted investments of $76.9 billion ($61.8 billion when bank deposits are excluded). These investments are composed mostly of bank liabilities, Treasury securities, other bonds, and stocks. Direct investment in the United States has constituted a rather minor share of OPEC's foreign assets. Only $4.8 billion in direct investments have been identified, and a large share of that is accounted for by the Kuwaiti purchase of Santa Fe International in 1981. Other placements in the United States consist largely of prepayments for military purchases and the liabilities to OPEC of companies other than banks.

This leaves a further $226.8 billion invested outside the United States and the Eurobanking market. These investments took various forms, including equities, property holdings, and loans to developed and developing countries (this includes concessional aid provided to developing countries) and were thus considerably larger than OPEC's holdings of claims on the United States. Loans to international organizations and purchases of gold amounted to $24.5 billion, and $15.3 billion was placed in sterling bank deposits and other investments in the United Kingdom.

Along with size and location another important characteristic of OPEC investments is the distribution of their maturities. The choice between various investments is guided by such factors as relative risks, rates of return, and liquidity of the claims. Long-term claims usually offer higher returns but are more subject to capital risks and are less liquid than short-term claims. Any investor faces this trade-off, of course, but there are two additional factors that, in the twelve to eighteen months immediately following a price shock, may temporarily cause the investment authorities in OPEC countries to favor short-term investments. First, there may be a lag before the countries realize that they will have sizable new surpluses, during which time they may prefer to put the money into short-term claims. Second, the inability to gather information quickly on long-term investments could also lead to temporary placement in short-term claims. These two factors probably explain much of the variation in the maturity distribution of OPEC's investments over the years (table 2-6). Short-term investments, largely bank deposits, have accounted for the most placements in the year immediately following each price shock, but a rapid and pronounced shift toward longer-term investments occurred in subsequent years, even when the annual surplus declined.[10] Thus new short-term investments accounted for 55.3 percent of identified OPEC investments in 1974 but amounted to less than one-third of new investments from 1975 to 1978. Short-term investments accounted for 68.4 percent of the identified financial surplus in 1979, but only 0.3 percent by 1981. Short-term investments declined sharply in 1982, although identified investments went virtually unchanged.

Some shift in the location of OPEC's investments has also occurred in recent years. This has been most noteworthy for short-term claims: the relative importance of deposits at banks in the United States and at foreign branches of U.S. banks has declined sharply since 1979 (table 2-7). The oil exporters as a group ran down their balances at U.S. offices of banks by $1.16 billion in 1980 (table 2-7), while their deposits at foreign branches of U.S. banks increased only $810 million. The corresponding figures for 1979 had been increases of $5.08 billion and $8.06 billion. Net purchases of Treasury bills and certificates were also smaller in 1980 than in 1979. These movements are striking; OPEC's short-term investments only fell from $37.4 billion in 1979 to $32.2 billion in 1980 (see table 2-6), while short-term investments in the United States or with U.S.

10. These figures exclude investments in short-term U.K. treasury bills and sterling bank deposits.

Table 2-6. *Distribution of OPEC's Net Short-Term Investments, 1974–83*
Billions of dollars unless otherwise specified

Distribution	1974	1975	1976	1977	1978	1979	1980	1981	1982	1983
Total short-term investments[a]	31.9	9.1	11.9	11.5	2.4	37.4	32.2	0.2	-20.5	-14.9
U.S.-based bank deposits and Treasury certificates	9.4	1.1	0.9	-0.5	-0.1	8.4	0.2	-2.6	5.0	-0.4
Bank deposits outside the United States	22.5	8.0	11.0	12.0	2.5	29.0	32.0	2.7	-25.5	-14.5
Identified surplus	57.7	37.5	39.0	38.5	15.0	54.7	94.0	57.2	-0.1	-9.9
Short-term investments as percentage of identified surplus	55.3	24.3	30.5	29.9	15.3	68.4	34.2	0.3	...	...

Source: Treasury Department data prepared by the Office of International Banking and Portfolio Investment.
a. Figures exclude investments in short-term U.K. treasury securities and domestic sterling bank deposits. Figures may not add because of rounding.

Table 2-7. *Distribution of OPEC's Net Short-Term Investments with U.S. Institutions, 1979–83*
Billions of dollars

Distribution	1979	1980	1981	1982	1983
Treasury bills and certificates	3.34	1.38	−0.52	0.38	−1.11
Deposits at U.S. branches of U.S. and foreign banks	5.08	−1.16	−2.05	4.66	0.68
Deposits at foreign branches of U.S. banks	8.06	0.81	−2.82	−6.44	−2.02

Sources: Foreign branch data are from "Geographical Distribution of Assets and Liabilities of Major Foreign Branches of U.S. Banks," Federal Reserve Board Statistical Release E.11 (various issues); other data are from the Office of International Banking and Portfolio Investment, Treasury Department.

institutions fell from $16.48 billion to $1.03 billion. Movement away from short-term claims in the United States and at U.S. banks abroad continued much more slowly in 1981. Because the decreases in American claims during 1982 and 1983 were a small fraction of the total drop in OPEC's short-term claims, it would appear that in relative terms the movement away from the use of American banks has finally ended. The 1982 data, however, must be interpreted carefully, because they include a large transfer of Venezuelan deposits from the Euromarkets to New York at the time of the Falklands War (see chapter 7).

Table 2-8 provides disaggregated data on the short-term flows of funds between OPEC and U.S. banks from 1979 through 1983. Only Middle Eastern producers ran down their short-term claims at both domestic and foreign branches of U.S. banks in 1980. As a group the others ran down claims on bank offices in the United States but increased deposits at foreign branches of U.S. banks to more than offset this decline. The picture is clouded further because Middle Eastern producers increased their holdings of long-term U.S. investments significantly in 1980 even as they moved funds out of U.S. banks; the inflow of long-term funds was some six times larger than the outflow of short-term funds. The other OPEC nations also increased their holdings of U.S. Treasury bonds and notes.

A partial explanation for such investment behavior during 1980 is that the U.S. freeze on Iranian assets caused OPEC nations to adjust their portfolios. All these countries presumably hold some of their balances in short-term claims to meet transaction and precautionary demands for money (for example, to pay for imports), and bank deposits are the most convenient instruments for such reserves. Frozen assets are no longer available for such use, but OPEC countries could lessen the impact of a freeze by one Western nation if they diversified placement of these

Table 2-8. *Changes in OPEC's U.S.-Related Portfolio Holdings, 1979–83*[a]
Millions of dollars

Holdings	1979	1980	1981	1982	1983
Middle East oil exporters[b]					
Treasury bills and certificates	3,552	51	1,088	62	−726
Other Treasury and federal agency securities	−1,097	9,122	12,964	7,383	−5,817
Corporate bonds	507	2,049	1,657	−597	−766
Corporate stocks	688	1,206	1,140	366	−807
Liabilities of domestic bank branches	4,233	−897	−2,551	425	247
Deposits at foreign branches of U.S. banks	5,328	−1,051	−2,490	−3,668	−1,942
Total[c]	13,210	10,480	11,808	3,971	−9,811
Other OPEC members[d]					
Treasury bills and certificates	−211	1,329	−1,608	317	−383
Other Treasury and federal agency securities	−141	516	−295	−665	−123
Corporate bonds	1	0	−2	6	−5
Corporate stocks	−16	−4	12	11	29
Liabilities of domestic bank branches	850	−263	498	4,239	435
Deposits at foreign branches of U.S. banks	2,733	1,861	−334	−2,776	−81
Total[c]	3,215	3,439	−1,689	1,132	−128

Source: Treasury Department data prepared by Office of International Banking and Portfolio Investment; and Federal Reserve Board, Statistical Release E.11, various issues.
a. Placements in the United States or at foreign branches of U.S. banks.
b. Iran, Iraq, Kuwait, Qatar, Saudi Arabia, and the United Arab Emirates. Also includes non-OPEC members Bahrain and Oman.
c. Figures may not add because of rounding.
d. Algeria, Ecuador, Gabon, Indonesia, Libya, Nigeria, and Venezuela.

deposits. Although Middle Eastern producers, who may feel that they are the most likely target of any future freeze, reduced short-term claims, the simultaneous increase in their long-term claims on the United States shows they were not overly concerned about the threat of a freeze. The actions of oil producers outside the Middle East indicated that they too might have wanted to move their short-term claims outside the United States.[11] Still, the overall effect was much milder than initially feared because both groups increased total claims on the United States during 1980.

A further drawdown of short-term claims with U.S. institutions occurred in 1981. Because of the small net additions to short-term claims worldwide in 1981 ($300 million according to table 2-6), however, the freeze was probably less important than that a number of non–Middle-Eastern producers had to draw down short-term claims to fund current

11. After all, the freeze only established that the United States could tie up deposits at foreign branches of U.S. banks when foreign governments cooperate. This issue of extraterritoriality was never ruled on in the courts, although most commentators believe the United States would have lost once the case was heard.

account deficits. Furthermore, the data from 1981 and 1982 also show the continued interest of the Middle Eastern countries in U.S. government securities. The sharp decline in holdings of Treasury securities in 1983 probably reflects Saudi Arabia's need to redeem maturing securities to cover its substantial deficit.

Despite the significant growth of placements in absolute terms, OPEC's foreign assets actually located in the United States (that is, excluding foreign branches of U.S. banks) as a share of the cumulative identified surplus peaked at 22.7 percent in 1976, fell continuously to 18.1 percent in 1980, and rose again to 21.7 percent in 1982. If foreign branches are included, the share declined continuously from 35.9 percent in 1976 to 26.4 percent in 1981 before bouncing back to 27.0 percent in 1982.[12] Both figures fell in 1983.

It is difficult to say that any one country or group of countries has replaced the United States in the investment portfolios of OPEC nations, especially since claims on the U.S. market remain far larger than those on any other nation. The other domestic markets most often mentioned as attractive to OPEC investors are the United Kingdom, West Germany, Switzerland, and Japan, with interest in Japanese and West German securities especially strong since the second oil shock. Great Britain, which received $7.5 billion of OPEC investments in 1974 (excluding Eurocurrency deposits), received only $7.8 billion more from 1975 to 1982 (table 2-5). OPEC claims on West Germany have increased considerably since the second oil shock; West Germany's accumulated gross liabilities to OPEC since 1974 were $9.6 billion at the end of 1978 and $22.4 billion by the end of 1982 (table 2-9). Loans to West German government authorities account for 61.3 percent of the claims. Interest in Switzerland appears to have been concentrated on bank-related investments. Deposits of the Middle Eastern nations with Swiss banks rose from $4.91 billion in 1978 to $6.56 billion in 1982, while fiduciary accounts rose from $3.90 billion to $11.90 billion over the same period (table 2-10). Finally, OPEC's interest in Japan suddenly seemed to blossom in 1980; it has been estimated that Arab investors accounted for one-half, or some $10 billion, of the net addition of $20.5 billion to yen assets held by foreigners in the first nine months of 1980.[13] Another source reported that OPEC investments in

12. Calculations are based on data in table 2-5 and in Statistical Release E.11 of the Board of Governors of the Federal Reserve System.

13. Stephen Bronte, "Petrodollar Sophistication Grows," *Middle East Economic Digest,* Special Report (December 1980), p. 10.

Table 2-9. *Distribution of OPEC Investments in the Federal Republic of Germany, 1974–82*[a]
Millions of deutsche marks

Distribution[b]	1974	1975	1976	1977	1978	1979	1980	1981	1982	1974-82
Private sector	3,323	3,545	2,268	4,100	1,692	3,117	4,889	2,924	-5,235	20,623
Long term[c]	1,524	2,308	1,071	1,850	1,906	1,817	2,898	2,590	-1,382	14,582
Direct investment	1,165	230	-11	-39	522	263	107	-63	55	2,229
Portfolio	280	597	550	884	659	335	993	1,360	258	5,916
Other	79	1,482	533	1,005	725	1,219	1,798	1,293	-1,695	6,439
Short term[d]	1,799	1,237	1,197	2,250	-214	1,300	1,991	334	-3,853	6,041
Banks	1,707	918	1,303	1,965	-481	1,049	2,175	127	-3,800	4,963
Enterprises and individuals	92	319	-106	285	267	251	-184	207	-53	1,078
Official	352	1,457	1,052	624	-780	-51	12,382	14,362	3,313	32,711
Total	3,675	5,002	3,320	4,724	912	3,066	17,271	17,286	-1,922	53,334

Source: Deutsche Bundesbank, *Statistical Supplements to the Monthly Reports of the Deutsche Bundesbank: Series 3, Balance of Payments Statistics* (August 1978, July 1982, August 1983).
a. A minus sign denotes a new outflow of funds.
b. Investment is classified as private or official according to the sector to which the German borrower belongs.
c. Long-term investments are those with original maturities of more than twelve months or for unlimited periods.
d. Short-term investments are those with original maturities of less than twelve months.

Table 2-10. *Liabilities and Fiduciary Accounts at Swiss Banks and Financial Institutions from Middle Eastern Nations, 1978–82*[a]
Billions of dollars

	1978	1979	1980	1981	1982
Bank liabilities	4.91	6.70	7.93	7.64	6.56
Fiduciary accounts	3.90	5.64	8.00	8.94	11.90

Source: Schweizerische Nationalbank, *Das Schweizerische Bankwesen* (Zurich: Orell Fuessli), various issues, 1978–82. All figures were reported in Swiss francs and converted into dollars at end-of-year exchange rates. Exchange rate data are from IMF, *International Financial Statistics,* vol. 37 (June 1984), p. 424.

a. Egypt, Iran, Iraq, Kuwait and other Persian Gulf nations, Libya, Saudi Arabia, Syria, and Yemen.

Japan reached $39 billion at the end of 1982, though a small decline was anticipated during 1983.[14]

The size and composition of OPEC's foreign investments have varied considerably during the decade since the first oil shock and will continue to vary in response to oil market conditions and the domestic development plans of individual nations. In particular, the current oil market glut has put considerable pressure on government revenues in all OPEC nations. This forced them as a group to run a sizable deficit in 1983 and, barring a sudden increase in oil demand, will lead to further current account deficits over the next several years. This, of course, implies that they will be drawing down foreign assets in the next few years.

The foreign assets of OPEC will still be sizable, however, and two questions concerning those investments continue to be important. First, to what extent can these nations intentionally or unintentionally affect international financial markets and thereby influence government policies through their foreign investments? Second, what will be the likely future investment behavior of those nations, especially Saudi Arabia, Kuwait, and the United Arab Emirates, that have accrued a sizable financial surplus and experience in investing in a variety of markets?

14. "Sumitomo Bank: Withdrawal of OPEC Funds Will Be $2.5B at Most," *Japan Economic Journal* (April 26, 1983).

CHAPTER THREE

Oil Shocks and International Financial Markets

THE 1973–74 oil price shock has become identified as the event that ended an idyllic post–World War II period of global financial stability and high economic growth. That characterization is scarcely true in the case of international financial markets, especially foreign exchange markets. The oil price shock did, however, lead to payments imbalances that further disconcerted policymakers dealing with the breakdown in the postwar rules of the game for international trade and payments. Indeed, the oil-related payments imbalances combined with other changes in the pattern of economic activity to restructure the international financial system.

The apparent financial stability of the postwar period was due to the Bretton Woods system of exchange rates pegged to gold. This system, established in the aftermath of World War II, functioned fairly well in its first two decades. But gradually, pegged rates came to mean unchanging rates. At the same time, rates of inflation began to vary considerably from country to country, which made currencies significantly overvalued or undervalued in comparison to the official pegged rates. The resulting pressures were expressed in such forms as the sterling crisis of 1967, the suspension of dollar convertibility into gold in 1971, and the decision of the Common Market countries in 1973 to float their currencies against the dollar. This last event, which occurred before the first oil shock, marked the end of pegged exchange rates, although this was not fully understood at the time. The central role of the U.S. dollar in the international monetary system and the relatively small role of foreign trade in the U.S. economy helped to insulate Americans from these developments. Yet for international financial markets and also for the conduct of macroeconomic policy, the demise of the Bretton Woods system was an event with implications as dramatic as those of the oil shocks.

The problems of the Bretton Woods system were caused by a fundamental conflict between the various countries' desires for independent national macroeconomic policies and the absence of clear responsibility for the exchange rate adjustments needed to equilibrate the system. The system was designed so that surpluses and deficits on current accounts would disappear quickly as governments made the interest rate adjustments necessary to counter incipient flows of funds in response to payments disequilibrium. It would be more accurate, however, to describe the system as putting pressure on deficit countries, except the United States, to move toward balance, while corresponding pressures on nations with surpluses were much smaller. Persistent payments imbalances magnified tensions within the Bretton Woods system, ultimately causing its demise and coloring later thinking on the appropriate response to oil-related payments imbalances.

Oil Shocks, Adjustment, and Payments Imbalances

Oil prices quadrupled in 1973–74 and doubled once again during 1979–80. Each round of price increases led to a transfer of real resources from oil consumers to oil producers equal to approximately 2 percent of world GNP.[1] At the time, it was hard to assess the impact of the increases on growth and inflation, but economists feared a period of stagflation whose length and severity would depend on the extent to which oil price increases pushed up other prices and wages.[2] Clearly, major adjustments would have to be made. But questions of what form those adjustments should take and under whose leadership they should be carried out were harder to resolve.

Four basic adjustment mechanisms were available to oil importers for responding to higher oil prices: energy adjustment, either by using less energy for a given amount of output or by switching to coal or some other non-OPEC source of energy; trade adjustment through expanding exports

1. A quick estimate of the income transfer involved can be obtained by comparing the share of world GNP received by the oil-producing nations before and after a price shock.

2. For a discussion of the impact on the U.S. economy, see the various studies in Knut Anton Mork, ed., *Energy Prices, Inflation and Economic Activity* (Cambridge, Mass.: Ballinger, 1979); and Congressional Budget Office, *The Effect of OPEC Oil Pricing on Output, Prices, and Exchange Rates in the United States and Other Industrialized Countries* (CBO, 1981).

or limiting imports; financial adjustment using capital flows from oil exporters to oil importers to fund payments deficits; and macroeconomic adjustment to limit energy demand by using monetary and fiscal policies to limit growth.[3] The first two are essentially long-term measures for permanent adjustment, though trade adjustment might improve the payments position in the short run, too. The other methods seemed able to yield temporary results in the interval during which more permanent structural adjustments were being made.

But at the time of the first oil shock these four options, even in combination, appeared insufficient for the smooth handling of payments imbalances. And the imbalances could not be ignored; persistent imbalances had, after all, hastened the downfall of the Bretton Woods system. Thus the notion arose that the elimination of any and all payments imbalances must be rapid, taking perhaps no longer than one or two years. Yet substitution of non-oil energy sources and the development of new, non-OPEC supplies of oil would be inadequate in so short a time, and the other methods faced objections at least as serious. It was feared that major oil producers (particularly Saudi Arabia, Iran, and Kuwait) would be unable to increase domestic spending rapidly enough for trade to play a major role in reducing Western balance of payments deficits. Furthermore, there was a payments deficit of industrial countries as a group vis-à-vis OPEC, which meant that trade between industrial countries might allow one deficit nation to improve its payments position, but only at the expense of other deficit nations. This would be an open invitation to the beggar-thy-neighbor trade policies that had caused such difficulties during the Great Depression. Because contractionary macroeconomic policies seemed to possess the same fault of leading to improvement in the payments position of one deficit nation at the expense of others, short-term financing of the deficits was the only remaining option. But this, too, seemed unlikely to succeed, because the payments imbalances promised to be much larger and more sustained than those previously experienced, even if the exact magnitude of the necessary financing was unclear.[4] The major concerns were whether the world financial system could safely

3. This four-way division is borrowed from Hollis B. Chenery, "Restructuring the World Economy: Round II," *Foreign Affairs*, vol. 59 (Summer 1981), p. 1107.

4. In a speech, Rimmer de Vries was able to cite an OECD estimate of a cumulative $300 billion OPEC surplus by the end of 1980 and a World Bank estimate of a $650 billion surplus. See "The Build-up of OPEC Funds," *World Financial Markets* (Morgan Guaranty Trust, September 23, 1974), p. 1.

handle such large imbalances, regardless of the source, and whether individual countries would always have access to necessary financing. The worries were amplified because no one was sure which institutions would handle the financing.

In general, the payments imbalances caused by the first oil shock were reduced more quickly than most observers had anticipated. As table 3-1 shows, the current account surplus (before official transfers) of the developing-country oil exporters reached $68.3 billion in 1974 but fluctuated near $35 billion the next three years before falling to a $2.2 billion surplus in 1978.[5] The second oil shock led to renewed concerns about financing as the surplus reached $68.6 billion in 1979 and peaked at $114.3 billion in 1980. But by 1982 these countries were again near balance, and they ran a deficit of $27 billion in 1983. Once the figures are adjusted for inflation, the surpluses following the second oil shock mimic the duration and real (inflation-adjusted) magnitudes of the surpluses following the first shock.

Still, a wide gap in the economic performances of the various non-OPEC nations appeared even as the current account balance between OPEC and non-OPEC nations was being restored. The seven larger industrial countries erased their deficits rapidly. Energy conservation and alternative sources of supply contributed more than had at first been anticipated, even though the United States essentially delayed its adjustment until after the passage of oil decontrol legislation in 1979. Energy adjustment was supplemented by OPEC's investment in these industrial nations and by rapidly expanded OPEC imports. Trade policies avoided extreme, beggar-thy-neighbor tactics as a means of adjusting to the oil shock, although one cannot deny the existence of aggressive trading behavior among Western nations. The speed of the adjustment in the larger industrial nations, however, was mostly attributable to contractionary macroeconomic policies that slowed growth and thus reduced imports and balance of payments deficits.[6] Monetary policy has been tight in the United States since late 1979, and for several years Europe and Japan felt obliged to

5. The IMF defines oil-exporting developing countries as those countries whose oil exports account for at least two-thirds of their total exports and amount to at least 100 million barrels a year (roughly equal to 1 percent of annual world oil exports). This definition, based on 1977–79 averages, includes all OPEC members except Ecuador and Gabon and adds Oman. All other developing countries are defined as non-oil developing countries.

6. Contractionary policies have been accused of damaging the growth prospects of less developed countries; see Chenery, "Restructuring the World Economy: Round II," pp. 1112–14.

Table 3-1. *Payments Balances on Current Account, 1973–83*[a]
Billions of dollars

Country group	1973	1974	1975	1976	1977	1978	1979	1980	1981	1982	1983[b]
Industrial countries											
Seven larger countries[c]	14.8	-2.7	24.9	10.1	10.4	36.2	6.9	-13.6	15.4	10.5	20.5
Other industrial countries	5.5	-8.1	-5.1	-9.6	-12.6	-3.5	-12.4	-26.6	-15.7	-14.1	-4.5
Developing countries											
Oil-exporting countries	6.7	68.3	35.4	40.3	30.2	2.2	68.6	114.3	65.0	-2.2	-27.0
Non-oil developing countries	-11.3	-37.0	-46.3	-32.6	-28.9	-41.3	-61.0	-89.0	-107.7	-86.8	-68.0
Total[d]	15.7	20.5	8.9	8.2	-0.9	-6.4	2.1	-14.9	-43.0	-92.6	-79.0

Source: International Monetary Fund, *Annual Report 1983* (Washington, D.C.: IMF), p. 18.
a. On goods, services, and private transfers.
b. IMF projection.
c. United States, Canada, Japan, West Germany, France, United Kingdom, Italy.
d. Reflects errors, omissions, asymmetries in statistics, and balance of listed groups with other countries (mainly the USSR and other nonmember countries of Eastern Europe).

pursue similar policies to protect the value of their currencies. Yet these policies were only partially a response to the effects of oil price hikes; the motivation behind monetary policy in several nations, particularly the United States and Great Britain, was to limit the inflation that resulted from the expansionary monetary policies of the 1970s.

The disappearance of their current account surpluses after the first oil shock proved that all OPEC nations could rapidly increase absorption of goods and services after an increase in income. The swing from large surpluses to deficits following the second oil price rise was caused more by a sharp drop in the demand for oil. Yet in both cases the disappearance of OPEC surpluses was translated largely into the reappearance of the traditional current account surpluses of the larger industrial countries. The smaller industrial nations seemed to experience a structural shift from surplus to deficit on the current account, while the non-oil developing countries went even further into deficit.

Several studies have provided a partial explanation of the divergent movements on the current accounts for different groups of countries by focusing on the distinction between temporary and long-lasting changes.[7] A country facing what it considered a temporary drop in income would initially borrow or run down past savings in an attempt to smooth its pattern of consumption gradually. This action shows up as a current account deficit; the larger the temporary drop in income, the larger the deficit. But this policy is no longer appropriate if the change is relatively permanent. In the face of a permanent drop in income, both current and future consumption must be reduced, which would cause the current account to move toward surplus. Similarly, permanent improvement in a country's economic position vis-à-vis the rest of the world could lead to an immediate and permanent increase in consumption. Expectations of a permanent improvement might even be so strong as to lead to an increase in the balance of payments deficit. This is particularly true if a country's natural resources suddenly become more valuable but developing them requires an increase in investment that exceeds the amount of funds available domestically. In this case it is an increase in investment, not consumption, that leads to the payments deficit. Finally, a country might also

7. See Jeffrey D. Sachs, "The Current Account and Macroeconomic Adjustment in the 1970s," *Brookings Papers on Economic Activity, 1:1981,* pp. 215–25; and Maurice Obstfeld, "Transitory Terms-of-Trade Shocks and the Current Account: The Case of Constant Time Preference," International Finance Discussion Paper 194 (Washington, D.C.: Federal Reserve Board, December 1981).

decide on political grounds to smooth the downward adjustment of consumption in response to unfavorable shocks by borrowing abroad.

The behavior of the industrial nations after 1973 seems to fit the theoretical model of adjustment to a permanent price shock. The industrial countries with the least dependence on imported oil, such as Norway and Canada, experienced the largest swings toward deficit on the current account. While these countries benefited from the oil price shocks, their deficits were caused by heavy borrowing in international markets to develop their natural resources.[8]

The story is somewhat more complicated for the non-OPEC developing countries. Within this group, too, a lower dependence on imported oil tends to be associated with a larger swing into deficit on the current account. Energy exporters could run deficits because of the need for foreign capital to develop their resources, while energy-poor nations in general had to cut back (relative to more favorably affected developing countries) from their previous levels of consumption and borrowing. But while developed countries as a group and non-OPEC developing countries as a group have a comparable dependence on imported oil, the deficit on the current account after the first oil shock worsened much more in the latter.[9] This difference is largely explained by the new availability of commercial finance to developing countries in the mid-1970s. Because the levels of debt outstanding at the start of the 1970s seemed relatively low in the developing countries, they were able to borrow to fill this "vacuum." Until the vacuum was filled, it was possible for the swing toward deficits on the current account to be greater in the developing countries.

The spending behavior of the OPEC nations, which differed markedly from many of the early predictions, is also roughly in line with the theory of current account behavior. Because they expected a permanent increase in the value of OPEC oil, they rapidly increased spending. The current account surpluses that piled up immediately following the two oil shocks were largely the result of domestic infrastructural constraints; countries as diverse as Saudi Arabia and Nigeria often needed to develop new harbors and roads before they could handle large-scale imports of consumer and capital goods. And even Saudi Arabia has used permanent adjustments of

8. Sachs, "The Current Account and Macroeconomic Adjustment in the 1970s," pp. 207–11. Dependence on imported oil is measured by the ratio of oil imports to GNP; the swing toward deficit is measured by the change in the ratio of the current account balance to GNP.

9. Ibid.

spending in addition to temporary reductions in its net foreign assets in responding to the current oil glut because it foresees the possibility that the current reduction in real oil prices may be permanent.[10]

Financing Payments Deficits

The theory of current account behavior implies the existence of a mechanism to adjust payments imbalances. One way to handle such imbalances would be through bilateral clearance systems in which each pair of countries agrees on how great an imbalance will be allowed in their bilateral trade and the surplus country provides the needed funding. Bilateral clearance systems, however, more often serve as a means of forcing bilateral trade to balance rather than providing funding to the partner "naturally" in deficit. In an integrated world capital market, on the other hand, the ability to run a trade deficit with a particular country depends not on the willingness of that particular country to fund the imbalance but on the willingness of investors in general. Thus a world capital market is a more efficient means of adjusting payments imbalances. But at the time of the first oil shock, it was not clear that an integrated world capital market existed. Most Western nations, in fact, were still involved in adjusting to the end of fixed exchange rates. It is necessary, therefore, to survey briefly the major changes that have taken place in the world financial system over the last decade.

Before the oil shocks, payments imbalances were characterized by surpluses in the industrial nations as a group offset by deficits in the non-oil developing countries; the figures for 1973 are fairly typical (see table 3-1). The size of these imbalances relative to income was smaller before 1973 than after. The Bank of England has calculated that the absolute sum of world current account surpluses and deficits (without regard to sign) has doubled from about 1 percent or 1.5 percent of the GNP of market economies to 2 percent to 3 percent of GNP since 1973–74.[11]

The new distribution of surpluses was in some ways the greatest threat to the use of financial adjustment. At the time of the first oil shock the OPEC nations were interested in investing in relatively few countries. The

10. The interrelationship of oil policy, development planning, and financial strategy in the OPEC countries is examined in much greater detail in chapters 5 through 7.

11. "Financing World Payments Balances," Bank of England *Quarterly Bulletin*, vol. 21 (June 1981), pp. 187–88.

flow of OPEC funds into the United States and West Germany seemed likely to exceed significantly the increase in American and German oil import bills, and Great Britain would probably receive funds sufficient to cover its deficits. But OPEC nations showed little desire to lend the requisite sums directly to other oil-consuming nations, developed or developing, partly because they lacked familiarity with those countries and partly because of the perceived risks of such lending. Thus some sort of intermediary would be needed to get funds from the surplus countries to oil-consuming nations. Banks, which had traditionally performed an intermediary role in domestic markets, were the only existing institutions that could easily assume this intermediary role in international markets. Yet because oil-consuming nations, particularly in the developing world, appeared to be greater risks than traditional bank customers, many feared that banks could not be depended on for large-scale recycling of OPEC surpluses or that such an intermediary role was undesirable.[12]

Such perceptions led to various proposals for multilateral funds to ease the recycling process. These proposals centered on establishing special mutual funds that would package various medium-term claims for resale to the OPEC nations.[13] To a certain extent these proposals favored the interests of the more advanced nations because they were designed to increase investment in new energy-saving technology in the West and to induce OPEC to share in the risk of lending to the many nations considered less creditworthy. It was suggested that some funds might consist entirely of government obligations, while others might guide OPEC surpluses into private investments, either by way of loans, purchases of equity, or participation in joint ventures. There were, however, major contradictions embedded in these plans. The proposals often assumed that the stronger Western nations would provide guarantees against inflation and exchange-rate fluctuations to the OPEC nations, but such guarantees would have

12. Even France, Italy, and Japan were at first listed among the nations that might have difficulties financing their deficits. See C. Dirck Keyser to Thomas D. Willett, "Contingency Planning: Consultations with Bankers," August 5, 1974, memorandum cited in appendix 8, "U.S. Government Studies, Analyses, Memoranda and Other Documents Discussing Concerns about, or Impact of OPEC Country Investments," *Federal Response to OPEC Country Investments in the United States*. Hearings before a Subcommittee of the House Committee on Government Operations, 97 Cong. 1 sess. (GPO, 1981), pt. 1, pp. 994–96.

13. One particular proposal received a fair amount of publicity. See Khodadad Farmanfarmaian and others, "How Can the World Afford OPEC Oil?" *Foreign Affairs*, vol. 53 (January 1975), especially pp. 215–22.

removed most of the element of risk sharing. Lower interest rates were also needed to encourage borrowing for investment, yet Western governments would then have had to provide guarantees or subsidies to satisfy OPEC's rate-of-return demands.

None of the proposals for mutual funds was realized, partly because the OPEC surpluses disappeared more quickly than was anticipated. Similar proposals appeared after the second oil shock and again proved unnecessary for the the same reason.[14] Some new multilateral programs for dealing with the surpluses eventually did take shape, however, mostly under the auspices of the International Monetary Fund. These included the oil facility (1974–75) and the Witteveen facility (established 1979), which borrowed from oil producers and lent the funds at below-market rates to the more seriously affected oil-consuming nations. The IMF also expanded the use of existing programs, such as the compensatory financing facility, by its members.

The main reason for the relative scarcity of special funds and programs, however, was the unexpected willingness of the banking system to intermediate between OPEC nations and the ultimate borrowers. This willingness was especially important for the non-oil developing countries. Before 1973, nations with surpluses tended to finance deficit nations directly through aid or foreign investment; after 1973, private capital markets funded most of these needs (table 3-2).

Although banks had not been the major source of funds in international markets before the 1970s, they were not complete strangers to foreign lending. The movement into international markets had begun after World War II, as large banks followed their multinational customers overseas. Several later developments favored a growing role for international banking markets in recycling surplus funds. One was the creation of Eurocurrency deposits, that is, currencies deposited with a bank office located outside the country issuing the currency. Although Eurocurrency deposits had existed before the oil shock, they became more important after 1973 because they allowed further margin for accommodation. OPEC preferences for bank claims in dollars no longer implied that American banks would bear all the risks of intermediation. Other important developments included reduced credit demands from the traditional domestic customers

14. For an example of such a proposal following the second oil shock, see Walter J. Levy, "Recycling Surplus Petrodollars via Internationally Issued Indexed Energy Bonds," *Middle East Economic Survey* (April 7, 1980), supplement, pp. 1–7.

Table 3-2. *Financing of Current Account Deficits in Non-Oil Developing Countries, 1973–82*
Billions of dollars

Source of financing	1973	1974	1975	1976	1977	1978	1979	1980	1981	1982
Current account deficit[a]	11.3	37.0	46.3	32.6	28.9	41.3	61.0	89.0	107.7	86.8
Financing through transactions not affecting net debt positions	10.3	14.6	11.8	12.6	14.4	17.9	23.9	24.1	28.0	25.1
Net unrequited transfers	5.5	8.7	7.1	7.5	8.2	8.2	11.6	12.5	13.8	13.2
Net direct investment flows	4.2	5.3	5.3	5.0	5.4	7.3	8.9	10.1	13.9	11.4
Use of reserves[b]	−10.4	−2.7	1.6	−13.0	−12.5	−17.4	−12.6	−4.5	−2.1	7.1
Net external borrowing	11.4	25.1	32.9	33.0	27.0	40.8	49.7	69.3	81.8	54.6
Official sources	4.9	6.8	11.7	10.5	11.4	13.8	13.3	17.6	23.0	19.5
Financial institutions[c]	9.8	18.6	23.2	21.5	14.7	25.6	35.9	53.3	52.5	n.a.

Source: IMF, *Annual Report 1983*, p. 33.

n.a. Not available.

a. Balance on goods, services, and private transfers (with sign reversed).

b. A minus sign indicates an accumulation of reserves.

c. This item is the sum of net long-term borrowing from financial institutions, exceptional financing, and "other net short-term borrowing." The IMF has described this sum as "a rough estimate, broadly consistent with national balance of payments statistics, of total net borrowing (short term and long term) from private banks."

of the banks and new forms for loan agreements. The use of margins over the London interbank offered rate (LIBOR) in pricing international loans reduced some of the risks for banks, which funded medium-term loans with shorter-term deposits whose price also was linked to LIBOR. Syndication of credits, with one or several large banks organizing loans and persuading other banks to participate, improved the prospects for countries that needed to borrow large amounts. Finally, cross-default clauses in loan agreements were instituted; under these clauses a country could be considered in default on all its loan agreements if it defaulted on any one of them. By giving all bank creditors essentially equal legal status, these clauses removed some of the threat of competition among banks to unload credits at the first sign of trouble.

A limited number of countries account for most of the recycling handled by banks. About 59 percent of foreign loans outstanding at the end of 1982 were made to developed countries.[15] Another 16 percent of the loans represented claims on major offshore banking centers, such as Singapore and Hong Kong. Thus 75 percent of bank lending was between developed countries or from developed countries to regional financial centers.

This lending is part of the recycling process, of course, but concern is usually focused on lending to developing countries and Eastern Europe. Table 3-3 presents data on the developing-country and Eastern European debtors to the Western banking system. Bank loans to developing countries increased particularly rapidly after the mid-1970s, rising from $127.7 billion at the end of 1977 to $362.7 billion at the end of 1982. Eastern European nations had borrowed $63.1 billion from banks at the end of 1982, although the rate of growth in their borrowings was much lower than that for developing countries. The ten largest borrowers accounted for 61.6 percent of this group's debt to Western banks, and the seven largest less developed countries accounted for 52.6 percent. With $62.9 billion in bank loans outstanding at the end of 1982, Mexico was the largest borrower, followed by Brazil with $60.5 billion of loans.

The magnitude of the risk inherent in loans to these countries depends to a large extent on their economic performance, which can be measured by such criteria as real income growth, export growth, and domestic investment and savings rates. On the basis of these criteria the major developing-country borrowers performed well until the end of 1979, although that impressive showing was due at least in part to the availability of bank

---

15. See Bank of England *Quarterly Bulletin*, vol. 23 (June 1983), table 13.1.

Table 3-3. *Bank Loans Outstanding to Eastern European
and Developing-Country Borrowers, December 31, 1977, 1980, 1982*
Billions of dollars

Country or group	1977	1980	1982
Eastern Europe[a]	40.2	70.1	63.1
Developing countries	127.7	279.6	362.7
Ten largest borrowers[b]	93.7	205.7	262.2
Mexico	20.3	42.5	62.9
Brazil	25.0	45.7	60.5
Venezuela	9.1	24.3	27.5
Argentina	4.9	19.9	25.7
South Korea	5.2	16.7	23.2
Soviet Union	11.7	13.4	14.6
Poland	8.8	16.2	13.9
Philippines	3.4	9.3	12.6
Chile	1.6	7.3	11.6
Yugoslavia	3.7	10.4	9.8

Source: Bank for International Settlements, *Maturity Distribution of International Bank Lending* (July 1978, July 1981, July 1983).

a. Includes Yugoslavia.

b. Among developing and Eastern European countries that are not financial centers; definition excludes Hong Kong and Singapore.

financing on easy terms.[16] After 1979, however, their situation deteriorated sharply, leading to reschedulings covering $111 billion of bank credits in 1983 alone.[17] High real interest rates and a slowing of trade damaged the prospects of all developing countries, and high oil prices hurt oil-importing countries. Mistakes in domestic policies also contributed to the debt crisis.[18] Finally, heavy reliance on short-term debt exacerbated the funding problems of less developed countries after 1982.[19]

Just as recycling OPEC surpluses was a key concern from 1973 until 1982, the debt crisis is likely to occupy the world's attention for a number

16. For a discussion of the performance of the largest developing-country borrowers, see Robert Solomon, "The Debt of Developing Countries: Another Look," *Brookings Papers on Economic Activity, 2:1981*, pp. 593–606.

17. "The Banks' Rescheduling Schedule," *Institutional Investor—International Edition* (September 1983), pp. 180D-82D.

18. For a discussion of the relative importance of domestic policies and external shocks in Latin America's recent difficulties see Thomas O. Enders and Richard P. Mattione, *Latin America: The Crisis of Debt and Growth* (Brookings Institution, 1984).

19. See John Calverley, "How the Cash Flow Crisis Floored the LDCs," *Euromoney* (August 1982), pp. 23–31; and Richard S. Dale and Richard P. Mattione, *Managing Global Debt* (Brookings Institution, 1983), pp. 11–13, 19–25.

of years. The connections between the current debt problems of developing countries and the disappearance of surplus OPEC funds are tenuous, however. Current account deficits have forced the OPEC countries to draw down their deposits at Western banks and have therefore removed one source of funds for international lending. Yet that need not lead to a global shortage of funds available to banks for lending, because by definition the disappearance of OPEC surpluses is matched by declines in developing country deficits or the reappearance of surpluses in the industrialized countries.[20] Rather, the debt crisis reflects the much-reduced willingness of banks to continue lending funds to developing countries whose prospects have become uncertain.

OPEC can still help support the global financial system. Nations such as Saudi Arabia and Kuwait may be able to lend additional funds to the International Monetary Fund and the World Bank, and those institutions could then relend them to developing nations. Arab banks, a small but important source of funds to several developing-country borrowers, could also participate more actively in reschedulings to ease the current problems, a possibility discussed in chapter 9.

OPEC Surpluses and Exchange Rates

The OPEC surpluses of the 1970s followed closely upon the switch from fixed to floating exchange rates. The concerns already present about the functioning of the international financial system were reinforced by fears that OPEC's financial decisions might either exacerbate or be influenced by fluctuations in the foreign exchange markets.

The links from foreign exchange markets to OPEC behavior have been very weak so far. First, OPEC used the Smithsonian realignment of exchange rates in 1971 as one justification for renegotiating its contract prices before 1973, although tight conditions in the oil market were actually the factor that forced the oil companies to yield. Second, when the dollar has been weak in foreign exchange markets, OPEC nations have discussed the possibility of accepting payment in dollars while pricing crude oil in a basket of currencies rather than in the dollar alone. By minimizing fluctuations in the purchasing power of a barrel of oil, such a

20. For example, the 1978 disappearance of OPEC surpluses was accompanied by large surpluses in Germany and Japan and an expanding role for their banks in the capital markets.

pricing mechanism could reduce the need for formal intra-OPEC negotiations to adjust oil prices to external conditions. This mechanism cannot help maintain real oil prices in a glutted market, however, without corresponding cutbacks in oil production. This need to adjust production has bedeviled all OPEC plans to adjust oil prices automatically to Western inflation and economic growth. It is conceivable, however, that a period of strong demand for OPEC oil coupled with a weak dollar could renew the demand for pricing oil in a basket of currencies.

Somewhat more attention has been devoted to the possible effects of OPEC financial decisions on foreign exchange markets. One worry was that OPEC might try to disrupt exchange markets by sudden transfers of funds from one currency to another; that concern is discussed in chapter 4. A more probable development is that the desire of OPEC states to diversify the currency composition of their financial holdings might gradually affect exchange rates—in particular, exchange rates between the dollar and the currencies of other industrial countries.

Foreign exchange markets, like all other markets, respond to changes in the supply and demand of commodities. In this case the commodities are dollars and other currencies. Studies have identified four aspects of OPEC behavior and of world oil trade that could potentially influence exchange rates: OPEC demand for assets denominated in dollars relative to the demand for dollars in Western portfolios; OPEC demand for American goods in relation to the demand for goods from other industrial countries; the speed with which OPEC surpluses disappear; and the relative dependence of Western nations on oil imports from OPEC.[21] These studies agree that the exchange rate value of the dollar should rise in the short run in response to OPEC balance of payments surpluses if the share of dollars in OPEC portfolios is greater than the share of dollars in non-U.S. portfolios. Whether the long-run value of the dollar after an oil shock will be higher than before the shock is unclear. These models do show, however, that the greater the OPEC preference for U.S. investments and goods and the lower the U.S. dependence on oil imports in relation to other oil con-

21. See Jerry Caprio and Peter B. Clark, "Oil Price Shocks in a Portfolio-Balance Model," International Finance Discussion Paper 181 (Washington, D.C.: Federal Reserve Board, June 1981); Paul Krugman, "Oil and the Dollar," Working Paper 554 (Cambridge, Mass.: National Bureau of Economic Research, September 1980); and Stephen S. Golub, "Oil Prices and Exchange Rates," Economic Journal, vol. 93 (September 1983), pp. 576–93.

sumers, the higher the final exchange rate of the dollar against other currencies.

These theoretical factors, which apply to real (inflation-adjusted) exchange rates, provide a partial explanation of the dollar's behavior in the 1970s. In particular, the shift from a strong dollar in 1975 to a weak dollar in 1978 may have been reinforced by the transition from large OPEC current account surpluses to an approximate balance. At the same time, it is clear that the conduct of American monetary policy has been far more important than the size of the OPEC surpluses or the behavior of OPEC investors in determining exchange rates. This has been especially true in the first part of the 1980s, when high U.S. real interest rates had a far greater effect on exchange rates than did OPEC investment decisions; the interest rates attracted funds from all parts of the world to the United States. Similarly, even though current OPEC deficits might put some mild pressure on the dollar because OPEC portfolios are heavily weighted toward the dollar, real interest rates and the prospect of large U.S. budget deficits will continue to have the largest impact on the dollar's value.

CHAPTER FOUR

Anticipated Threats from OPEC's Foreign Investments

OPEC INVESTMENTS led to some concern about their implications for Western economies. To a certain extent such worries have always existed about foreign investments, but they seemed more pronounced in the case of OPEC because of the amounts involved and because some oil nations tried to take economic action against the West. Members of the Organization of Arab Petroleum Exporting Countries, for instance, cut back production and instituted embargoes in response to the 1973 Arab-Israeli war, and Iran threatened to wage financial warfare on the United States during the hostage crisis. The concerns of Western nations are even more understandable when one considers that the oil price shocks are often thought to mark the end of an era of unchallenged Western (especially American) influence.

This chapter will evaluate the potential for financial disruptions emanating, intentionally or unintentionally, from actions taken by OPEC members collectively or individually. The focus will be on several scenarios that have generated the greatest concern: in particular, that the banks handling OPEC deposits might become overly dependent on those funds and might offer tempting targets should OPEC wish to exert pressure on the West; that sudden investment shifts from one currency to another could threaten the stability of the international financial system; or that OPEC countries might attempt to advance their national goals through investments in strategic industries.[1] On the other hand, the West itself might be able to exercise some leverage on OPEC nations because their investments are located in Western financial markets.

---

1. Discussion of the potential use of OPEC aid for political leverage will be delayed until chapter 8.

Table 4-1. *Investment Position of the Oil Exporters in the United States and at U.S. Banks, December 1982, 1983*[a]
Billions of dollars

Distribution	December 1982	December 1983
Treasury securities	41.40	40.39
Bills and certificates	7.88	6.77
Bonds and notes	33.52	27.97
Federal agency securities	6.04	5.65
Corporate bonds	5.92	5.15
Corporate equities	9.61	8.83
Bank liabilities	16.90	17.58
Other nonbank liabilities	5.43	4.28
Other U.S. government liabilities[b,c]	4.64	4.55
Direct investment[b]	4.38	5.03
Total investments in United States	94.31	85.81
Deposits at foreign branches of U.S. banks	20.83	18.81
Total	115.14	104.62

Sources: Data from Treasury Department, Office of International Banking and Portfolio Investment, prepared June 26, 1984; and Federal Reserve Board Statistical Release E.11 (March 14, 1984, and June 15, 1984).
a. OPEC nations plus Bahrain and Oman unless otherwise noted.
b. OPEC nations only.
c. Position, which consists of cumulative flows beginning in 1972, primarily includes prepayments for U.S. exports.

OPEC Investments and World Markets

One way of measuring the potential for disruptions from OPEC financial actions is to compare the size of the investments with the size of the markets in which they have been placed—for example, the market for U.S. government securities. The size of markets that involve securities with similar maturities, liquidity, and so forth must also be taken into account because world financial markets are fairly well integrated now, and that integration of markets may diminish or magnify the effects of disruptions on a particular market. Table 4-1 provides information on OPEC investments in U.S. and related international banking markets at the end of 1982 and 1983.

Absolute figures, such as the $94.3 billion of investments in the U.S. market or $37.7 billion at bank offices in the United States and at foreign branches of U.S. banks, can sound large and worrisome, but again it is important to remember the size of the relevant markets. For instance, OPEC had accumulated $41.4 billion in U.S. Treasury bills, certificates, notes, and bonds by the end of 1982. Yet total foreign holdings of marketable and nonmarketable Treasury securities equaled $149.4 billion at the end of 1982, while the total public debt then outstanding was $1.197 trillion.[2] Thus OPEC held less than 3.5 percent of all Treasury securities. This market is known for its depth and its large number of participants, and the power of OPEC to affect it would seem small. Even the fact that most of the OPEC purchases of Treasury securities were made by Middle Eastern members does not affect this result. Furthermore, the already limited role of OPEC investors in this market had declined by the end of 1983.

OPEC influence in U.S. stock and bond markets would seem even smaller. Equity portfolios totaled $9.6 billion at the end of 1982, and direct investments totaled $4.4 billion, amounts that are miniscule compared to the $1.72 trillion total value of corporate equities at that time. OPEC held $12 billion of non-Treasury bonds (that is, corporate, state, municipal, and agency issues) at the end of 1982 out of a total of $449.4 billion in state and local government securities and $570.9 billion in corporate bonds outstanding.[3] In these markets too the size of OPEC holdings declined during 1983 (table 4-1).

OPEC's threat to U.S. banks seems similarly limited. Its deposits at bank offices in the United States were $16.9 billion at the end of 1982; for a more comprehensive measure, OPEC deposits at bank offices in the United States and at foreign branches of U.S. banks amounted to $37.7 billion at the end of 1982. The deposits were placed mostly with the larger U.S. banks; they pale in comparison to the $802 billion of liabilities as of the same date at the domestic branches alone of the largest banks.[4] Nor does the concentration of OPEC deposits in the largest U.S. banks change the story significantly. As of March 31, 1981, Middle Eastern oil exporters held $19.8 billion at domestic and foreign branches of the six largest U.S. banks, which was 6.03 percent of the total $328.5 billion deposited at these banks on the same date.[5] The exposure of the next

---

2. Board of Governors of the Federal Reserve System, *Bulletin* (December 1983), p. A31.

3. Data on the value of equities and bonds outstanding in the United States are from Board of Governors of the Federal Reserve System, "Flow of Funds Accounts, First Quarter 1983," p. 56.

4. Board of Governors of the Federal Reserve System, *Bulletin* (February 1983), pp. A18, A20.

5. *Federal Response to OPEC Country Investments in the United States*, Hearings

fifteen banks was even smaller. Including non–Middle Eastern OPEC deposits would not significantly affect these results; over two-thirds of the OPEC deposits originate with Middle Eastern members.

OPEC investments are probably most concentrated in the Eurobanking market. Between 1974 and 1982 OPEC nations added $94.3 billion to their deposits in Eurobanking markets (see table 2-5). They probably had no more than $5 billion in Eurocurrency deposits at the end of 1973, which implies that they had no more than $100 billion at the end of 1982.[6] Total Eurocurrency liabilities in the main financial centers had reached $1.25 trillion by December 1982.[7] This measure of gross Eurocurrency liabilities includes interbank deposits, however, and a measure that excludes interbank deposits is preferable. A good estimate of the net size of the Euromarket is $850 billion, which implies that OPEC supplied a little under 12 percent of net Euromarket funds. Although this might at first appear to be a high concentration, there are several mitigating factors. These OPEC deposits involve more than one depositor, and in fact OPEC members with smaller reserves (for example, Nigeria, Ecuador, and Venezuela) keep most of their funds in the Euromarket. More importantly, that market has connections to all the main domestic banking markets in the West, and most Euromarket banks are actually branches of parent banks located in domestic markets, such as the United States or West Germany. Just as the funding of a Euromarket branch cannot be treated in isolation from the global funding operations of the parent bank, it would be a mistake to treat the 12 percent share of OPEC deposits in the funding of Euromarket

---

before a Subcommittee of the House Committee on Government Operations, 97 Cong. 1 sess. (GPO, 1981), pt. 1, p. 248.

6. The estimated $5 billion value of OPEC Eurocurrency deposits at the end of 1973 is obtained as follows: Susan Bluff (*OPEC Surplus* [New York: Bankers Trust Company, 1981], p. 9) has estimated that the OPEC members with positive net foreign assets had $15.4 billion of net foreign assets then; the debtors also had some assets. Use $17 billion as an estimate of gross assets. Then $2.5 billion is accounted for by deposits at banks in the United States and $5.8 billion by non-bank liabilities or other U.S. government liabilities, once one subtracts cumulative 1974–82 flows into those items, shown in table 2-5, from investment positions at the end of 1982, shown in table 4-1. Investments in U.S. corporate bonds, stocks, and Treasury securities were several hundred million dollars (see tables 2-5 and 4-1). Thus about $8 billion is left to be divided among all other investment instruments, and $5 billion seems a reasonable amount for Eurocurrency deposits.

7. This is the amount of foreign-currency-denominated liabilities of commercial banks within the reporting area of the Bank for International Settlements. See BIS, *Fifty-Third Annual Report* (1983), p. 112.

branches as equivalent to a reliance on OPEC deposits for 12 percent of the global funding needs of the parent firm.[8]

Another question of considerable interest is the share of these deposit liabilities denominated in dollars. According to data from the Bank for International Settlements, dollar-denominated claims accounted for 77.7 percent of Eurobanking liabilities at the end of 1982.[9] It is reasonable to assume that dollar-denominated claims held a similar share in OPEC Eurocurrency deposits, which would imply that these nations held $78 billion in Eurodollar deposits at the end of 1982. Some portion of other OPEC non-U.S., nonbanking investments are also probably denominated in dollars. The consensus seems to be that about 65 percent of the investments (that is, excluding foreign aid) are in dollars, which implies that OPEC nations added $220 billion to their net holdings of dollar-denominated investments from 1974 to 1982 and perhaps $250 billion to gross holdings.[10]

Partly because common estimates of the total dollar-denominated OPEC investments are so much larger than the $94.3 billion of identified OPEC investments in the United States, some people have wondered whether considerable U.S. placements might be going unnoticed. Indeed, if all dollar-denominated OPEC placements were in the domestic U.S. market, the market might be overly dependent on OPEC funding. But around $78 billion of dollar-denominated deposits are probably in the Eurobanking market alone, and dollar-denominated Eurobond issues account for some of the $103 billion of investments in other developed and nonmarket economies between 1974 and 1982 (see table 2-5). Rather, it is the gap between the $393.5 billion of identified investments and the at most $440 billion of investable OPEC funds at the end of 1982 that places an upper limit on hidden investments. The actual amount that could be in the United States is much smaller.

Furthermore, the conduits most commonly mentioned for disguising OPEC funds are relatively unimportant. Several Caribbean financial cen-

8. For example, the data presented earlier in this chapter on American bank liabilities to OPEC showed that deposits of Middle Eastern OPEC nations accounted for only 6 percent of the deposits of the largest banks.

9. There were $1.249 trillion of foreign-currency-denominated liabilities outstanding at Western commercial banks at the end of 1982, including $971 billion of dollar-denominated liabilities. See BIS, *Fifty-Third Annual Report*, p. 112.

10. This figure is applied to the total OPEC surplus minus foreign aid, not to identified investments.

ters have been particularly emphasized, with the Netherlands Antilles figuring most prominently. Federal government statistics indicate that foreign branches of U.S. banks had $2.61 billion in liabilities outstanding to the Netherlands Antilles at the end of 1982; bank offices within the United States had a further $3.63 billion, but $2.79 billion was in the form of liabilities to their own Netherlands Antilles offices.[11] Because of its tax laws and banking confidentiality, Luxembourg has also been suggested as a haven for such funds, yet foreign branch liabilities to Belgium and Luxembourg totaled only $4.86 billion at the end of 1982 and the liabilities of U.S. offices a further $2.71 billion, including $829 million to their own offices in Belgium and Luxembourg. Switzerland was the only substantial source of claims: $13.36 billion at foreign branches, and $29.37 billion at offices in the United States, including $1.98 billion to their own offices.

Before correcting for possible double counting, then, a total of $56.4 billion in claims from Switzerland, Luxembourg, and the Netherlands Antilles were outstanding at U.S. banks at the end of 1982. If all of this represented OPEC money, it would entail a significant underreporting of OPEC interest in the United States, especially vis-à-vis banks. A number of facts, however, militate against such an interpretation. First, Switzerland and Luxembourg are both important banking centers, and while some of these funds may represent hidden investments, it is unlikely that a large share represents hidden OPEC investments: these banks also handle funds from European and other clients trying to evade taxation or exchange controls or merely seeking greater privacy. Second, Swiss fiduciary accounts from Middle Eastern sources totaled $11.90 billion at the end of 1982 (see table 2-10). If one uses this $11.90 billion figure as an upper limit instead of the $42.73 billion outstanding to Switzerland at domestic and foreign branches of U.S. banks, the size of possible disguised OPEC investments via Switzerland is dramatically reduced. Third, Luxembourg, Switzerland, and the Netherlands Antilles do not appear to be important channels for hiding OPEC purchases of stocks and bonds because net purchases from 1974 to 1982 by these countries were very small.[12]

---

11. Data on the liabilities of foreign branches of U.S. banks are available in *Statistical Release* E.11 of the Federal Reserve System (December 15, 1983). Data on the liabilities of bank offices located in the United States (including branches of foreign banks) are available in *Treasury Bulletin* (Winter 1983), p. 96.

12. Gross purchases and sales were much larger, of course. See *Treasury Bulletin*, various issues.

These data suggest that hidden OPEC investments in the United States are small. If it were assumed that all the money in Swiss fiduciary accounts from Middle Eastern sources were placed with U.S. banks and that all U.S. bank liabilities to Belgium, Luxembourg, and the Netherlands Antilles (excluding liabilities to a bank's own branches) represented OPEC money, then $22.1 billion in OPEC deposits with U.S. banks would have gone unreported. Although this would increase the estimated exposure of U.S. banks at the end of 1982 from the identified $37.7 billion to approximately $60 billion, it would still be small in comparison to the $802 billion in domestic claims. In any case, it is likely that only a small fraction of that $22.1 billion represents bank liabilities to disguised OPEC investors. And the potential for hidden investments in most other U.S. financial markets is even smaller. These investments are probably concentrated in real estate (where the participants in a transaction are perhaps unaware of reporting rules or the transaction may be too small to require reporting) and are mostly transactions by private investors from the OPEC nations.

Potential Control of U.S. Industries

One of the issues often raised by foreign investment in the United States is the possibility of foreign control over strategic sectors or companies in the U.S. economy. This issue has come up repeatedly in regard to OPEC investments in the United States and is worth some discussion.

Financial instruments can be divided into two categories for discussions of controlling interest. The first includes government securities, corporate bonds, bank deposits, and commercial paper. These kinds of financial claims do not provide a vote in or control of management decisions and are therefore not relevant to a discussion of direct OPEC control (indirect control through the threat of financial disruptions is considered in the next section). The second category includes direct investments, property, and portfolio holdings of stocks. Ownership in any of these forms includes some measure of control (except in rare cases where stock may not carry voting rights).

In the United States, any holdings of less than 10 percent of a company's capital are defined as portfolio investments, while holdings of 10 percent or more are defined as direct investments. The 10 percent criterion is an arbitrary standard intended to reflect differences in the degree of control.

Investments in which there are no public issues of shares, particularly real estate investments, are also classified by the same standard. The major real estate investments by OPEC governments or their private citizens are usually covered by statistics on direct investments.

OPEC private and public-sector investors had portfolio holdings of U.S. equities worth $9.6 billion at the end of 1982, almost all in the hands of Middle Eastern investors; direct investment was $4.4 billion. These are not significant shares of the overall U.S. market. The investments have been focused on the larger U.S. companies, but OPEC members have rarely made large investments in any one firm, apparently because of the legal requirement that holdings of 5 percent or more of outstanding shares by any controlling group must be disclosed to the Securities and Exchange Commission. Kuwait has been the most active in purchasing U.S. stocks and has portfolios managed by a number of U.S. banks. Government investors in Saudi Arabia and the United Arab Emirates have also purchased American stocks, but on a much smaller scale.

Confidential information on Kuwait's five portfolios with Citibank was leaked to the press in early 1981.[13] These five portfolios, which at that time had a market value of $3.7 billion, represented a major part of Kuwait's investments in U.S. stocks, although smaller portfolios were probably maintained at other financial firms. The investments were well diversified, representing from 1 percent to slightly over 2 percent of the common stock of a number of large U.S. companies. Investments related to natural resources included $457.2 million in oil stocks and a further $90.2 million in oil service firms. Still, the amounts involved hardly gave Kuwait control over any single company. Although this information seemed to confirm that diversified stock purchases by OPEC members did not involve any particular control of the U.S. economy, newspaper articles worried that a more aggressive strategy that could upset the stock market was soon to be implemented. The supposed strategy was to trade blocks of 10,000 shares that move up and down within a two- to three-point range in

13. See Dan Dorfman, "Kuwait Oil Profits Buy $7 Billion Worth of U.S. Securities," *Washington Post*, May 31, 1981, and "Kuwait Puts Citibank on Investment Hot Seat," *Washington Post*, June 7, 1981. It was later reported that most of the Citibank portfolio was moved to Morgan Stanley and that Chemical Bank may have become manager of the rest. See "Bankers Say Kuwait Spurned Citibank, Shifting $4 Billion to Morgan Stanley," *Wall Street Journal*, September 15, 1981. These articles are reprinted in *Federal Response to OPEC Country Investments in the United States*, pt. 1, pp. 382–85.

a given week. Citibank was to implement this strategy by selling at a high price and buying the block back when the security's price had dropped two to three points. Furthermore, one Kuwaiti official had suggested that Citibank turn over 5 percent of the portfolio every week, which would have been a significant increase in activity. Although the article editorialized that these suggestions "would surely accelerate ulcer-producing yo-yo moves in the marketplace,"[14] it is more likely that block trading in response to price changes would lead to more trading within a narrower band. After all, price fluctuations should be smoothed not exaggerated when rising stocks are sold sooner and falling stocks bought sooner. This strategy would be difficult to implement successfully, however, because the portfolio manager would have to identify market turning points. As for the proposal for faster turnover in the portfolio, it would probably have no particular effect on market variability.

Almost by definition, direct investments are more likely to involve the problem of foreign control than portfolio investments. OPEC total direct investment has been relatively small, however, despite its concentration on real estate, finance, and energy. Although foreign purchases of real estate have occasionally generated intense interest, they are insignificant. OPEC investors have purchased hotels, shopping centers, and one resort island, but many of these purchases have been made by private investors, and no one investor has much money in U.S. property. In particular, the concern that investors from Middle Eastern oil-exporting nations have acquired large amounts of agricultural land is not supported by the available data. At the end of 1982 they held only 38,300 acres (ownership of U.S. agricultural land by all foreign investors totaled 13.5 million acres, slightly more than 1 percent of all privately owned U.S. agricultural land).[15]

Investments in banking have always attracted attention, yet in this sector, too, OPEC purchases have not involved a significant share of any local market, let alone of state or national markets. Besides, a number of state and federal agencies already must review such investments before they are completed.

14. Dorfman, "Kuwait Puts Citibank on Investment Hot Seat."

15. Canadian, British, and Hong Kong investors accounted for 7.86 million acres, or almost 60 percent of foreign holdings; see Federal Reserve Bank of Chicago, *International Letter* (July 29, 1983), pp. 2–3.

Purchases of energy-related industries cannot be dismissed quite as quickly. Unlike most other OPEC direct investments, energy investments have usually involved governments rather than private individuals, and thus contain the potential for conflict between American energy security and OPEC energy strategies. Kuwaiti investments in the energy sector have excited the greatest concern. In 1981 the Kuwait Petroleum Corporation (controlled by the Ministry of Oil) announced plans for three large energy investments in the United States: a refinery joint venture with Pacific Resources in Hawaii ($185 million); an exploration venture with AZL Resources ($50 million); and the $2.5 billion acquisition of Santa Fe International.[16] Still, such investments, even in combination with Kuwait's portfolio holdings, do not involve significant control of the energy sector of the U.S. economy.[17]

Purchases of defense-related companies also would pose problems, but so far no such purchase has been identified. In fact, the case that has gathered the most attention involved a private individual's stake in Whittaker Corporation, which conducted about 5 percent of its business with the Department of Defense, although only 1 percent required security clearances. The Department of Defense already has procedures in place for judging any foreigner's influence on U.S. companies working on defense contracts. Furthermore, regardless of the location of ownership of a firm, only those employees with clearances actually have access to restricted

16. The venture with Pacific Resources was never realized. Chapter 6 discusses these particular investments within the context of the Kuwaiti investment strategy.

17. Various interesting side issues were involved in the Santa Fe case. One of these involved C. F. Braun, a subsidiary of Santa Fe that had done contracting work at nuclear facilities. The work had centered on the design of buildings that would house other companies' nuclear technology, however, rather than on the nuclear technology itself. This issue was resolved by having those subsidiaries placed in a blind trust so that the Kuwaiti government earned the profits of C. F. Braun without having management control. Braun also withdrew from another such design contract.

The second issue involved Santa Fe International's ownership of mining leases on federal lands. The issue centered on whether there were reciprocal rights for American companies in Kuwait, which is the criterion stated in the Mineral Leasing Act of 1920. Santa Fe leases would be void if Kuwait was not ruled a reciprocal country (for details, see *Federal Response to OPEC Country Investments in the United States*, pt. 2). So far the Department of the Interior has forbidden Kuwaiti investors to acquire new energy and mineral leases on federal lands, but the status of earlier leases is unresolved; see "Kuwaitis Barred from Acquiring Federal Leases," *Wall Street Journal*, March 11, 1983.

information, so it is difficult to see how stock purchases would make access to secret information any easier.[18]

Overall, then, one must conclude that OPEC investments have not led to significant control of any market, industry, or sector in the U.S. economy.

Possibilities for Disrupting Financial Markets

Observers have often speculated that market disruptions could emanate from OPEC financial decisions and have considered how financial markets would respond. Such disruptions could occur in two basic ways: first, deposits could be abruptly withdrawn from American bank branches here and abroad to be transferred to dollar claims outside the United States and its financial institutions; second, sizable dollar holdings might be switched into other currencies. In discussing either possibility it is simplest to assume that the OPEC nations act as a group. Although such coordination is unlikely, this assumption provides an upper limit on the magnitude of the threat.

If OPEC nations decided to move their deposits simultaneously from domestic and foreign branches of U.S. banks to Eurodollar deposits at non-U.S. banks, American banks would somehow have to borrow dollars to continue funding their previously contracted loans. But OPEC's actions would have changed only the distribution of dollar liabilities, not their net amount, so a clear source of funds would be available. The non-American banks to which OPEC transfers the deposits would suddenly have more funds than they need at the going interest rate—exactly the amount, in fact, that the American banks would want to borrow. The necessary funds would be available through the Euromarkets.

That is the basic scenario, to which a number of details can be added. There is no reason to presume that the average interest rate would change one way or the other, although certain inefficiencies are present in the system. The American banks might have to pay a slightly higher rate, the OPEC nations would probably receive a slightly lower rate (non-American banks could not immediately use the funds for their own customers), and the non-American banks would charge a small fee, perhaps 0.1 percent,

---

18. For details on Department of Defense procedures and the Whittaker Corporation's contracts, see *Federal Response to OPEC Country Investments in the United States*, pt. 3.

Table 4-2. *Maturity Distribution of OPEC Dollar Deposits at Foreign Branches of U.S. Banks, End of 1980*

Maturity	Percentage of total
Less than three days	21
Three days to one month	31
One month to three months	26
Three months to six months	16
Six months to one year	4
Over one year	2

Source: *Federal Response to OPEC Country Investments in the United States,* Hearings before a Subcommittee of the House Committee on Government Operations, 97 Cong. 1 sess. (Government Printing Office, 1981), pt. 1, p. 240.

for an interbank transaction.[19] Thus two groups would suffer in the long run: American banks would be at a slight competitive disadvantage against non-American banks, and OPEC nations would receive a lower interest rate on their holdings.

The amounts involved and the speed of transfer would also be important. The greater the sums involved, the larger the margin accruing to the non-American banks and the greater the loss that American banks and the OPEC nations would suffer. The losses for OPEC could be considerable. There are reports that OPEC had to accept lower-than-market rates of return in 1974 when its desire to hold deposits was greater than banks' desire to issue such liabilities.[20] Furthermore, there are limits on how fast OPEC nations could transfer their money. Table 4-2 presents data on the maturity distribution of dollar deposits at foreign branches of U.S. banks at the end of 1980; the present distribution of OPEC deposits probably does not differ significantly. If so, only 21 percent of the deposits could be moved in three days and only 52 percent within a month. Thus of the $37.7 billion in OPEC holdings at American banks, less than $8 billion would be involved in the first three days, an amount which would be relatively easily handled in a $1.25 trillion market.

19. A General Accounting Office study cited a loss to American banks of a few basis points (hundredths of 1 percent) or a few thirty-seconds of a percent above the cost of direct OPEC deposits. See *Are OPEC Financial Holdings a Danger to U.S. Banks or the Economy?* EMD-79-45 (GAO, June 11, 1979), p. 20.

20. A standard discount of 0.5 percentage point and a top figure of 6 percentage points are quoted in a memorandum reprinted in *Federal Response to OPEC Country Investments in the United States*, pt. 1, p. 1000. Further references to below-market rates for OPEC deposits in 1974 appear in memorandums cited on pages 984 and 993 of the appendixes.

It is also unlikely that individual banks would be affected. OPEC deposits were only 6.03 percent of total deposits for the six largest U.S. banks in March 1981, and the share for other banks was even smaller.[21] The funds that OPEC could move within three days amount to no more than 1.5 percent of the total deposits at these banks, which makes it highly unlikely that individual banks would be in trouble. The Federal Reserve System could use discount window lending to support them during the transition if there were any problems. Furthermore, with only a few banks heavily involved, the situation should be easy enough to monitor.

Banks, of course, can and do have other means of protecting themselves from such withdrawals. They hold some assets, such as Treasury bills and government bonds, that can quickly be liquidated, and their capital base helps to guarantee solvency against any sort of shock. Banks also match the maturities of assets and liabilities to a certain extent, although assets on average have a longer maturity than liabilities. Furthermore, bank examinations check whether a bank has an excessive reliance on any one source of funds. Apparently, dependence on OPEC deposits has never landed a bank on the problem list.[22]

Although it is possible that because of OPEC moves other investors might also withdraw funds from U.S. banks, that threat would also be ameliorated by market forces. Non-American banks would be unable to use all funds, deposit rates would be bid down, and the transfer would be halted. Of course, non-OPEC sources might not move funds. For example, nothing in particular happened when OPEC countries ran down deposits at U.S. banks in 1980. Therefore, one must conclude that because of the relatively small size of available OPEC bank deposits, a shift of dollar deposits from U.S. banks to other banks would be easily digested. Market mechanisms should undo most of the transfer, while current central bank powers should be sufficient to handle any problems during the transition.[23]

The financial effects of a simple shift from U.S.-based dollar claims to non-U.S.-based dollar claims are small enough that an OPEC decision to

21. GAO, *Are OPEC Financial Holdings a Danger to U.S. Banks or the Economy?* p. 20.

22. *Federal Response to OPEC Country Investments in the United States*, pt. 1, p. 248.

23. A similar story is applicable to the government securities market. Because of the relatively small amounts involved and because the Federal Reserve is already constantly involved in the secondary market and could use its powers to aid that market, it is unlikely to come under pressure through OPEC actions.

make such a shift in order to exert pressure on the United States is unlikely. A decision to abandon the dollar would thus appear to be the more threatening disruption. It would involve more financial variables, would lead to more uncertainty, and would probably require a coordinated Western response. Of course, such a transfer is also the least plausible possibility, because it would impose high costs on OPEC. Most of the funds would have to be moved into Western markets and Western currencies because of their sheer magnitude, and even then only a small part could be moved at the current market exchange rate. OPEC nations would thus suffer losses on all the dollar holdings they were unable to move and would have to pay transaction costs on the holdings they did manage to move.

Actual movement of OPEC claims might take months or OPEC might only threaten to move out of the dollar. Yet a threat would have almost the same effects as an actual transfer in the short run because the uncertainty induced in the market could lead other investors to sell dollars. Most of the effects on the dollar and on OPEC investors would be felt the first day, even if the move were to take place over a long period of time: interest rates would probably increase, the dollar would fall, and the value of OPEC holdings would be diminished. The West is already probably able to deal with such a disruption. Formal agreements that specifically refer to OPEC investment moves would be difficult to negotiate, but the major Western governments would be able to cooperate quickly and effectively without new agreements. Because an appreciating exchange rate vis-à-vis the dollar would reduce exports and employment in Western countries, they would use such measures as capital controls or would lower the interest rates available to foreign depositors to limit the damage. Central banks already have a number of other mechanisms, such as currency swaps or credit lines, that could be used to limit the consequences of such currency transfers on exchange rates and the money supply.[24] These mechanisms, however, should be used in conjunction with exchange rate changes; the costs to OPEC of disruptive funds transfers would otherwise be too small. The Federal Reserve System also has powers it could use to support American financial markets, and other central banks have the necessary powers to protect their own financial systems and to work with the Federal Reserve to preserve international financial arrangements. A

24. The financial policies available to U.S. and foreign monetary authorities to counter any actions to destabilize the dollar are discussed in more detail in Arthur I. Bloomfield and Richard C. Marston, "Policies for an OPEC Dollar Run," *Journal of Post-Keynesian Economics*, vol. 3 (Spring 1981), pp. 299–311.

complete move out of the dollar by OPEC or by a single nation such as Saudi Arabia or Kuwait would be a serious matter, but the Western nations would have both the incentives and mechanisms for working together.

A small adjustment in currency holdings of the OPEC nations would theoretically have some effects on foreign-exchange markets, but these effects would probably go unnoticed amid the daily trading. If such movements were announced after they were completed, there would be little reason for other investors to alter their currency holdings solely because of OPEC's past activities. If, however, these movements appeared to be politically motivated and to presage further OPEC movements, then the standard scenario unfolds once more.

One further option available to U.S. authorities for countering any intentionally disruptive OPEC capital movements is a freeze implemented under the International Emergency Powers Act. The United States has implemented financial freezes several times in the past and there is no reason to doubt that it would be willing to do so again.

The Freeze on Iranian Assets

Among OPEC nations, only Iran has threatened to withdraw funds from U.S. banks in the hope of damaging the United States. Although the threat was made shortly after the seizure of the U.S. embassy and American hostages in Tehran, U.S. concerns began as the shah's government was falling, almost a year before the hostage seizure and asset freeze. While politicians worried about the loss of a pro-Western state in the strategic Gulf region, banking officials were concerned about loans outstanding to Iran from American banks.

Although Iran had accumulated a surplus of about $26 billion from 1974 to 1978 (see table 2-4), various Iranian banks and ministries had continued to borrow for domestic projects. In early 1979 the banks began to reevaluate their exposure and the possibility of calling in loans to Iran because its new government issued public statements bringing into question its responsibility for the loans, even though it continued to make timely payments.

Once American hostages were seized on November 4, 1979, various ways of maintaining pressure on Iran were discussed, especially political and economic methods that would delay the need for military action. Although a freeze on Iranian assets was among the policy options presented to President Carter in the days immediately following the seizure, the first economic measure to be used was an embargo of Iranian oil that went into effect on November 12. The freeze on assets was not implemented in the first few days because it was thought that several months would be required before it affected Iran—no one expected the hostage crisis to last that long—and treasury officials felt the freeze might cause other nations to doubt the security of U.S. banks and dollar assets.[25]

Yet only ten days into the hostage crisis the Treasury Department assented to a freeze. This policy change was apparently triggered by Foreign Minister Bani-Sadr's announcement that Iran intended to withdraw its money from U.S. banks, an amount the Iranian government estimated at $12 billion.[26] Early on the morning of November 14, President Carter froze all assets of the government of Iran in the United States and under the control of U.S. banks, businesses, and individuals outside the United States.

The exact rationale of the American government is murky. A White House statement issued in conjunction with the executive order freezing the assets cited only one purpose: "to insure that claims on Iran by the United States and its citizens are provided for in an orderly manner."[27] Administration officials are said to have concluded that Iran's plan to withdraw its funds was based on political rather than financial considerations and that Iran "decided to opt for the propaganda benefits of a public announcement." It was also reported that Treasury Secretary G. William Miller had confirmed that the Iranians "made no immediate move to withdraw their assets in the hours after the announcement, which was received in Washington about 5 a.m. Noting this, the administration took several hours to notify allied and oil-producing nations, especially Saudi Arabia, before Mr. Carter signed the order freezing the assets soon after 8 a.m."[28]

Furthermore, Robert Carswell (then deputy secretary of the treasury) emphasized the desire to obtain the release of the hostages and to protect

25. The Treasury's contingency planning for a freeze to protect bank claims had begun in February 1979, although it was then viewed as unnecessary. See *Iran: The Financial Aspects of the Hostage Settlement Agreement*, House Banking, Finance and Urban Affairs Committee, 97 Cong. 1 sess. (GPO, 1981), pp. 3–6.

26. "Bank Account Moves by Iran, U.S., Are Seen Setting Bad Precedents," *Wall Street Journal*, November 15, 1979.

27. *New York Times*, November 15, 1979.

28. Terence Smith, "Carter's Strategy in Iran," *New York Times*, November 15, 1979. European markets were already open, and Iran could have tried moving the funds because 5 a.m. Washington time would have been 10 a.m. in London.

property claims of U.S. individuals and corporations. He said that the resources immediately available to Iran for an attack on the dollar were $1 billion to $2 billion. Thus the "risk of Iran destabilizing the dollar with that level of resources was not significant," but the "threat to the dollar was presented to other nations as a major reason for action."[29]

Other official statements were less clear in their evaluation of the significance of Iran's threat. During congressional testimony, Under Secretary of the Treasury Anthony Solomon cited the hostage seizure and "an intent to damage or destroy the dollar" as factors guiding the administration's decision. He described the freeze as a response to "an announced hostile explanation for the funds and the intent to inflict political damage and monetary and financial damage."[30] Whether Solomon felt that Iranian actions could have damaged the dollar or whether the threat merely provided a convenient excuse to implement a freeze went unasked and unanswered at these hearings. Karin Lissakers, on the other hand, has asserted that what triggered the freeze was "fear that a sudden withdrawal of those assets might set off a major currency and banking crisis for the United States" and quoted Solomon as saying, "our central concern that morning was the dollar, not the banks." She continued that "the Saudis urged the administration to blame the freeze on the threat to the dollar, not on the seizure of the hostages," but this leaves unresolved the question of whether U.S. officials seriously believed in a threat to the dollar.[31]

Overall, the delayed response of the administration seems to show that it doubted the existence of a serious direct threat. It is, however, conceivable that government officials were worried that the lack of a strong U.S. response would damage the government's credibility on other policy matters, in particular, the monetary measures adopted barely one month earlier to control money growth and inflation and to support the dollar.

Legally the freeze was important because it attempted to extend U.S. jurisdiction to liabilities of foreign branches of U.S. banks, an action that ran counter to the belief that Eurodollar deposits were under the legal authority of the country in which they were placed. This extraterritorial

29. Robert Carswell, "Economic Sanctions and the Iran Experience," *Foreign Affairs*, vol. 60 (Winter 1981–82), p. 258.

30. *International Financial Conditions*, Hearings before the Subcommittee on International Finance of the Senate Committee on Banking, Housing and Urban Affairs, 96 Cong. 1 sess. (GPO, 1980), pp. 17, 18.

31. Karen Lissakers, "Money and Manipulation," *Foreign Policy*, no. 46 (Spring 1982), pp. 107, 112, 114. The source for her quotation of Under Secretary Solomon was not identified.

Table 4-3. *Estimates of Iranian Assets Blocked on November 14, 1979*
Millions of dollars

Assets	Estimate of November 19, 1979	Census of October 25, 1980
Total investment in the United States	3,684	4,451
U.S. government securities	1,235	1,274
Corporate stocks and bonds	35	65
Commercial bank liabilities	1,426	1,177
Other investments[a]	988	1,935
Gold held in the United States	638	636
Assets blocked abroad	4,523	4,609
Banks	4,523	4,546
Nonbanks	n.a.	63
Total	8,845	9,696

Source: *Federal Response to OPEC Country Investments in the United States*, pt. 1, p. 176.
n.a. Not available.
a. Includes nonbank liabilities and U.S. government accounts.

control tied up an additional $4.5 billion of Iranian deposits (see table 4-3). As a result, Iran was unable to make loan payments and was declared in default. There was a flurry of lawsuits: Iran attempted to use the courts to free the claims with U.S. institutions outside the United States, and American corporations filed lawsuits worldwide to attach Iranian assets to ensure payment of their own claims against Iran. The legality of the freeze on claims in U.S. institutions abroad remains untested because none of these cases was ruled on.

The hostages were released in January 1981. A major part of the negotiations by this time had centered on resolving the various financial claims and counterclaims. The final agreement was that Iran's $2.35 billion in gold at the Federal Reserve Bank of New York and approximately $5.5 billion in deposits at foreign branches (this included fourteen months of interest) were to be transferred to an escrow account of the Algerian government at the Bank of England. From that account, $3.6 billion was to be used to pay off Iran's debts to syndicates that included U.S. banks, the country was to receive $2.8 billion, and $1.4 billion was to remain to settle other U.S. bank claims against it.[32] A second account, opened with a deposit of $1 billion, was to be used to pay off the nonbank claims

32. Statement of Warren Christopher, former deputy secretary of state, in *The Iran Agreements*, Hearings before the Senate Committee on Foreign Relations, 97 Cong. 1 sess. (GPO, 1981), pp. 59–60.

adjudicated before a special panel. Whenever this second account dipped below $500 million, Iran was supposed to restore it to that level; it was therefore dubbed the "bottomless pitcher" account.[33] The settlement left unanswered the question of whether Iran's actions actually posed a threat to individual U.S. banks, to the dollar, or to the domestic or international financial system.

Table 4-3 lists two estimates of the Iranian assets blocked on November 14, 1979. The first was prepared five days after the freeze; the second is from a Treasury Department census conducted almost a year later. The Iranian assets totaled $9.7 billion, $4.6 billion of which were blocked abroad. Bank liabilities amounted to $5.7 billion of the total. The discrepancies between estimates are relatively unimportant and would not have altered the evaluation of the overall threat. The actual sizes are relatively minor for any of the markets. In particular, the $5.7 billion of liabilities at branches of U.S. banks was a small part of their total liabilities, even if all of the funds could have been withdrawn immediately.[34]

Any fear of damage to the dollar appears unjustifiable. Admittedly, the value of the dollar had been under some pressure on foreign exchange markets before the October 6, 1979, change in Federal Reserve procedures was implemented.[35] But Iran did not have $12 billion of deposits that it could move quickly, and the effects of a move of only several billion dollars would probably have been small for a foreign-exchange market whose U.S.-based traders alone had $32 billion in contracts that changed hands every day.[36] The value of the dollar did drop slightly in trading that day. The Iranian announcement was made just after European markets opened, and the U.S. response took three hours. During this time, perhaps in anticipation of a $12 billion transfer, the dollar dropped from 1 percent to 2 percent against most currencies, but recovered about half of its value by the close of European trading when it became obvious that no unusual

33. Ibid., p. 31.
34. An earlier announcement by Foreign Minister Bani-Sadr that referred to $12 billion of Eurodollar deposits at U.S. banks appears mistaken and may have meant $12 billion in deposits at all banks. Iran had $8.04 billion of deposits at non-U.S. banks at the end of 1979 according to the Bank for International Settlements, *Maturity Distribution of International Bank Lending* (July 1980).
35. Those new procedures focused on monetary aggregates rather than interest rates as a way of controlling money growth.
36. Based on data for March 1980 reprinted in Federal Reserve Bank of Chicago, *International Letter* (October 7, 1983), p. 1.

amounts of dollars were being exchanged.[37] It recovered most of the rest of its value the next day, once the details of the freeze were known. Thus even Iran's much overstated figure of an immediate $12 billion transfer did not cause undue pressure in the market before the freeze was announced. The small decline in the dollar's value in anticipation of the transfer demonstrates how difficult it would be for an OPEC nation to make a financial threat without suffering from its own decision.

Another possible result of Iran's action was that individual banks may have been endangered as a result of large loans to Iran or a heavy reliance on Iranian deposits. But loans seem unlikely to have led to serious problems for the banks. The settlement at the end of the crisis included $3.6 billion to pay off all loans from all syndicates that included U.S. banks. At least ten American banks were involved, so any loss, although painful, should have been manageable. Bank of America, Chase Manhattan, and Citibank also had made nonsyndicated loans worth $1 billion.[38] Yet some of that amount would have been recovered in court proceedings against Iran and through the attachment of Iranian assets.

The possibility that deposit withdrawals would have harmed individual American banks seems almost as remote. Speculation here centered on the Bank of America, which was reported to have bid aggressively for Iranian deposits. Most other American banks had lost Iranian deposits since the revolution, and the most likely target of Iranian wrath, Chase Manhattan, had very few left by November 1979. Though no official figures were published for individual banks, it has been reported that Bank of America had approximately $3 billion of Iranian deposits at overseas branches, and that Iran had deposits of $400 million at both Chase Manhattan and Citibank.[39] Even Bank of America should have found the loss of Iranian deposits manageable, albeit embarrassing, given that it had $89.3 billion in total deposits at the end of 1980.[40]

For all these reasons, it seems rather unlikely that the Iranian case

37. "Currency Trading in Turmoil," *New York Times*, November 15, 1979.

38. Peter Truell, "Banks Pressured to Boost Interest on Iranian Funds," *Wall Street Journal*, February 1, 1983.

39. Lissakers, "Money and Manipulation," p. 112; Truell, "Banks Pressured to Boost Interest on Iranian Funds."

40. Press reports did not mention that American banks had any problems getting funds the day of the freeze, even during the hours between the Iranian threat and the U.S. freeze. The data on Bank of America's total deposits are from *American Banker*, March 5, 1982, p. 65.

presented a situation in which the financial system or individual banks were dangerously exposed. The only real commercial threat cited, the possible nonpayment of loans, is irrelevant to the analysis of OPEC investments abroad. Furthermore, analysis of the statements and behavior of American officials and institutions at that time indicates that they, too, considered the threat minimal. The freeze seems to have been a response to a political problem.

Summary

OPEC's foreign assets, though considerable, pose little threat to American or Western interests. The investments have not led to significant control of any economic sector or of the funding sources of the financial sector. Any OPEC nation would have difficulty using its foreign investments to manipulate the West. The diversification of investments, the limits on how much can be quickly moved, the structure of financial markets themselves, and central bank procedures combine to limit the threat. Western nations also have some reverse leverage on OPEC because those OPEC members with the largest financial claims are most dependent on Western markets for maintaining the value of the investments. In many ways the freeze of Iranian assets has made the reverse leverage of the United States more credible.

One can imagine unlikely situations in which one of the states with significant surpluses would threaten to pull its funds out of the United States solely for political reasons. For instance, after an extreme change of government, a nation might not be particularly worried about the value of its claims. The United States would then have to use its existing powers, including currency swap lines and the Federal Reserve's lender-of-last-resort capability, to supplement market forces. But there would be little reason to fear the results of a freeze used in response to such hostile threats. Existing powers should therefore be sufficient for the monetary authorities, especially when supplemented by the threat of such a freeze.

CHAPTER FIVE

Saudi Arabia's Investment Strategy

SAUDI ARABIA has indisputably emerged as a major figure in the world financial system during the past decade. A cumulative current account surplus of $160 billion from 1974 to 1982 (this includes government and private-sector claims) has given the country both potential influence on the financial system and a stake in its smooth functioning. At the same time its expanded role has focused attention on Saudi financial moves and on the Saudi Arabian Monetary Agency (SAMA), the institution that manages the bulk of the government's foreign assets. Some of this attention is generated by purely commercial interests, since SAMA's holdings represent one of the largest single sources of funds in the world. Yet occasionally there have been concerns premised on a belief that the investments are highly variable or that they respond to interests different from (and perhaps inimical to) those of Western nations. The huge inflow of funds generated by the second oil shock is typical of the changing economic factors that could lead to a change in strategy, while the continuing Arab-Israeli dispute or the Iranian freeze are potentially significant political factors. The heavy reliance of Middle Eastern nations on placements in the United States has declined somewhat, but the question of whether this indicates major shifts in strategy is much more difficult to answer. This chapter examines that question by focusing on Saudi investments during the 1974–83 period.

The Size of Saudi Arabia's Foreign Investments

Saudi Arabia is by far the largest holder of foreign assets among the OPEC nations, having added about $160 billion to its net holdings of foreign assets between 1974 and 1982 (see table 2-4). Low demand for oil has recently forced the nation to draw on its holdings, however, and by one estimate the current account deficit reached $20 billion in 1983.[1] Still, after including the $5.08 billion of net foreign assets of SAMA and the Saudi commercial banks at the end of 1973,[2] net government and private-sector foreign holdings should be $145 billion at the end of 1983.

The Saudi government controls the bulk of the foreign investments. SAMA directly controlled $134.02 billion near the end of September 1983, its gross holdings of foreign assets having reached $140.97 billion toward the end of 1982.[3] The Saudi Fund for Development appears to be the other main government agency with overseas assets. It had disbursed $1.39 billion of its own loans and administered another $249 million of loans for the government by the end of 1981.[4] Other government agencies may have small amounts invested overseas. Private-sector holdings have also grown rapidly in recent years. Commercial banks held $17.76 billion in gross foreign assets at the end of 1982 and $16.02 billion in net foreign assets; the figures had fallen to $16.32 billion and $15.06 billion, respectively, at the end of September 1983.[5] Other private sources could account for another $6 billion to $8 billion in overseas investments. Overall SAMA controlled 84 percent of Saudi Arabia's foreign assets in mid-1983, other government agencies perhaps 2 percent, and the private sector almost 15 percent.[6]

Economic Factors Guiding Investment Policy

Three broadly defined sets of of factors provide most of the economic explanation of OPEC investment decisions, regardless of country. Tradi-

1. As estimated by Wharton Middle East Economic Service and reported in "Oil Exporters Head for Huge Deficit," *Middle East Economic Digest* (November 18, 1983), p. 2.

2. International Monetary Fund, *International Financial Statistics, 1983 Yearbook* (IMF, 1983), p. 439.

3. The dates are approximate because Saudi statistics are prepared according to lunar months, not according to the Gregorian calendar; see IMF, *International Financial Statistics*, vol. 37 (June 1984), pp. 386–87.

4. Organization for Economic Cooperation and Development, *Aid from OPEC Countries* (Paris: OECD, 1983), p. 59.

5. IMF, *International Financial Statistics*, vol. 37 (June 1984), pp. 386–87.

6. This assumes SAMA holdings of $135.5 billion, private sector holdings (including commercial banks) of $23 billion, and other government holdings of $3.5 billion.

tional financial variables, such as risk and rate of return, are important, but oil policy and development plans usually provide the bounds within which financial influences operate. It is the interaction among these economic factors and between economic and political influences that distinguishes one OPEC country from another.

Oil policy imposes different constraints on Saudi financial decision-makers than on financial officials in other OPEC nations because Saudi oil policy itself reacts to different conditions than do the policies of the other nations. Saudi Arabia plays a pivotal role in world oil markets because it comes closer than any other nation to being able to influence the price of oil: it has substantial oil reserves, which will last well into the twenty-first century, and the ability to adjust production over a broad range. Thus Saudi Arabia should be more conscious of the effects of its oil policies on both current revenues and the long-run value of its oil reserves, although political influences can also be important because Saudi decisionmakers operate under conditions of great economic uncertainty.[7] These economic and political influences combine to cause oil production and revenues to vary considerably, as table 5-1 shows. Production increased rapidly from 1970 to 1973 and did not fall below 7.08 million barrels a day between 1973 and 1981. Yet in order to limit the erosion of OPEC prices for crude oil, the Saudis had to shift from producing 9.82 million barrels a day in 1981 to only 5.53 million barrels a day in 1983.[8] These production adjustments, aimed at moderating movements in prices, often compound the direct effect of higher or lower oil prices on revenues and thereby increase the discrepancy between revenues and spending.

Development factors are also important to investment policy. Although Saudi Arabia is often characterized as a low absorber of revenues, both expenditures and the growth rate of spending have been quite high (table 5-2). At the time of the first oil shock the country was at a very early stage of development, so the first two development plans (1970–75 and 1975–80) emphasized high growth rates in all sectors and the elimination of physical constraints. Accordingly, Saudi Arabia devoted large sums to building domestic infrastructure and to providing social services. It also

7. For a comparison of economic and political models of OPEC behavior, see Theodore H. Moran, "Modeling OPEC Behavior: Economic and Political Alternatives," *International Organization*, vol. 35 (Spring 1981), pp. 241–72. For a look at the various economic and political elements in Saudi Arabia's oil policy, see William B. Quandt, *Saudi Arabia's Oil Policy* (Brookings Institution, 1982).

8. Data for 1983 are from *Middle East Economic Digest* (June 15, 1984), p. 68.

Table 5-1. *Saudi Arabian Oil Production and Revenues, 1970, 1973–82*

Year	Crude oil production (million barrels a day)	Oil export revenues (billions of dollars)
1970	3.79	2.20
1973	7.60	7.82
1974	8.48	31.14
1975	7.08	29.72
1976	8.58	38.78
1977	9.20	43.96
1978	8.30	37.82
1979	9.53	58.65
1980	9.93	102.01
1981	9.82	113.23
1982	6.48	75.84

Sources: Production data are from Saudi Arabian Monetary Agency, *Annual Report 1401 [1981]*, pp. 138–39; and "Saudi Policy Aims at Consolidation after a Decade of Rapid Expansion," *IMF Survey* (November 21, 1983), p. 366. Revenue data are from IMF, *International Financial Statistics, 1983 Yearbook* (IMF, 1983), p. 439.

used a significant portion of its oil revenues for military expenditures. The Third Plan (1980–85) represented something of a change in development policy because one of its explicit objectives was to promote structural change in the economy. This restructuring was most evident in plans for "maximizing domestic value-added from crude oil production through domestic hydrocarbon industries" and for reducing the "percentage share of physical infrastructure in total investment after completion of the continuing commitments from the Second Plan period."[9] Preliminary information on the Fourth Plan indicates that these priorities will be unchanged.[10] Whatever implications the reorientation of Saudi development plans might have had for government expenditures, however, have been obscured by the sharp change in oil market conditions.

Saudi oil and development policies influence financial decisions both directly and indirectly. The direct effect is probably clearest because any surplus of revenues over expenditures must be invested and any deficit must be covered by drawing on interest or principal from the reserves. Between 1973 and 1982 Saudi Arabia had a current account surplus in every year except 1978, and even that deficit was only $2 billion after including official transfers. The government, however, has run budget

9. Saudi Arabian Ministry of Planning, *Third Development Plan, 1400–1405 A.H./1980–1985 A.D.*, pp. 16, 17.

10. Finnan Barre, "Saudis to Encourage Private Investment," *Financial Times*, December 8, 1983.

Table 5-2. *Saudi Arabian Government Revenues and Expenditures,*
Fiscal Years 1975-76 to 1984-85
Billions of dollars

Fiscal year	Revenues	Expenditures
1975-76	29.3	23.2
1976-77	38.4	36.3
1977-78	37.2	39.4
1978-79	39.7	44.6
1979-80	62.8	56.0
1980-81	104.7	71.2
1981-82	107.8	83.4
1982-83	71.7	71.0
1983-84	53.6	63.6
1984-85[a]	60.9	74.0

Source: Revenue and expenditure figures before the 1981-82 fiscal year are from Saudi Arabian Monetary Agency, *Annual Report 1401 [1981]*, p. 14; figures for the 1981-82 and 1982-83 fiscal years are from "Saudi Policy Aims at Consolidation after a Decade of Rapid Expansion," *IMF Survey* (November 21, 1983), p. 367; and figures for fiscal years 1983-84 and 1984-85 are from Edmund O'Sullivan, "Saudi Budget Signals a Thaw," *Middle East Economic Digest* (April 6, 1984), pp. 47-48. All figures were denominated in Saudi riyals. They were converted into dollars at end-of-calendar-year exchange rates (for example, 1975 exchange rate for fiscal 1975-76 figures), except that 1984-85 data were based on the May 1984 exchange rate. Exchange rate data are from IMF, *International Financial Statistics* (July 1984), p. 389.
a. Data for fiscal year 1984-85 represent budgeted amounts.

deficits several times. The one in fiscal year 1977-78 was $2.2 billion; it rose to $4.9 billion in fiscal year 1978-79 (table 5-2).[11] Indeed, the Saudi budget deficits might have been very large after 1979 had the second oil shock not intervened. Even during the brief crunch in 1978 and 1979, severe measures, such as slowing down payments and restricting departments to 70 percent of their originally budgeted amounts, had to be taken to control the deficit.

There is little question that after several years of large surpluses the Saudis once again now face a period of sizable budget deficits. Although Finance Minister Aba al-Khail had insisted early in 1982 that "We will not cut our spending and we will not take from our reserves" for the fiscal year 1982-83 budget, those goals proved unattainable.[12] Government revenues during this period equaled $71.7 billion (table 5-2). Had Saudi Arabia not cut its spending from the originally budgeted $91.2 billion, the country would not only have used all of its interest income but also as much as $20 billion of the principal of its foreign holdings to cover budgeted expendi-

11. These budget deficits may not include all Saudi spending on foreign aid. The current account figures, however, include foreign aid grants.
12. Reported in *Middle East Economic Digest* (April 2, 1982), p. 33.

tures.[13] The Saudis, however, did cut spending during the year, and on-budget expenditures (which excludes most foreign aid) totaled $71 billion (table 5-2). They probably spent several billion dollars on unreported foreign aid. In other words, they matched on-budget spending to the level of their revenues and were forced to use some of the principal of the foreign investments to cover off-budget expenditures. Apparently spending began to exceed revenues in the second half of 1982, because SAMA's holdings of foreign assets actually peaked at that time.[14]

The gap between revenues and expenditures widened in fiscal year 1983–84. The budget allowed expenditures of $74.4 billion and projected revenues of $64.4 billion, including $43.9 billion of oil income and $13.0 billion of investment income.[15] This implied a budget deficit of $10 billion. The Saudis cut spending further during the fiscal year because oil revenues fell short of expectations. They were still able to keep deficits to $10 billion, but revenues were only $53.6 billion and expenditures were $63.6 billion (table 5-2). Furthermore, because there may be as much as $5 billion of unreported foreign aid expenditures, the government faced an actual shortfall of at least $15 billion during that fiscal year. Nor does the government foresee much relief in fiscal year 1984–85; it has allowed for a $13.1 billion deficit (table 5-2). Deficits of this magnitude have forced a reconsideration of current and future spending plans, reflected partly in the sharp drop in actual expenditures and partly in plans to rely more heavily on the private sector for domestic development.[16] In any case, reserves will probably have to be drawn upon substantially over the next few years, particularly if spending is hard to control, as some have argued, or if the oil market does not recover quickly.

Saudi oil policy and development plans also indirectly affect the management of financial reserves in the sense that the reserves must be struc-

13. The original 1982–83 budget provided for spending 313.4 billion riyals; see "Saudi Budget Shifts Emphasis from Infrastructure to Human Resources," *Middle East Economic Digest* (April 30, 1982), p. 17. All figures in riyals were converted into dollars at the rate prevailing at the end of 1982; see IMF, *International Financial Statistics, 1983 Yearbook*, p. 439.

14. They had reached $145.1 billion at the end of the third quarter of 1982 before beginning their decline; see IMF, *International Financial Statistics*, vol. 37 (January 1984), p. 381.

15. Edmund O'Sullivan, "Saudi Budget Signals a Thaw," *Middle East Economic Digest* (April 6, 1984), pp. 47–48. All amounts were originally stated in riyals and then converted into dollars at the exchange rate prevailing at the end of 1983.

16. See Barre, "Saudis To Encourage Private Investment," and Carla Rapoport, "Saudi Arabia Plans to Widen Industry Base," *Financial Times*, January 23, 1984.

tured to be available for future needs. The relevance of such planning is clear in the current oil and budget situation. Fortunately, the Saudis seem to have followed just these sorts of guiding principles even when the previous budget situation might have made it seem unlikely that they would actually use their foreign claims to fund domestic spending.

One aspect of such planning might involve a target level of reserves. Finance Minister Aba al-Khail has stated in the past that Saudi Arabia wanted a surplus "at the very least equivalent to twice our annual foreign exchange needs."[17] Dr. Ahmad al-Malik, then director general of the SAMA Foreign Department, said that SAMA's priorities were to use its sizable surplus to promote domestic development and "protect the value of its own assets."[18] Abdul-Aziz al-Quraishi, then governor of SAMA, has likewise emphasized that Saudi Arabia "will need an increasing amount of resources for investment within the country"[19] and that "SAMA, as custodian of the financial assets for the government, has an obligation to maintain the value of these assets."[20]

This emphasis on eventually using the funds for domestic spending led to a desire for safe, short- and medium-term claims.[21] Much of the short-term investment, perhaps $50 billion as of the end of 1982, has been in the form of bank deposits, usually in the Euromarkets because the interest rates are higher than in domestic American and European markets.[22] Some

17. Quoted in "Why the Free-Spending Saudis Must Keep Their Oil Flowing," *Business Week* (July 27, 1981), p. 41. Saudi foreign exchange outflows totaled $80.5 billion in 1981 for imports of goods and services and foreign aid; see IMF, *International Financial Statistics, 1983 Yearbook*, p. 443.

18. Reported in "Mideast Financial Surpluses and Recycling," *Middle East Economic Survey* (July 6, 1981), p. i.

19. "Lifting the Veil in Saudi Arabia," *Euromoney* (April 1979), p. 60.

20. "An Interview with the Head of SAMA," *Institutional Investor—International Edition* (August 1980), p. 92.

21. According to Quraishi, "we do not wish to commit our funds to very long-term periods. However, we have taken advantage of market opportunities and we have a fairly good mix of short-term and medium-term maturities." See "Lifting the Veil in Saudi Arabia," p. 60.

22. Saudi Arabian claims on European, Canadian, and Japanese banks totaled $16.26 billion in December 1977 and rose to $41.83 billion at the end of 1982; see Bank for International Settlements, *Maturity Distribution of International Bank Lending* (July 1978 and December 1983). The U.S. Department of the Treasury only reports statistics that aggregate the holdings of the Middle Eastern oil exporters. There were $15.50 billion of Middle Eastern deposits at foreign branches of U.S. banks and $6.43 billion of deposits at domestic branches of U.S. banks at the end of 1982; for offices in the United States, data were prepared by the Office of International Banking

government securities are also attractive. For example, U.S. Treasury bills and medium-term notes (one- to four-year maturity) could be liquidated immediately, although notes would have some capital risk.[23] Most other investments, however, are less well designed for meeting the additional Saudi criterion of protecting the value of the assets. The capital risk involved in ten-year bonds is considerable during a period of volatile interest and inflation rates, and, despite being based on physical rather than paper assets, stocks have also shown considerable volatility.

Diversification has also been mentioned by the Saudis as an important factor in their investment decisions.[24] This is a standard investment criterion, of course, because a properly designed portfolio can reduce risk while improving the expected rate of return. Diversification can take many forms, both within and across currencies, but the Saudis consider the range for diversification across currencies to be severely constrained. First, most countries offer limited markets or control capital inflows more than the United States does. The Saudis also seem to feel constrained by the currency denomination of their exports and imports. Because crude oil exports are priced in dollars, they feel that investments should largely be in dollars; then any drop in dollar receipts from oil can be partially replaced by the dollar returns from investments. A major share of imports is also priced in dollars, which also leads to a large share of dollars in the optimal portfolio. Pricing exports and imports in dollars is partially a Saudi decision, but it also reflects the large role of the dollar in world trade and payments.

The rate of return is mentioned less often as a Saudi investment criterion. The occasional references that do exist are usually used to justify oil price rises, such as Quraishi's statement that "the rise in the price of oil does not offset the loss on dollar assets resulting from dollar depreciation."[25] Deemphasizing rates of return in public statements probably reflects the Saudi preference for passive rather than active portfolio man-

---

and Portfolio Investment of the Treasury Department; other data are from Federal Reserve Board, Statistical Release E.11, December 15, 1983. Combined, these probably included $10 billion of Saudi deposits at domestic and foreign branches of U.S. banks. Most of these claims would be held by SAMA or other government agencies.

23. Capital risk is the risk that the price of a security when liquidated will be different from the face value because of movements in market interest rates that had occurred since the time of purchase.

24. "Mideast Financial Surpluses and Recycling," p. i, and "Lifting the Veil in Saudi Arabia," p. 57.

25. Ibid., p. 60.

agement. It may also reflect some discomfort with the conflict between the style of Western financial claims and the Islamic prohibition on receiving interest. Borrowers coming to SAMA for cheap funds, however, have usually been disappointed.

Finally, an awareness of the effects of their decisions on the world economy has supposedly influenced Saudi financial decisions. For example, they might intentionally invest in weak currencies or weak economies. Financial needs, such as preserving the value of foreign claims, may also have led occasionally to more moderate oil policy decisions. Typical of such comments is that of al-Quraishi in 1979: "Saudi Arabia has always acted in a responsible manner and has not done anything that would destabilize the international foreign exchange markets, even though this has often been at great national loss."[26]

Thus seven economic factors potentially affect Saudi investment policy: oil policy, development policy, protecting the value of the claims, diversification, liquidity, rate of return, and the health of the world economy. The next section will explore the relative importance of these economic factors and their possible interaction with Saudi political goals.

Investments in America

As oil revenues began pouring into Saudi coffers following the 1973 price shock, SAMA first faced the serious problem of what to do with the excess funds. Saudi surpluses promised to be considerable, yet the structure of oil markets and the world economy meant that standard methods for eliminating the surpluses, such as appreciation of the currency or a cutback in exports, would only exacerbate the short-term problem. New development plans, which would lead to increased imports, were also feasible, but gearing up for such spending would take time. Thus the only immediate choices concerned how to manage the funds.

In the early months of 1974 the Saudis followed very conservative procedures, relying mostly on short-term dollar and Eurodollar claims. Because countries had always relied on gold and on liquid claims, primarily dollars and to a lesser extent sterling, as a way of holding their

26. Ibid., p. 59. Most Saudi and OPEC statements bemoaning losses on foreign assets because of depreciation and inflation neglect the fact that nominal interest rates are higher on those currencies whose value is expected to decline because of inflation or depreciation.

reserves, SAMA's choices were in line with traditional central bank practices for maintaining the value of the reserves. These preferences were reinforced by the limited availability of short-term claims in other currencies and Eurocurrencies, while the sheer size of dollar markets made it less likely that SAMA's placements would affect market rates of interest. Furthermore, at a time when many financial institutions looked shaky, SAMA relied on its familiarity with American and British institutions and the New York and London markets.

These economic factors, combined with Saudi Arabia's traditional political ties to the United States, made it natural that SAMA should look toward the dollar as the primary currency for investing its surpluses. It soon became clear, however, that bank deposits alone would be an insufficient instrument. The banks had more Saudi deposits than they wanted and thus began to quote the Saudis lower rates on new deposits than other depositors received. The Saudi decision to make deposits in a limited number of banks would have exacerbated this tendency.[27] The Saudis thus sought other secure financial instruments and began to focus on the debt obligations of Western governments. Although SAMA also appears to have been interested in British and German government debt, most of the initial efforts were directed toward the United States, and it began buying U.S. Treasury bills and certificates.

In December 1974 the United States agreed to handle some SAMA purchases of Treasury securities through a special arrangement involving the Federal Reserve Bank of New York as an agent of the Treasury Department.[28] This agreement, which was eventually extended to all govern-

27. Most references only indicate that OPEC countries had such problems with placing bank deposits. It seems logical to assume that Saudi Arabia was among the OPEC countries with such problems, given the size of its surpluses and its limited list of approved banks. References to OPEC rates as much as 6 percentage points below market rates are from memoranda quoted in *Federal Response to OPEC Investments in the United States*, Hearings before a Subcommittee of the House Committee on Government Operations, 97 Cong. 1 sess. (GPO, 1981), pt. 1, pp. 984, 993, 1000. The magazine *Arab Banking and Finance* recently assembled an unofficial list of fifty-eight banks with deposits from SAMA, including twelve U.S. banks, ten Japanese banks, and five U.K. banks. See "SAMA's Secret Agents," *Arab Banking and Finance* (August 1983), pp. 21, 23.

28. See memorandum, Jack F. Bennett to the secretary of state, "Special Arrangements for Purchase of U.S. Government Securities by the Saudi Arabian Government," February 6, 1975, reprinted in "The Washington-Riyadh Financial Axis," *International Currency Review*, vol. 14 (July 1982), pp. 17–18.

ments and central banks,[29] applied to securities with a maturity of one year or more, and established a tranche of Treasury securities supplemental to the regular auctions whose price was determined by those auctions.[30] This add-on facility was designed to minimize the impact of Saudi purchases and sales on the prices of particular issues of Treasury securities. It included a provision under which SAMA (and other monetary authorities) had to give two days' notice of any sales made prior to maturity so that the Treasury could repurchase the securities at the then prevailing market rate. No specific amounts of purchases were pledged under the agreement. Furthermore, Saudi Arabia was able to use normal market channels to purchase additional Treasury and agency securities.

This particular mechanism for handling purchases of medium-term Treasury securities, and more generally the significant Saudi purchases of short- and medium-term U.S. government obligations, has generated considerable discussion over the years. The Treasury Department has argued that there is no special economic benefit accruing to SAMA through using the add-on facility rather than securities brokers, and except for SAMA's small savings on commissions, this is true. The benefit to the United States through improved control of government securities markets is also small. There is a separate question of the confidentiality of data on Saudi portfolio investments in the United States, which are published in an aggregate figure with all other Middle Eastern oil producers. This confidentiality is not part of the add-on agreement. Instead it reflects U.S. laws that seek to avoid publishing investment data that would provide information on the holdings of individual investors.[31] Government investors have

---

29. U.S. General Accounting Office, *Are OPEC Financing Holdings a Danger to U.S. Banks or the Economy?"* EMD-79–45 (GAO, June 11, 1979), pp. 10–11.

30. The Treasury Department first determines the amount of its financing needs and the maturity of the securities. The standard procedure for Treasury security auctions then requires large bidders, mostly brokers and dealers in securities, to enter bids for the securities, while smaller purchasers, basically individuals, are allowed to enter noncompetitive bids. The accepted competitive bids are used to determine an average security yield that applies to all noncompetitive tenders. This average yield is also applied to securities in the supplemental tranche.

31. The two laws pertaining to this case are the Survey Act of 1976 and the Bretton Woods Agreement Act. A discussion of the legal basis for the confidential treatment of investment data is contained in *The Operations of Federal Agencies in Monitoring, Reporting on, and Analyzing Foreign Investments in the United States*, Hearings before a Subcommittee of the House Committee on Government Operations, 96 Cong. 1 sess. (GPO, 1979), pt. 2, pp. 226–35.

been responsible for the bulk of the investments from several of the Middle Eastern oil-exporting countries in bank deposits and U.S. Treasury bills.[32] To the extent that confidentiality increased Saudi Arabia's American investments and thereby lowered the cost of funding, the arrangements have been advantageous to the United States. The net effect on U.S. interest rates or economic activity probably has been negligible.

Saudi Arabia has also purchased large amounts of U.S. government obligations outside the add-on facility. The overall Saudi interest in U.S. government securities seems to have been guided mostly by the desire to protect the value of foreign assets; the risk to principal is small. The liquidity of these investments has also meshed well with potential Saudi development needs. In fact, Saudi Arabia appears to have relied heavily on its maturing Treasury obligations to fund the budget deficits of 1978 and 1979. To a lesser extent the purchase of Treasury securities might have been a response to relative rates of return. If, as reported, OPEC Eurodollar deposits occasionally earned rates as much as 6 percentage points below the interbank rate, the rate of return on Treasury securities became attractive. Similarly, the large purchases of Treasury bonds in 1980 and 1981 by Middle Eastern oil exporters (of which a large share probably represented purchases by SAMA) have provided very high real rates of return combined with liquidity and safety.

Since the mid-1970s SAMA has also been interested in the obligations of U.S. corporations. Most of this investment has been in corporate bonds, sometimes in private placements tailored specifically for SAMA. Originally investments were restricted to AAA-rated firms, but that requirement has eased somewhat.[33] Seven years, however, is still reported to be the longest maturity SAMA is normally willing to consider. Corporate placements have included $650 million of debt from American Telephone and Telegraph Company and its subsidiaries, $300 million from International Business Machines Corporation, $200 million from U.S. Steel Corporation, and over $500 million in oil company debt.[34] Such bonds provide

32. At the end of 1978, official investors accounted for 70 percent to 80 percent of outstanding liabilities to Middle Eastern nations reported by U.S. banks and brokers, including Treasury bills held in custody. The five countries are Iran, Iraq, Kuwait, Saudi Arabia, and the United Arab Emirates. See *The Operations of Federal Agencies in Monitoring, Reporting on, and Analyzing Foreign Investments in the United States*, pt. 2, p. 248.

33. "Lifting the Veil in Saudi Arabia," p. 60.

34. "Royal Resources: Saudi Central Bank is Secretive, Conservative, and Enormously Rich," *Wall Street Journal*, March 13, 1981.

high, safe, and regular income, while the term is short enough that illiquidity should not pose any problems. SAMA has also purchased small amounts of stocks, but participates in this market indirectly through discretionary portfolio managers.[35]

Saudi investments in the United States and in dollars have been considerable, and Saudi Arabia has placed a somewhat greater emphasis on the U.S.-based investments than have most other OPEC producers. Thus in early 1979, Finance Minister Aba al-Khail was able to state that the proportion of Saudi assets in the United States was 44 percent to 45 percent.[36] The proportion of OPEC's cumulative identified investments placed in the United States at that time was only 20.4 percent (32.1 percent if deposits at foreign branches are included).[37] Because this high reliance on the United States and the dollar existed at a time when the dollar was experiencing considerable pressure on foreign exchange markets, observers kept predicting an OPEC, especially SAMA, move out of the dollar. Political justifications, especially after the freeze on Iranian assets in November 1979, were also available. Finally, beginning in 1980, SAMA made several large and highly publicized placements outside the United States and outside the dollar, characterized by one editorial as part of "the big OPEC pull-out."[38]

SAMA and the Deutsche Mark

West Germany had been identified early as one of the countries likely to attract OPEC investments. Yet the amount that had actually entered West German capital markets stayed small for several years following the first oil price shock: net investment flows from OPEC between 1974 and 1978 equaled only DM 17.63 billion, or $9.64 billion (see table 2-9). Although further investments were almost surely made in deutsche mark-denominated deposits and bonds in the Euromarket, the limited OPEC investment was noteworthy, especially the minimal investment in German government securities.

35. "Mideast Financial Surpluses and Recycling," pp. i–ii.

36. "Lifting the Veil in Saudi Arabia," p. 59.

37. See table 2-5 and Board of Governors of the Federal Reserve System, Statistical Release E.11, December 20, 1979.

38. "The Big OPEC Pull-out," *Euromoney* (July 1980), p. 5. The article itself was much milder than its title would indicate.

That situation changed suddenly in early 1980 when SAMA began direct placements with the West German government. New placements continued into 1981 when it was announced that Saudi Arabia had actually extended DM 5.5 billion of credits directly to the West German Ministry of Finance in 1980, that a further DM 5.5 billion would be extended directly in 1981, and that additional funds might be channeled into West Germany through the commercial banks.[39] Furthermore, it has been reported that having agreed to help finance West Germany's 1982 deficit if necessary, Saudi Arabia was again called on for substantial loans.[40] Contrary to earlier forecasts of a large-scale withdrawal from the dollar in favor of the mark, these purchases of German securities do not appear to represent a radical change in strategy. Nevertheless, it is important to describe the mixture of economic and political factors facing Saudi Arabia and West Germany that prompted the transaction.

Somewhat ironically, before 1980 the strength of the mark was the greatest barrier to Saudi investments in it. That strength was based on the tight monetary policies of the Bundesbank and on the basic strengths of the West German economy. Saudi Arabia and other OPEC members were very interested in deutsche mark-denominated claims for a share of their holdings because of these economic factors, but suitable deutsche mark-denominated claims were scarce. The German stock market is thin compared to U.S. markets because large blocks of the stock of most major companies are owned by the banks. For similar reasons the market for corporate bonds is circumscribed. Three main forms of investment remained: government obligations, domestic bank deposits, and Euromark claims. Any of these probably would have been attractive investments to SAMA; as one article described it, Saudi Arabia had been "hankering after an opportunity" to diversify into German securities.[41]

But at that time the West German authorities were unwilling to let foreigners purchase significant amounts of marks. A strong mark did provide certain benefits, especially in the battle against inflation, but the authorities feared that currency appreciation resulting from foreign purchases would adversely affect the competitiveness of German exports and

39. "West Germany to Borrow $2.75 Billion from Riyadh to Finance Deficit," *Middle East Economic Survey* (January 19, 1981), p. 1.

40. "Bonn Has Budgetary-Support Pledge," *Middle East Economic Digest* (February 12, 1982), p. 40; *Financial Times*, August 23, 1982, p. 1.

41. Sarah Martin, "How Germany's Cash Mountain Crumbled," *Euromoney* (March 1981), p. 38.

thus German employment. In fact, consultative arrangements between the government and German banks were designed to limit foreigners' purchases of marks and mark-denominated securities. Meanwhile, the German Capital Markets Subcommittee, an unofficial group of representatives from six leading German banks and the Bundesbank, had been encouraging Germans to lend outside of Germany in order to reduce the upward pressures on the mark.

This situation was changed dramatically by the second oil shock, which hit the German economy suddenly and very hard. The German government seemed only mildly concerned about financing at the start of 1980. In January a new gentleman's agreement between the Bundesbank and the banks had even further restricted the sale of mark-denominated claims to foreigners by agreeing that all new debt certificates sold to nonresidents would have at least five years to maturity.[42] But by March the bonds needed to have only two years remaining to maturity. Meanwhile, ballooning government budget deficits had prompted a willingness to accommodate the long-standing Saudi interest in German government securities. As Germany's current account position worsened, further measures were taken to increase capital flows into the mark. In November the restriction on bonds was relaxed so that securities with at least one year remaining to maturity could be purchased by nonresidents, and in December the Capital Markets Subcommittee decided to halt new bond issues in deutsche marks and private placements by nonresidents, which would decrease the outflow of capital from the mark.[43]

The long-repressed Saudi demand for deutsche mark-denominated claims proved convenient for West Germany in the early 1980s. Saudi Arabia bought DM 11 billion in German government notes directly and made further purchases through banking channels. The continued Saudi interest in these claims helped support the value of the mark because Germany's capital account remained under pressure even as its current account improved.

A variety of factors led the Saudis to respond favorably to the new German willingness to borrow from SAMA. Most important was their view that both Germany and the mark continued to be good investments. The offer of government securities also meshed well with SAMA's standard view of what sort of securities should be purchased to protect the

42. See OECD, *Financial Market Trends* (December 1980), p. 17.
43. Ibid.

value of the claims. The rate of return was also attractive, although Saudi Arabia has been reported to have balked at least once at a sale with insufficiently high yield.[44] Furthermore, the massive amounts of new funds flowing into SAMA during 1980 and 1981 contributed to its need to diversify within and outside the dollar. Finally, it had become clear during the course of 1980 that Saudi Arabia could make such a move without affecting the dollar and the value of its accumulated dollar holdings.

This analysis has scarcely referred to political factors that could help explain SAMA's interest in German claims, but two potential political motivations clouded much of the early discussion. One possibility was that the move into the mark was a political response to the American freeze of Iranian assets; but the continued, indeed increased, Middle Eastern purchases of U.S. Treasury bonds during 1980 and 1981, which presumably included sizable purchases by SAMA, rule that out. The other concern was that the investments represented an attempt to persuade West Germany to drop its long-standing refusal to sell Leopard 2 tanks to Saudi Arabia. This political motivation could not have been very important to the Saudis, however, for the purchases of German securities were sizable despite clear official signals that West Germany will not sell the tanks. It is also unlikely that SAMA made these investments to shore up the mark because its stake in the mark was small.

The best explanation of the Saudi and German attitudes toward deutsche mark-denominated investment centers on economic not political factors: for Germany, a sudden need for funds, and for Saudi Arabia, a large demand for secure claims at attractive interest rates. The likely future course of Saudi interest in the mark is unsure. The rapid disappearance of their surplus removes any pressure to find outlets for new funds. Germany's need for funds is also diminishing; the pressure on its balance of payments has eased considerably, although the value of the mark has stayed low because of high dollar interest rates. The recent investments are not likely to foreshadow a large role for the deutsche mark in SAMA portfolios at the expense of the dollar.

The Lure of Japan

In recent years Saudi Arabia and other OPEC members have concluded a variety of investments in Japan, in sharp contrast to the lack of interest in Japanese investments in the years immediately after the first oil shock.

44. Martin, "How Germany's Cash Mountain Crumbled," p. 44.

The small role of the yen and of investments in Japan during the 1970s probably reflected a lack of familiarity with Japanese institutions and the Saudis' perceptions of the risk of such claims. Because of an almost complete dependence on imported energy, the majority of which was crude oil, Japan was perhaps the industrial nation most affected by the oil price increases. Japanese banks were not major forces in international banking then, and had to pay a "Japan rate" for Euromarket funding in 1974 that included premiums of up to 1 percentage point over the funding costs for other banks. This situation settled down quickly, because Japan weathered the first oil shock as well as (perhaps better than) any other industrial nation. But OPEC interest in yen-denominated investments appears to have been minimal in the mid-1970s despite the sales efforts of Japanese security firms.[45]

Saudi Arabia made a $1 billion loan to Japan in 1974, but after that its interest seemed largely limited to dollar deposits with a few of the largest banks and to purchases of dollar-denominated Eurobonds of Japanese companies.[46] Gradually, however, SAMA and other OPEC authorities became interested in yen investments. The first OPEC moves came in the late 1970s when Kuwait, acting through its London investment office, entered the Japanese stock market.[47] SAMA made its first tentative moves in the fall of 1979, and by the spring of 1980 it had clearly become very interested in yen-denominated investments.

A number of factors help to explain the timing of the Saudi move. By the late 1970s the "Japanese miracle" was gaining worldwide recognition, and Japan had emerged as one of the more attractive places to invest. Although the second oil shock briefly renewed concerns about Japanese vulnerability, by the start of 1980 the country seemed to have weathered the second oil shock equally well. During the mid-1970s, however, Japan's economic success had led to large payments surpluses, an appreciation of the yen, and pressures for further appreciation. Thus at that time Japan was concerned with discouraging inflows of capital and chose to restrict capital movements through a mixture of regulations, administrative guidance, and special programs. The net effect was to lower the

45. See Stephen Bronte, "Petrodollar Sophistication Grows," *Middle East Economic Digest* Special Report (December 1980), p. 10.
46. See Marjorie Boardman, "Entering the Japanese Market," *The Middle East* (March 1982), p. 76.
47. Bronte, "Petrodollar Sophistication Grows," p. 10; and Boardman, "Entering the Japanese Market," p. 76.

returns on the limited number of available financial instruments to levels below those possible on investments in other currencies.

The second oil shock caused a major change in Japanese attitudes. Expansionary fiscal policy led to large budget deficits that combined with heavy dependence on imported energy to generate large deficits on both its current and capital accounts. After running down its reserves to support the yen in 1979, the government had little choice but to seek capital inflows. On March 2, 1980, the Finance Ministry instituted a series of measures designed to encourage capital inflows and discourage outflows. Two of these measures were particularly important for Middle Eastern investors. The first exempted foreign central banks, governments, and international organizations from interest rate restrictions on free-yen (non-resident) deposits. This liberalization significantly changed the economic incentives facing foreign central banks.[48] Previously, free-yen deposits had paid the ceiling rate of 5.5 percent; immediately after the reform the new rate attained 13 percent, the level prevailing in the short-term "gensaki" market.[49] The second measure was permission for Japanese companies to float yen-denominated private placements abroad, thus providing corporate bonds that had previously been virtually unavailable.

These measures served to increase OPEC (and non-OPEC) investments in Japan and were of critical interest to SAMA. The only previous options in the Japanese market available to SAMA were stocks and the gensaki market, which provides a way of holding short-term yen and involves sale and repurchase agreements on already-issued government bonds.[50] It provides a source of short-term yen investments with no capital risk, even though the underlying securities have longer terms to maturity. SAMA's first yen investments apparently had been in the gensaki market, though for relatively small amounts: a total of ¥50 billion ($213 million) from November 1979 to April 1980.[51] The gensaki market was probably too short-term for SAMA's tastes, however, and could also make the agency appear as too active because securities are both bought and sold by the

48. OECD, *Financial Market Trends* (December 1980), p. 18.

49. Bronte, "Petrodollar Sophistication Grows," p. 10.

50. In this market the lender agrees to buy a bond today at a price $P1$ and sell on a future date at price $P2$; the return is determined by the price difference.

51. "SAMA to Purchase Japanese Equity," *Middle East Economic Survey* (March 30, 1981), p. 1. All yen amounts in this section are converted at ¥235 per dollar. This was the rate at the end of 1982 and is approximately the average rate prevailing since that time. See IMF, *International Financial Statistics*, vol. 36 (December 1983), pp. 246–47.

lender to the gensaki market. The free-yen deposits, roughly comparable to U.S. certificates of deposit, offered SAMA the opportunity to place money passively in yen accounts for three- to twelve-month periods.[52] By the end of 1980 it had deposits of ¥698 billion ($2.97 billion) at Japanese banks, the largest amount of any oil country.[53] This figure probably has not changed very much since then.

Next SAMA moved into Japanese government securities. In one sense this began with the gensaki market investments from November 1979 to April 1980. These repurchase agreements reportedly were replaced in April 1980 by an informal agreement for the Bank of Japan to sell SAMA ¥50 billion ($213 million) of medium-term government securities every month.[54] No details were announced officially, but the deal reportedly involved bonds with either a three-year maturity or with a repurchase agreement at the end of three years.[55] The Japanese government later agreed to let the agency buy the necessary foreign exchange for the bonds directly from the Bank of Japan.[56] SAMA has also been able to purchase government bonds from the Ministry of Finance and from securities companies, although the former has rarely been used. There were, for example, only four purchases reported from September 1981 to May 1982, totaling ¥120 billion ($511 million).[57] Purchases of government bonds through securities companies totaled slightly over ¥440 billion in 1981 and approximately ¥250 billion in the first ten months of 1982.[58] Purchases of government bonds through the three channels reportedly totaled ¥2,700 billion ($11.49 billion) as of March 1983.[59] Purchases apparently

52. There is no maximum time limit on such deposits; however, deposits over one year are rare in any currency.

53. According to Nihon Keizai Shimbun, reported in "SAMA Gets a Yen for Japan," *Middle East Economic Digest* Special Report (May 1981), p. 29.

54. *Middle East Economic Survey* (March 30, 1981), p. 1; "SAMA Gets a Yen for Japan," p. 29.

55. Bronte, "Petrodollar Sophistication Grows," pp. 10–11.

56. "SAMA Gets a Yen for Japan," p. 30. Thus SAMA paid for the yen securities with dollars of an equivalent amount, which the Bank of Japan itself then converted into yen.

57. ¥20 billion in both September 1981 and October 1981, a further ¥20 billion in January 1982, and ¥60 billion in May 1982. See "Finance Ministry Directly Issues Government Bonds for Saudi Arabia," *Japan Economic Journal*, November 10, 1981; and *Middle East Economic Digest* (June 4, 1982), p. 60.

58. "Saudi Cuts Buying of Japanese Bonds," *Japan Economic Journal*, November 9, 1982.

59. The estimate that cumulative purchases of government bonds equalled ¥2,700 billion fits well with the previously mentioned reports of ¥120 billion bought through

were suspended from May until November 1983, however, at which time SAMA purchased ¥5 billion ($21 million) in three-year bonds directly from the Ministry of Finance.[60]

It has also been reported that SAMA allocated $1 billion in March 1981 for the purchase of Japanese equities. The purchases were to be carried out by two British merchant banks: Baring Brothers and Robert Fleming and Company. Simultaneously the agency gave managers of its U.S. and Swiss portfolios permission to enter the Tokyo market on a discretionary basis.[61] Once again prior action by the Japanese Ministry of Finance may have encouraged the move; restrictions on foreign investments had been significantly eased as of December 1, 1980.[62] The underlying strength of the Japanese economy and of its multinationals in world markets would have made equities an attractive investment, while the prospect of continuing large Saudi surpluses also favored a move into world equity markets. The decision to enter Japanese equity markets may also have been due in part to the Saudi perception that any further buying on Wall Street would generate political resistance in the United States, whereas domestic resistance was absent in Japan.[63] It is still unclear whether significant Saudi purchases of Japanese equities have taken place.

SAMA made its first major purchase of yen-denominated Japanese corporate bonds in April 1981 in a ¥10 billion ($43 million) deal with Kawasaki Heavy Industries and thus finally took advantage of the second of the special measures from March 1980.[64] No other completed private placements of straight bonds with SAMA have since been reported, although they have almost surely occurred. The Japanese Ministry of Finance also has allowed certain quasi-government corporations to issue yen-denomi-

---

Ministry of Finance channels, ¥1,800 billion from the Bank of Japan (¥50 billion a month from April 1980 to March 1983), and ¥690 billion from the market. The ¥2,700 billion estimate is contained in "Saudi Arabia Halts Purchase of Japanese Gov't Bonds," *Japan Economic Journal*, March 8, 1983.

60. "Saudi Begins Curtailing Purchase of Gov't Bonds," *Japan Economic Journal*, May 10, 1983; and Yoko Shibata, "SAMA Back in the Japanese Bond Market," *Financial Times*, December 13, 1983.

61. "The Saudis Edge into Equities—in Japan," *Business Week* (April 13, 1981), p. 127.

62. OECD, *Financial Market Trends* (November 1981), p. 49.

63. SAMA did already have U.S. stock portfolios under the discretionary management of New York firms.

64. "Kawasaki HI Secures Yen Fund from SAMA," *Japan Economic Journal*, April 21, 1981.

nated, government-guaranteed bonds directly to Saudi Arabia. The first such deal involved a Japan Air Lines placement for ¥10 billion ($43 million) late in 1981.[65] In one of the most interesting deals to date, it was reported in early 1982 that SAMA had been negotiating convertible bond issues: ¥20 billion ($85 million) in Sony bonds and ¥10 billion ($43 million) in Honda bonds, both with 10-year maturities and a 5.6 percent interest rate coupon. Although the negotiations were broken off at that time because of news leaks, the placements were eventually made.[66] Future deals for convertible bonds are unlikely, however, because of unwanted publicity and changing economic factors. In particular, since late 1982 the marked softening of oil demand has forced Saudi Arabia to begin running down its foreign holdings. Equities and convertible bonds and even longer-term straight bonds are less liquid and carry a greater risk to the preservation of the principal of the investment than do shorter-term securities. Straight bond deals with maturities between three and five years would mesh better with SAMA's current needs.

It is unclear whether Saudi investments in yen securities will increase further. In early 1981 it was reported that SAMA had decided to place 15 percent of its total funds in yen, approximately $20 billion,[67] but the agency apparently stopped short of that target. SAMA has around $11.5 billion of Japanese government bond holdings, $3 billion of yen deposits, and $200 million to $300 million worth of corporate and quasi-government bonds, or around $15 billion of yen holdings, and there may be some small amounts of equities and Euroyen deposits. The disappearance of the surplus can account for part of the shortfall: the agency has apparently been reluctant to alter its past placements before they mature, and any new investment usually comes out of maturing securities or from entirely new funds. The relatively low level of Japanese interest rates in comparison to

65. "SAMA Gets a Yen for Japan," p. 30.

66. A convertible bond includes the option for the buyer to convert the bond's principal into a certain amount of equity at certain dates in the future. The number of shares, evaluated at stock prices at the time of issue, usually involves a discount of 10 percent to 20 percent on the bond principal; the larger the discount, the less the incentive for conversion and the higher the necessary interest payments. These issues supposedly involved low discounts, which would encourage conversion.

Japanese newspaper stories on the prospective transactions that appeared in January mistakenly reported the deals had been completed. The mere publication of the articles led to a postponement. "SAMA Purchases Convertible Bonds of Sony and Honda," *Japan Economic Journal*, January 26, 1982; and "Converts to the Japanese Way," *Eight Days* (February 20, 1982), p. 60.

67. "SAMA Gets a Yen for Japan," p. 30.

U.S. rates also explains some of the shortfall. Finally, it may just take time until SAMA feels comfortable enough with investments in Japan, a country with which it has no historical ties, although trade ties have increased dramatically. But yen investments amounting to 15 percent of the SAMA portfolio remain plausible.

The Saudi Role in IMF Financings

Probably the largest commitment of Saudi funds in a single transaction occurred in May 1981, when SAMA and the International Monetary Fund concluded a large-scale borrowing agreement.[68] That deal generated considerable comment, both on economic and political grounds. The political questions centered on Saudi power within the IMF in general and Palestine Liberation Organization (PLO) membership in particular, while economic interest focused on the size of the loan and the use of the Special Drawing Right (SDR) to denominate it.[69]

The loan was indeed large. SAMA agreed to loan up to SDR 4 billion in the first year of the commitment and up to SDR 4 billion more in the second year. The possibility of further commitments in the third year was left for later discussions and was to depend on Saudi Arabia's reserves and balance of payments position. Drawings were made for six years, and ninety days' notice was required before any drawing. The IMF agreed to draw SDR 1 billion in the first year and not more than SDR 4 billion in any year without SAMA's approval. The interest rate, computed semiannually, was based on the weighted average rate of five-year government securities in each of the component currencies of the SDR.

Whether any feature of the loan other than its size should have attracted so much attention is questionable. Saudi lending to the IMF was scarcely a new phenomenon. There had been two loans totaling SDR 2.25 billion

68. "Enlarged Access Policy in Effect with Signing of Saudi Agreement," *IMF Survey* (May 18, 1981), pp. 149, 156.

69. The Special Drawing Right is a composite currency in which IMF transactions are denominated. Since January 1, 1981, it consists of 0.54 dollar, 0.46 deutsche mark, 34 yen, 0.071 pound sterling, and 0.74 French franc. It was originally designed to give a 42 percent weight to the dollar, 19 percent to the mark, and 13 percent to the pound, French franc, and yen, but the exact percentages vary with exchange rates. As of April 30, 1981, 1 SDR was worth $1.19858.

under the 1974 and 1975 oil facilities, SDR 1.85 billion of which had been repaid by May 1981.[70] Saudi Arabia had also granted a credit line of SDR 1.93 billion to the supplemental financing facility, and had accepted SDR 397 million in claims on the two facilities because of transfers from the Deutsche Bundesbank in November 1980.[71]

Thus from SAMA's point of view, lending to the IMF represented additional funds to an old investment outlet. In addition, the SDR was not a new currency to SAMA, and acceptance of it was guided by SAMA's evaluation of the SDR's component currencies. Even the scale of the IMF loan did not represent a new opportunity for currency diversification. By 1981 Saudi Arabia either had access to the government securities market or had made loans on a direct government-to-government basis in all of the component currencies of the SDR, except perhaps the French franc. Finally, the rate of return was the same as the composite rate SAMA could expect from investments in the underlying currencies. Thus, while the attractive rates on the IMF loan encouraged Saudi participation, they hardly represented a new financial opportunity. Nor would the IMF loan have provided much protection against asset freezes, for the amounts involved are small compared to Saudi budgetary requirements.

The loan was also in line with IMF policy of enlarged access, under which it could borrow funds sufficient to bridge any payments difficulties likely to occur before the next increase in quotas.[72] The payment of interest at market rates was similar to the provisions of the supplemental financing facility and also corresponded to increased IMF emphasis on market-related pricing of loans to its members, a movement favored by the United States.

The complaints that the loan would give Saudi Arabia undue political influence within the IMF seem unjustified. These complaints are usually tied to the almost simultaneous doubling of the Saudi quota, which gave it the sixth largest voting power in the IMF. Still, its 3.43 percent share of total votes falls far short of the 15 percent necessary for a veto on deci-

---

70. The oil facilities had borrowed SDR 6.9 billion from sixteen nations (six OPEC members, five other energy exporters, and five nations blessed with strong currencies). The funds were used to finance oil-related adjustment in developing countries. The loans had a longer term than usual IMF lending. See IMF, *Annual Report 1982* (IMF, 1982), p. 115, table I.9.

71. Ibid., pp. 115–16; and IMF, *Annual Report 1981* (IMF, 1981), pp. 90–91.

72. Ibid., p. 82.

sions.[73] Undoubtedly a certain amount of political prestige was gained from the loan, but the other political benefits were miniscule.[74]

Overall, four factors were probably influential in determining the Saudi loan. One was the favorable Saudi payments position, which not only made such a large loan possible but even encouraged SAMA to pursue such an investment. Second, the loan yielded high safe returns comparable with those received on the large Saudi investments in American, German, and Japanese government issues. A third factor was probably the feeling of a constraint on some of its purchases of direct government issues; OPEC investments in the United States generated considerable, often unfavorable, publicity, while investment opportunities in West Germany and Japan could disappear if those countries' exchange rates improved and their governments decided external financing was no longer necessary. Finally, because economic factors were favorable, providing such funding to the IMF at commercial rates was a low-cost way of demonstrating general Saudi support for the third world and a larger IMF role in the adjustment process.

Investments in Energy-Related Industries

One of the lingering fears about OPEC strategy has been that one or several of the nations might invest their surplus funds in ways that would extend their influence on the oil market itself or on other energy-related industries. Some observers treated the various Kuwaiti joint ventures and purchases of American companies in 1981 as the vanguard of a Saudi movement toward direct investments in energy-related industries. Such a movement within SAMA's own funds, however, seems unlikely because it would be incompatible with the agency's stated guidelines and with its actions since the oil shocks. Financially, such investments would be very risky and would increase the Saudis' already high dependence on oil market developments, a combination SAMA has never countenanced. Nor would such investments fit with the agency's almost complete avoidance of stock portfolios, let alone direct investment. Other Saudi agencies,

73. Ibid., p. 77.

74. Observer status for the Palestine Liberation Organization at the IMF was viewed by many as the goal of Saudi Arabia and other Arab members, yet Saudi Arabia entered into the loan agreement even though no concessions were granted on the issue.

however, could implement such actions as part of the country's oil or industrial policy.

Saudi Arabia's industrial policy is based on the nation's comparative advantages: energy and to a lesser extent capital. That policy aims at diversification of the economic base, especially through the development of hydrocarbon-based industries.[75] Development could proceed via any of five routes: moving downstream into refining and petrochemicals; processing gas as an energy source or feedstock; developing energy-intensive industries, such as smelting; developing industries that can exploit their connections to and from the oil industry; and moving upstream into energy exploration and drilling.[76]

Current long-range planning in Saudi Arabia includes all five options, but limits upstream energy investments to Saudi Arabia's own territory. There are two main components to the industrialization plans. First, under the aegis of the Royal Commission for Jubail and Yanbu, two new industrial cities are being developed through a management contract with the Bechtel Corporation. Jubail's design includes petrochemical complexes, oil refineries, a steel mill, and related service industries, along with the housing and the infrastructure for a city of 300,000 by the year 2000. Yanbu, on the Red Sea coast, would have a similar mix of industries and should attain a population of 150,000 by 2010. The second part of the plan involves Petromin's gas gathering, treatment, and transmission project, which supports the activities at Jubail and Yanbu by providing ethane as a feedstock and energy source.[77]

A variety of products are planned for the complexes, as table 5-3 shows. Even those projects coming on line by the mid-1980s represent an ambitious attempt to break into world petrochemical markets. Saudi Arabia, however, has structured the commercial and financial arrangements in a very conservative manner. Seven of the projects are fifty-fifty joint ventures between the Saudi Arabian Basic Industries Corporation (SABIC) and non-OPEC corporations; the eighth is a cooperative venture with the governments of Kuwait and Bahrain. A large share of the marketing and distribution of the products will be handled by the foreign non-OPEC

75. Saudi Arabian Ministry of Planning, *Third Development Plan*, p. 17.
76. The last of these options does not actually involve industrialization.
77. See Hugh George Hambleton, "The Saudi Petrochemical Industry in the 1980s," in Ragaei El Mallakh and Dorothea H. El Mallakh, eds., *Saudi Arabia: Energy, Developmental Planning, and Industrialization* (Lexington, Mass.: D.C. Heath for Lexington Books, 1982), pp. 52-53.

Table 5-3. *Planned Saudi Arabian Petrochemical Production*
Thousands of metric tons per year

Product	No foreign partner	Foreign partner								
		Mobil	Shell	Exxon	Dow[a]	Celanese/ Texas	Taiwan Fertilizer	Mitsubishi Consortium	Mitsubishi Consortium	Bahrain/ Kuwait[b]
Ethylene	...	450	...	...	500	...	...	...	...	...
Low-density polyethylene	...	200	656	260	...	...	...	130	...	...
High-density polyethylene	...	90	...	...	150	...	...	300	...	...
Ethylene glycol	...	220	454	...	...	...	...	...	...	...
Ethylene dichloride	...	...	377	...	...	...	...	...	...	...
Caustic soda	...	...	295	...	...	...	...	...	...	...
Styrene	...	...	281	...	...	...	...	...	...	...
Ethanol	...	...	...	...	...	650	...	...	...	...
Methanol	...	...	...	...	...	...	...	...	600	1,000
Urea	300[c]	...	...	...	...	...	500	...	...	...

Source: Data from Saudi Arabian Basic Industries Corporation reported in *Middle East Economic Digest* Special Report (November 1983), p. 28.
a. Formerly a joint venture between Saudi Arabian Basic Industries Corporation and Dow Chemical. Plans to produce polyethylenes were scrapped after Dow pulled out. For details see *Middle East Economic Digest* (January 7, 1983), p. 37.
b. This product is a joint venture with the governments of Bahrain and Kuwait. It will also produce 1,000 tons of ammonia a year.
c. A separate joint venture with domestic private partners.

partners in those seven projects. The main Saudi contributions are the natural gas feedstocks, low-cost and virtually complete electricity, water, and port facilities, and favorable financing from the Public Investment Fund of much of the foreign partner's share of the capital costs.[78] Saudi Arabia has also entered into two joint-venture refineries: a Jubail-based partnership with Shell and a Yanbu-based joint venture with Mobil. Each will produce 250,000 barrels a day of refined products. Petromin is responsible for the 50 percent Saudi share in these projects.[79]

Planning Minister Hisham Nazer has indicated that the Saudi goal is to supply 5 percent to 6 percent of world demand for certain basic petrochemicals.[80] Implementation of Saudi plans for refineries and petrochemical plants may not require large foreign investments because the marketing responsibility for the complexes is assigned largely to foreign partners.[81] Nonetheless, Planning Minister Nazer and Oil Minister Ahmed Zaki Yamani have recently indicated that the Saudis would be interested in ventures outside their territory.[82] Saudi Arabia could, for example, buy into existing petrochemical plants in the West and agree to supply them with basic petrochemicals from plants currently nearing completion in Jubail and Yanbu. These overseas joint ventures could replace parts of the projected complexes at Jubail and Yanbu; this would benefit the Saudis by enabling them to avoid the relatively high costs of constructing new chemical plants in the Middle East,[83] and by reducing fears that their petrochemical production could be frozen out of world markets because of growing protectionist tendencies.

78. Crude oil entitlements are a further incentive for the foreign firms. For details on the various projects see Hambleton, "The Saudi Petrochemical Industry in the 1980s," pp. 51–75; and "SABIC Aims for the Top," *Middle East Economic Digest* Special Report (November 1983), pp. 6, 8, 28.

79. See "What Future for Arab Refiners?" *Middle East Economic Digest* (February 3, 1984), pp. 20–23.

80. "Saudis Give a Hint of Possible Joint Ventures Abroad," *Petroleum Intelligence Weekly* (January 17, 1983), p. 1.

81. This contrasts with the original Kuwaiti decision to market on its own the products from Kuwaiti plants. Kuwaiti investments are discussed in chapter 6.

82. "Saudis Give a Hint of Possible Joint Ventures Abroad," *Petroleum Intelligence Weekly* (January 17, 1983), p. 1.

83. These costs are 35 percent to 67 percent higher than in Western Europe, according to figures from Shell International Chemical Company reported in Hambleton, "The Saudi Petrochemical Industry in the 1980s," p. 54. See also Carla Rapoport, "Saudi Petrochemicals Must Be Sold at Fair Prices, Says Regan," *Financial Times*, October 27, 1983; and "Saudis Raise Petrochemicals Issue," *Middle East Economic Digest* (October 28, 1983), p. 3.

The Saudi petrochemical complexes could also prove attractive to the West. The feedstock for the plants is relatively cheap because the best alternative use for Saudi natural gas is to flare it at its source. Some existing Western plants would have to be scrapped, but U.S. companies will be least affected by Saudi moves into petrochemicals because transportation costs will tend to prevent the Saudis from supplying the American market. Finally, the Saudis remain unlikely to enter exploration or drilling ventures outside their own country. All these factors combine to make it unlikely that Saudi investments in hydrocarbon-based industries would pose a threat to Western economic security.

An Evaluation of Saudi Investment Behavior

Details on four broad categories of SAMA's foreign investments and on SABIC's domestic industrialization program make it possible to identify the underlying factors that explain most of the Saudi investment strategy.[84] Seven plausible economic influences are oil policy constraints, development needs, liquidity, safety, rate of return, diversification, and a concern for the world economy. Potential political factors have included the American freeze of Iranian assets, the Middle East conflict, third world solidarity, a desire for leverage on Western policies, use of Saudi financial power to consolidate its oligopolistic oil market position (a quasi-economic factor), and international prestige. The previous analysis favors the conclusion that Saudi investment strategy has been based largely on conservative economic factors.

Oil policy has had the most obvious impact on financial decisions because Saudi efforts to influence oil markets have generated the buildup of funds and have often created substantial pressure for SAMA to seek new investment outlets. Spending requirements have had a mostly indirect role in investment decisions because the Saudis chose liquid and safe investments in anticipation of future spending needs.

Liquidity and safety, the hallmarks of a conservative strategy, seem to have been the most important determinants. These two factors are hard to separate in many Saudi investments. The choice of currency of denomination shows this tendency, because most investments have been in dollars,

---

84. As indicated earlier, foreign aid will be discussed in a separate chapter because, almost by definition, it involves noneconomic factors.

with small but significant shares in marks and yen. The choice of financial instruments points to the same conclusion: bank deposits and government bonds are very liquid and safe; limited amounts of funds were placed in stocks, which, though liquid, involve significant capital risk; and even the less liquid corporate bonds involved at most a medium-term commitment to top-rated borrowers. The loan to France, reportedly $4 billion, also fits in well with this interpretation, given the high standing of French borrowers in the financial markets.[85]

The rate of return on investments does not appear to play as prominent a role in Saudi decisionmaking as considerations of liquidity and safety. Yet the interest rate is hardly irrelevant. Except for the six to twelve months immediately following the first oil shock when its investment options were largely limited to bank deposits, SAMA probably has not accepted below-market interest rates. The interest in U.S. Treasury bills, which pay several hundred basis points less than Eurodollar deposits, provides one example of the relative importance of safety and rate of return. SAMA has reportedly approved a fairly restricted list of banks for its deposits. Sometimes these banks have been unwilling to absorb new SAMA deposits and have therefore quoted lower rates to discourage the business. In such conditions Treasury securities provide attractive rates of return, given the limitations imposed by safety considerations. Yen-denominated investments also suggest the relative importance of safety and rate of return in Saudi investment decisions. Even after it was clear that Japanese institutions were safe, no major Saudi investments in yen securities were reported until reforms had liberalized the deposit markets and led to a sharp rise in interest rates to market levels. Basically, the rate of return seems to enter into all investment decisions, but only after the criteria of liquidity and safety have screened the investment.

Diversification has also been one of the key words in the Saudis' own statements. The size of the financial flows, a consequence of Saudi oil policy, has provided the greatest impetus for diversification, especially in the first few years after the second oil shock. Diversification has taken several forms, both within and between currencies. The currency diversification has attracted considerable attention, but only the move into the yen reflected any change in Saudi policy. SDR diversification has been minimal and in any case has existed since 1974. The Saudi interest in deutsche marks probably had been present since 1974 but could only be realized in

85. Felix Kessler, "France Welcomes $4 Billion Saudi 'Gift,' But Many Ask What Price Tag Will Be," *Wall Street Journal*, December 27, 1982.

1980, when soaring budget deficits and a falling mark made it necessary to open German capital markets to all investors. The timing of German investments therefore seems to have been determined more by German government decisions than by a switch in Saudi strategies. The diversification of financial instruments within currencies has been more gradual, but investments are still limited largely to bank deposits, government securities, and corporate bonds. A large-scale move into equities has often been predicted but has not occurred. Nor is it likely to occur in the near future because revenue needs and liquidity and safety considerations make it inappropriate.

The role of the last economic factor, a concern for the health of the world economy, is hard to evaluate. This might have motivated some of the oil policy decisions and thus increased the funds available for investment.[86] An examination of individual investments usually yields other factors that better explain the placements. For example, the IMF loans, especially their magnitude, can be explained by considerations of safety and rate of return. Yen and deutsche mark investments likewise were motivated by the attractive opportunities those investments provided, not by a desire to help support those currencies. There is a chance that concerns about the dollar's health may occasionally have affected SAMA, because the large share of dollars in SAMA's portfolio has led to an acute awareness of the need to sustain the dollar's value. Indeed, SAMA might otherwise have been tempted in late 1978 to move a small amount of its portfolio out of the dollar. Yet even at that time other factors generated more serious constraints. Saudi budget deficits meant that SAMA was drawing down its claims during this period, so new investments were unlikely. In addition, the dollar's weakness meant that those nations with strong currencies were unwilling to open their markets to foreign investors. Recently, of course, Saudi Arabia has benefited from the very high real rates of return on the dollar investments in its portfolio. More generally, Saudi imports and exports are structured in such a way that SAMA needs mostly dollars in the "consumption" part of its portfolio dedicated to balancing expenditure demands and income shortfalls.[87] Even in the "investment" part of the portfolio, dollar claims should be large because a

86. It is not even clear that the health of the world economy was an independent factor in oil policy decisions; Saudi economic interests and world economic interests coincide to a certain extent on questions of oil pricing.

87. Though the Saudis could decide to accept and receive a larger share of payments in currencies other than the dollar.

large share of world financial claims is denominated in dollars. Thus in some senses a large dollar involvement is inevitable.

These economic criteria explain a very large share of Saudi investment behavior, but two particular classes of investments, foreign aid and the Iraqi loans, are not amenable to economic analysis.[88] Both were strongly motivated by domestic security considerations. But otherwise political factors have played only a marginal role in the Saudi investment strategy. This is best demonstrated by an examination of the placements most often cited as proof of the importance of political factors. Saudi interest in third world solidarity can explain the country's patterns of foreign aid, for example, but does not explain SAMA's pattern of investments, even the IMF loan. Saudi Arabia's financial assets have not increased its influence on Western political decisions, though its importance as an oil exporter has forced Western governments to consider Saudi attitudes and needs in forming policy on energy security or the Middle East. Of course, chapter 4 has already demonstrated why the structure of world financial markets would make it difficult and costly for any OPEC nation to disrupt them in an attempt to influence Western political decisions.

The freeze on Iranian assets has had little effect on the U.S.-based investments of OPEC investors from the Middle East; given Saudi Arabia's large share of Middle East surpluses, it seems logical to conclude that it must have been a major source of the Middle Eastern purchases of Treasury securities in 1980 and 1981. At the same time the new financial needs of West Germany and Japan following the second oil shock prompted those nations to open up their markets to foreign investments, an opening that permitted the Saudis to realize a long-standing interest in marks and an evolving desire for yen. Access to markets and considerations of liquidity, safety, and rate of return are sufficient to explain large purchases of U.S. Treasury securities simultaneous with major flows into West Germany and Japan. Obviously this conclusion does not agree with the arguments that have been made to link the freeze with SAMA's interest in mark and yen investments.

Even more prevalent was the fear that Saudi Arabia might use its financial wealth to consolidate its oligopolistic oil market position. This could occur plausibly in one of three ways: using the assets as a buffer for riding out oil market downturns, purchasing controlling interests in energy indus-

---

88. See chapters 7 and 8 for discussions on OPEC loans to Iraq and foreign aid, respectively.

tries, or making loans to other oil exporters that would enable them to survive market downturns without increasing production or cutting prices.

Obviously the reserves have functioned as a buffer in those years that the Saudis used the interest income (and sometimes part of the principal) to cover budget deficits. But the ability to support oil prices in glutted markets by liquidating foreign assets to cover spending needs is counterbalanced by the fact that Saudi Arabia eased the upward pressure on oil prices when it originally ran the surpluses. As for the second method, Saudi Arabia has not attempted to use investments in energy industries as a means of consolidating its oil market power. The current industrialization strategy does call for investment in domestic petrochemical complexes, and the Saudis are planning for a small but noticeable role in world petrochemical markets. These investments, however, might even weaken Saudi Arabia's influence in the world oil market because they essentially require it to increase the supply of natural gas, a competitive fuel.

The Saudis might also have tried to use their financial wealth to strengthen their oil market position through loans to other third world oil exporters. There was speculation throughout 1982 and into early 1983 that they would make a $1 billion loan to Nigeria, but no loan of that scale was made;[89] rumors of a smaller loan still exist. Saudi Arabia did agree to reduce its output in August and September of 1984 below the levels agreed to in OPEC's production sharing system, and to let Nigeria increase production by an equivalent amount.[90] In late 1982 it was reported that Saudi Arabia had offered Mexico a $12 billion loan at below-market interest rates, presumably with the hope of fostering future cooperation, but that Mexico had turned down the offer.[91] It is unlikely, however, that the Saudis considered making so large a loan, which would mostly have been used to pay off bank loans coming due in the second half of 1982. Although neither Mexico nor Nigeria appears to have received loans, Saudi Arabia has dedicated some of its oil revenues to noncommercial uses in its foreign aid program and the probable loans to Iraq, so the potential for political investments in the third world is not entirely absent.

89. See Charles Grant, "Nigeria on the Brink," *Euromoney* (April 1983), p. 133.

90. "OPEC Price Unaltered; Saudis Helping Nigeria," *New York Times*, July 12, 1984.

91. "Saudi Support for Mexico Reported," *Middle East Economic Digest* (September 24, 1982), p. 67; and William Chislett, "Mexico 'Turns Down Saudi Offer of Loan,'" *Financial Times*, October 4, 1982.

That leaves only two other noneconomic considerations: a desire for international prestige and a desire for confidentiality. International prestige has undoubtedly been attained, but it has mostly been a product of the SAMA emphasis on conservative economic factors. The desire for secrecy on individual deals may occasionally have postponed or canceled some transactions. More importantly, the general confidentiality of investments in America may encourage SAMA to increase its investments by some small amount or to make investments through U.S. institutions rather than through third-party transactions. Of course such confidentiality is a normal concern for individual investors.

The evidence favors the conclusion that the Saudi investment strategy has followed a conservative course dictated largely by underlying economic factors. Shifts in strategy have mostly been small and gradual, although the composition of new flows has varied somewhat more as it responds to opportunities for foreign investments in Western nations. The Saudis are now experiencing a medium-term downswing in the oil market and thus are likely to draw on their reserves over the next several years. A shift in strategy is unlikely, however, because the other factors guiding that strategy have not changed.

CHAPTER SIX

Kuwait's Investment Strategy

MORE THAN TWO DECADES before the first oil shock, the Kuwait Investment Board was established in London to advise Kuwait on the disposition of its surplus oil revenues.[1] The average current account surpluses were small in those years, of course, and interest income was not a major source of government revenue. That situation has changed significantly in the last decade. While crude oil remains the ultimate source of the nation's economic strength, foreign investments have become an important source of income, providing earnings equivalent to 78.6 percent of oil and gas export revenues in 1982. The government investment income was equal to 54 percent of oil and gas revenues in fiscal year 1982–83.[2]

Kuwait has become an active and sophisticated participant in financial markets around the world, and its financial strategy is of considerable interest. The most important reason for such interest is the estimated $68 billion of foreign claims under government control at the end of 1983.[3] Kuwait is therefore the only OPEC nation besides Saudi Arabia whose holdings are large enough to have a potential influence on the world financial system. The Kuwaiti surplus also seems more permanent than the surplus of any other OPEC nation.

Individual Kuwaiti investment activities have also attracted considerable attention because of the belief that they are precursors to actions of other Gulf states. For example, Kuwait was the first OPEC nation to make purchases of Japanese stocks; other states soon followed. The 1981 series

1. See M. W. Khouja and P. G. Sadler, *The Economy of Kuwait: Development and Role in International Finance* (London: MacMillan, 1979), pp. 195–96.
2. See Kuwaiti data published in "Kuwait Adopts Measures to Adjust to the Impact of Reduced Oil Revenues," *IMF Survey* (August 8, 1983), pp. 236–38.
3. See later sections for construction of this estimate.

of energy-related direct investments in the American market was also cited as a preview of future investments by other OPEC nations. Whether or not such energy investments are indeed pursued by others, it is important for discussions of energy security to know the motivation and likely magnitude of Kuwait's energy investments.

Finally, Kuwait seems to be evolving from an economy based almost wholly on oil exports to one in which the export of capital and financial expertise plays an equal role. This process is an integral part of the Kuwaiti development strategy and has potential ramifications for the size and nature of the country's investments. Because Kuwait's strategy has also been offered as a development model for the other Gulf states with surpluses, it is important to determine what factors argue for and against such a strategy.

Economic Factors Guiding Investment Policy

It is tempting to assume that Kuwait should pursue an investment policy similar to that of Saudi Arabia. After all, a quick inspection seems to reveal the same underlying conditions—location on the Persian Gulf, low population, dependence on oil, and large foreign exchange reserves. Yet those surface similarities hide very real differences in the economic situations of the two countries.

These differences are most obvious in Kuwait's role in the oil market. Kuwaiti oil exports have declined sharply since reaching 2.93 million barrels a day in 1972.[4] Domestic crude oil production fell to 822,000 barrels a day in 1982, and exports declined to 369,000 barrels of crude oil and 354,000 barrels of refined oil a day. Thus Kuwait's share of world crude oil markets has sharply contracted. At the lower production level Kuwait has oil reserves that should last into the twenty-second century and thus a substantial interest in the long-term commercial prospects for oil.[5] Yet the country would find it difficult to affect market conditions by increasing production; its feasible production range is only a small fraction of the conceivable Saudi range. Kuwaiti financial planners therefore do not face the same revenue swings (in absolute terms) from attempts to

4. Central Bank of Kuwait, *Quarterly Statistical Bulletin* (April–June 1983), p. 39.
5. "Kuwait Adopts Measures to Adjust to the Impact of Reduced Oil Revenues," p. 237.

moderate oil price increases, and the pressure to find new investment outlets quickly after an oil shock is reduced.

On the other hand, Kuwait can cut production drastically during an oil glut as part of a concerted OPEC effort to support the official price. In doing so it will experience only minimal pressure on financial policy because development needs also impose fewer constraints on its financial decisions than they do in other OPEC nations. Kuwait's small land area and population reduce development demands, and a higher percentage of the required infrastructure was in place at the time of the first oil shock. Although spending on social services and basic utilities has increased rapidly in the last decade, the margin between oil revenues and development expenditures was large enough that even the 1982–83 and 1983–84 budgets have not required the government to use more than half of the income from investments, and the 1982 current account surplus almost matched receipts on foreign investments.[6] The budget for fiscal year 1984–85 follows the same pattern.[7]

Kuwaiti financial decisions have therefore been made in an environment relatively free of pressures from either short-term oil market phenomena or basic development needs. The Kuwaitis should, then, have more control than most OPEC nations over the size of the surpluses, and longer-term considerations should play a greater role in investments. It is interesting to consider briefly those long-term factors that should guide the decision on the optimal surplus and the extent to which they have affected Kuwaiti decisions.

Economic theory argues that policymakers should maximize some standard such as the present value of wealth or consumption and that the optimal size of the surplus is merely one of the results of such an analysis. The only major source of wealth in Kuwait is crude petroleum, and any oil production in excess of current expenditure requirements represents the transformation of oil wealth into non-oil wealth in the form of foreign investments or investments in domestic industrialization. Such a transformation should occur only if the rate of return on the alternative investments exceeds the rate of return on oil in the ground.[8]

6. Ibid., pp. 237–38.
7. Shakib Otaqui, "Kuwait's Budget: Can It Revive the Economy?" *Middle East Economic Digest* (April 27, 1984), p. 18.
8. There is an extensive literature on the optimal management of an exhaustible resource. For a relatively untechnical discussion, see Robert M. Solow, "The Economics of Resources or the Resources of Economics," *American Economic Review*,

Such theoretical guidelines, while hard to implement, do seem to be in the background of Kuwaiti discussions, and two policy decisions have probably been heavily influenced by these arguments. The first is Kuwait's current oil production ceiling of 1.25 million barrels a day (mbd), less than 40 percent of the 1972 production peak of 3.28 mbd.[9] Without this production restraint, which seems to have been guided by arguments that oil in the ground yields better returns than financial investments, the cumulative surplus would have been much larger. The second decision is the 1976 creation of the Reserve Fund for Future Generations, which is routinely described as an exchange of oil and financial assets. By law this fund receives at least 10 percent of oil revenues each year, and neither the interest payments nor the principal of the fund may be consumed before 2001.[10] Even these decisions are somewhat contradictory applications of the guidelines because one decreases the surplus and the other mandates continuous "surpluses" for the long-term investment account. It is nearly impossible to identify other situations in which the theoretical guidelines may have been a factor.

There are several more prosaic justifications for the investments. The so-called international finance option, for instance, is one of the few practical ways of diversifying the economy. More direct Kuwaiti management of its funds could not only lead to a higher return on investments but also provide increased skills and new employment opportunities for the local population. A related explanation is that foreign assets, especially direct investments, allow Kuwait to enter industries with ties to crude oil production and enhance the value of its oil assets. None of these alternative motivations exactly contradicts the theoretical model. Yet it is interesting to note that even those who use the terminology of the theoretical guidelines usually start with the assumption that Kuwait *must* run surpluses. Thus two Kuwaiti economists have written: "Being a surplus

---

vol. 64 (May 1974), pp. 1–14. For a technical discussion see Stephen W. Salant, "Staving Off the Backstop: Dynamic Limit Pricing with a Kinked Demand Curve," in Robert S. Pindyck, ed., *Advances in the Economics of Energy and Resources*, vol. 2 (Greenwich, Conn.: JAI Press, 1979), pp. 187–204; and D. M. G. Newberry, "Oil Prices, Cartels, and the Problem of Dynamic Inconsistency," *Economic Journal*, vol. 91 (September 1981), pp. 617–46.

9. Central Bank of Kuwait, *Quarterly Statistical Bulletin* (April–June 1980), table 16; and Shakib Otaqui, "Investment Income Keeps Kuwait's Spending on Course," *Middle East Economic Digest* (March 19, 1982), p. 17.

10. Khouja and Sadler, *The Economy of Kuwait*, p. 202; and *Middle East Economic Digest* (April 2, 1982), p. 19.

economy, it is natural that capital outflows would represent the major function [of Kuwait]. . . . The real issue is not whether Kuwait should or should not play an international financial role, by necessity she has to."[11] Thus, even though it is plausible that financial incentives are necessary for Kuwait to increase oil production in those years when surpluses are already quite large, it is difficult to argue that a small increase in the real rate of return on financial instruments (perhaps 1 to 2 percentage points) would measurably affect the level of oil production. The recent demonstration that real oil prices cannot increase forever without serious effects on the level of production and revenues has also lessened the importance and urgency of extra financial incentives.

Given the size of the surplus, a number of economic factors could have determined its placement. Even with the low production of recent years Kuwait has used only half its interest income to cover budget deficits; it apparently has no plans to dip into the principal of its reserve funds anytime soon.[12] Liquidity is therefore not a major concern of the Ministry of Finance, and holdings of highly liquid bank deposits and U.S. Treasury certificates could be small. Safety should be a major concern, however, if these reserves are indeed viewed as a pension fund for the decades after the oil runs out.

The rate of return is another potentially important factor for Kuwait. The absence of short-term fiscal demands on the surplus has allowed the Kuwaitis to choose long-term investments, such as stocks, bonds, and direct investments, that tend to offer higher returns at the expense of some risk to the principal of the investment if liquidated quickly. This strong emphasis on the rate of return shows up in other forms. For example, the Kuwaitis have expressed an especially strong interest in equities, based on the belief that claims on real assets should be the best hedge against inflation. For the same reason, property holdings have played a small but noticeable role in the official portfolio. Medium-term bonds have played a large role because they have paid high interest rates even after adjusting for inflation.

Kuwait also seeks diversification. Its preference for longer-term invest-

11. Hazem El-Beblawi and Erfan Shafey, "Strategic Options of Development for Kuwait," *IBK Papers*, no. 1 (Kuwait: The Industrial Bank of Kuwait, July 1980), p. 23.

12. Kuwaiti law also makes it illegal to tap the investments of the Reserve Fund for Future Generations before 2001, which leads to an emphasis on long-term investments for that particular account.

ments means that its holdings of medium- and long-term investments may be comparable in magnitude to those of SAMA, leading to extra pressure to diversify currencies and borrowers within that portion of the portfolio. There are, however, a number of reasons why Kuwait cannot diversify too far from the dollar. As Abdlatif al-Hamad, then minister of finance and planning, summarized, "The dollar being the largest trading currency, and the U.S. economy being the largest, and the dollar-denominated invest-ment instruments being the biggest in number and variety, it's a natural thing that the percentage of the dollar, in relation to other currencies, is that much greater."[13]

Several other economic factors have played an ambiguous role in Kuwaiti investment decisions. The first is the complementarity between individual investments and Kuwait's crude-oil-based economy, since such complementarity has been cited as a justification for running a surplus. The second is the possibility that financial decisions were influenced by concerns for the health of the world economy. A third is that management control is important because Kuwait has acquired large stakes in several firms.

Thus the seven economic factors that may possibly have conditioned Kuwait's foreign investments are the absence of short-term constraints, itself a function of Kuwait's development needs and oil market role; the rate of return; safety; diversification; complementarity; concerns about the health of the world economy; and a desire for management control. Politi-cal criteria may also have influenced the investment pattern. For example, some have feared that energy investments could be used to strengthen Kuwaiti or OPEC influence in world oil markets. The investments also may have responded to regional or third world concerns, or they may have been used to secure political ties that could protect Kuwait against Iraqi and Iranian claims on its territory. The following sections assess the rela-tive importance of these economic and political factors for Kuwait's for-eign investment decisions.

Size and Distribution of the Government Portfolio

The inevitable first task in an analysis of the Kuwaiti investment strategy is to quantify the size of government holdings. Table 2-4 in chapter 2

13. David Ignatius, "Kuwait's $70 Billion Finance Minister," *Wall Street Journal*, November 25, 1981.

showed that, based on current account data, the public and private sectors together had added $80.6 billion to their net holdings of foreign assets between 1974 and 1982. At the end of 1973 the net holdings of foreign assets by the central bank were $500 million and those of the commercial banks $1.2 billion, while government assets in 1972 (the last year this item was reported) were $2.4 billion, including $364 million in foreign assets at the central bank.[14] Other financial institutions and other private-sector corporations and individuals also probably had small net holdings of foreign assets before 1974. Total net holdings of foreign assets at the end of 1982 were probably between $85 billion and $87 billion.[15]

The exact distribution between public and private sectors is unavailable. Perhaps the lowest estimate of public-sector holdings is that provided by the minister of finance to the Kuwaiti National Assembly, who said the government's foreign investments were $51 billion at the end of 1981.[16] That estimate seems too low, especially in light of other data and other Kuwaiti statements. Jassem Al-Khorafi, chairman of the Financial and Economic Affairs Committee of the National Assembly, stated that government reserves equaled $66.7 billion at the end of 1981 and had increased to $71.6 billion at the end of 1982,[17] although that figure may include some local investments.

This study will use an estimate of $64 billion for the government's net holdings of foreign assets as of the end of 1982.[18] This figure does not

14. International Monetary Fund, *International Financial Statistics, 1983 Yearbook* (IMF, 1983), p. 325.

15. That is, $80.6 billion accumulated by all sectors between 1974 and 1982, central bank holdings of $500 million and commercial bank holdings of $1.2 billion at the end of 1973, between $1.5 billion and $2 billion of other government holdings at the end of 1973, and between $1 billion and $2.5 billion of other private holdings at the end of 1973.

16. "Kuwait's Investments Abroad Top $50 Billion, Finance Minister Says," *Wall Street Journal*, October 26, 1982. The minister of finance's estimate probably excluded the substantial foreign holdings of the government-owned Kuwait Petroleum Corporation.

17. "Kuwait's Reserves Given as $72 bn in 1982," *Middle East Economic Survey* (June 6, 1983), p. B5.

18. That figure has been obtained as follows. First, it is assumed that net foreign holdings are around $86 billion, an estimate from the middle of the range provided earlier. Those net holdings include $6 billion of net foreign holdings by the central bank and $3.3 billion at commercial banks and other financial institutions (see IMF, *International Financial Statistics, 1983 Yearbook*, p. 325). This leaves $76.7 billion to divide between other government holdings and nonfinancial private-sector holdings. These are assigned 75 percent to the government and 25 percent to the private sector,

attempt to assign any part of the foreign holdings of financial institutions or nonfinancial corporations to the government, even though the government owns shares in most of those companies. The continued balance of payments surplus during 1983 means that the government's net holdings of foreign assets probably had increased to approximately $68 billion by the end of 1983.[19]

One of the most striking facts about this government portfolio is the minimal amount held in short-term securities. Investments in bank deposits and U.S. Treasury bills (including any holdings in central bank reserves) were probably about $12 billion at the end of 1982, or approximately ten months of import cover.[20] This implies that over 80 percent of the government's foreign assets are in longer-term holdings; a figure of $52 billion can be used for such holdings as of the end of 1982. Disbursements to Iraq probably represented approximately $5 billion by the end of 1982.[21] Another $3 billion includes such items as loans to the IMF, central bank holdings of gold, concessional loans by the Kuwait Fund for Arab

---

based on investment income data from the balance of payments for the years 1980 to 1982 (see Central Bank of Kuwait, *Quarterly Statistical Bulletin* [April–June 1983], table 42). This implies that at the end of 1982 the government (excluding the central bank) had $57.5 billion of net foreign assets, $63.5 billion if the central bank is included.

19. The 1983 current account surplus was KD 1.53 billion, or $5.26 billion at the average 1983 exchange rate. See Shakib Otaqui, "Kuwait: Emerging from the Gloom," *Middle East Economic Digest* (June 22, 1984), pp. 26–30; and IMF, *International Financial Statistics*, vol. 37 (July 1984), p. 282. Using the 75 percent–25 percent split between government and private-sector holdings implies that the government's holdings increased $3.95 billion.

20. Private and government holdings of deposits at Canadian, Japanese, and European banks totaled $12.21 billion as of December 1982; see Bank for International Settlements, *Maturity Distribution of International Bank Lending* (December 1983). Holdings of Middle Eastern OPEC nations in the United States at the end of 1982 included $7.1 billion of Treasury bills and certificates along with $6.4 billion of bank deposits. They also held $15.5 billion at foreign branches of U.S. banks, for a total of $29 billion; see data from the Office of International Banking and Portfolio Investment, Department of the Treasury, September 9, 1983; and Federal Reserve System, Statistical Release E.11, December 15, 1983. At least $4 billion of these holdings can reasonably be assigned to Kuwait, for $16 billion in total holdings of short-term instruments. The previous estimate of a government share of 75 percent in overall holdings can then be applied to the $16 billion figure.

21. Commitments may have reached $8 billion. The loans to Iraq are included here as part of the investment portfolio because Kuwait's own balance of payments figures do not subtract these loans before determining the annual current account surplus. See the section on Iraq in chapter 7 for further information on the recent Arab loans to Iraq.

Economic Development, and occasional government-to-government loans on nonconcessionary terms.[22] The remaining $44 billion probably includes $26 billion of equity holdings and $18 billion of bonds.[23] The foreign equity holdings include stocks, direct investments, and property. Although this category lumps together a wide variety of investment claims, they do have one common element: all present some voting power, though the percentage and actual power are small in most cases. Bond investments do not offer such opportunities to affect the borrower's actions.

The government was supposed gradually to transfer management of its reserves to the new National Investment Authority, but that change is unlikely to affect the basic tenor of investment policy. That authority, which is chaired by the minister of finance and has representatives of the minister of oil and of the central bank, was largely a response to the national assembly's desire for a centralized authority that would also be more responsive to the assembly.

Equity Investments

Whether in the form of stocks, real estate, or direct investment, equities represent the sort of tangible assets that the Kuwaitis consider ideal for preserving capital in the long run while offering high rates of return. The range of investment opportunities also expands considerably for an investor willing to consider equities because real estate and direct investments can be made almost anywhere if liquidity is not a pressing concern. Over the years Kuwait has pursued equity investments worldwide, and its hold-

22. The Kuwait Fund had made net disbursements of $1.4 billion by the end of 1981, according to Organization for Economic Cooperation and Development, *Aid from OPEC Countries* (Paris: OECD, 1983), p. 46. The Central Bank of Kuwait lent SDR 685 million to the IMF's oil facility, all of which was repaid by May 1983, and SDR 325.1 million (around $351 million) was outstanding to the IMF's Supplementary Financing Facility as of April 30, 1983. See IMF, *Annual Report 1983*, pp. 125–26, tables I.9 and I.10.

23. This 60–40 division between equity and other holdings in the long-term portfolio accords with the supposed 1974 decision of Kuwait to allocate its general reserve fund in this ratio; see Khouja and Sadler, *The Economy of Kuwait*, p. 200. It also fits roughly with comments made to the author in interviews with bankers in 1982 and 1983, but there has been some variability in estimates of components of the portfolio. The highest estimate of equity holdings was contained in an article that referred to the "$48,000 million in equities that Kuwait is thought to have invested abroad"; see *Arab Banking and Finance* (July 1982), p. 56. Even if this figure includes both public and private claims, it still far exceeds other estimates of Kuwait's equity involvement.

ings now range from fertilizer factories in Pakistan and oil refineries in Malaysia to steel plants in West Germany and office buildings in London. Yet the United States, Great Britain, West Germany, and Japan account for almost all of Kuwait's equity investments because most investment opportunities are still in the industrial nations.

Khaled Abu Suud, financial adviser to the emir of Kuwait, estimated in late 1979 that Kuwait then held $20 billion of long-term investments in the United States,[24] which implies, in light of the sixty-forty split between equities and bonds in the long-term portfolio, that Kuwait already held as much as $12 billion of U.S. equities and property in 1979. Kuwait's equity investments have probably risen since then to $14 billion, or over 50 percent of its global equity portfolio.

The first American investment to attract considerable attention was the $17.4 million purchase of Kiawah Island resort in 1974. Although that deal stoked fears of Arabs buying up substantial amounts of American property, real estate investments do not represent a major share of the portfolio. Total American real estate investments by Kuwait have been placed as high as $500 million, but a recent Department of Commerce study listed only five U.S. real estate transactions by Kuwaiti government-owned or government-controlled entities from January 1974 to June 1981. The four investments for which prices were given had a total value of $59.4 million at the time of transaction.[25] In any case, real estate investments have been a small percentage of Kuwait's American investments and an extremely small percentage of the value of American real estate. These investments have largely been in hotels and other commercial properties, usually in the South or West. Undeveloped land is rarely bought except in conjunction with Kuwaiti plans to build on the site.

Portfolio holdings of stocks are far more typical of Kuwait's American investments.[26] Although disclosure is not required for most of Kuwait's

24. This figure includes equity and bond instruments and may also include some dollar-denominated Eurobonds issued by American corporations. See Bill Paul, "Power Broker: Kuwait's Money Man Favors U.S. and Stocks in Placing Oil Billions," *Wall Street Journal*, October 9, 1979.

25. International Trade Administration, *Direct Investment in the United States by Foreign Government-owned Companies 1974–1981* (Department of Commerce, March 1983), appendixes B, D. This study only used publicly available reports and thus may not have included all direct investments reported to the Department of Commerce's Bureau of Economic Analysis.

26. The United States defines holdings of less than 10 percent of the shares outstanding in a company as portfolio holdings, 10 percent or more as direct investment.

American portfolio, some information was revealed in 1981 about the Kuwaiti portfolios managed by Citibank.[27] At that time Citibank managed a number of portfolios for Kuwait, including five equity portfolios. The value of the equity portfolios was $3.7 billion as of November 28, 1980, while the remaining portfolios were valued at $3.3 billion. There was considerable trading in the Citibank portfolios, although this could have been trading in either bonds or stocks. Much more detailed information was revealed on the two largest portfolios: their market value was $2.43 billion as of December 1980, and they included 196 firms in a wide range of industries. Energy companies accounted for 22.6 percent of the two portfolios (table 6-1), but there were also large holdings in the health, information processing, and utility sectors. Most of the holdings were less than 1 percent of a company's outstanding stock, but in two cases the ownership exceeded 2.5 percent (Atlantic Richfield and American Telephone and Telegraph). Table 6-2 lists the ten largest holdings in the two portfolios.

The rest of Kuwait's U.S. stock portfolio probably follows a similar pattern, although the emphasis on energy may be slightly smaller. Almost all the holdings represent less than 5 percent of a company's stock because U.S. law requires public disclosure of holdings above that level. The investments were built up gradually after the first oil shock, and by late 1979 Kuwait held between $1 million and $50 million of the stock of most of the top 500 U.S. corporations, according to Khaled Abu Suud, adviser to the emir of Kuwait.[28] Net investment in American stocks has probably slowed during the past two years because the 5 percent disclosure standard may be discouraging investments in some companies. However, it seems reasonable to assign a value of $11 billion to Kuwait's portfolio holdings of U.S. stocks at the end of 1982.[29]

Many of the remaining investments in the United States are direct investments in energy-related companies. The Kuwait Petroleum Company (KPC) has been the principal in most of these deals, which are a relatively recent development. In 1980 Kuwait offered to buy 14.6 per-

27. Dan Dorfman, "Kuwait Oil Profits Buy $7 Billion Worth of U.S. Securities," *Washington Post*, May 31, 1981; and Dorfman, "Kuwait Puts Citibank on Investment Hot Seat," *Washington Post*, June 7, 1981.

28. Paul, "Kuwait's Money Man Favors U.S. and Stocks in Placing Oil Billions."

29. This contradicts U.S. Treasury figures, which provide an estimate of $9.6 billion for equity holdings by OPEC at the end of 1982 (see table 4-1). Capital gains can explain some of the difference.

Table 6-1. *Distribution of Two Kuwaiti Portfolios of U.S. Stocks*

Sector	Value[a] (millions of dollars)	Share of two portfolios (percent)
Autos, durables	54.6	2.25
Chemicals	107.7	4.43
Electrical machinery	148.4	6.11
Electronics	44.1	1.81
Finance, banks	66.3	2.73
Finance, insurance	52.5	2.16
Food, beverage, tobacco	133.8	5.50
Food service	46.2	1.90
Forest products	62.4	2.57
Health	246.1	10.13
Information processing	224.6	9.24
Metals	71.3	2.93
Miscellaneous nondurables	165.7	6.82
Oil service	91.2	3.75
Oil companies	457.2	18.81
Retail sales	127.0	5.23
Transportation	64.8	2.67
Utilities	190.7	7.85
Miscellaneous common stock	75.3	3.10
Mutual funds	0.7	0.03
Total	2,430.6[b]	100.00[b]

Source: Dan Dorfman, "Kuwait Oil Profits Buy $7 Billion Worth of U.S. Securities," *Washington Post*, May 31, 1981.
a. Applying December 1980 prices to equity holdings as of April 4, 1981 (this is the method used in the original article).
b. Figures may not add because of rounding.

cent of the common stock of Getty Oil Company for $982 million, but the offer was rejected.[30] Early in 1981 KPC announced plans for a joint venture with Pacific Resources Incorporated for the operation of its Hawaiian refinery, under which KPC was to take a 50 percent stake (worth $185 million) and to guarantee 50 percent of the refinery's crude oil supply requirements. This agreement was never completed.[31] KPC also entered into an exploration joint venture with AZL Resources Incorporated for $50 million. The largest direct investment was the $2.5 billion takeover of

30. "KPC Gets Ready to Join the Oil Majors," *Middle East Economic Digest* Special Report (May 1982), p. 14; and "How Kuwait Widens Its Portfolio," *Middle East Economic Digest* (February 20, 1981), p. 6.
31. "KPC Enters Euro-Oil Market," *Middle East Economic Digest* (February 4, 1983), p. 25.

Table 6-2. *Ten Largest Holdings in Two Kuwaiti Portfolios of U.S Stocks*

Company	Number of shares[a]	Percent of company shares outstanding	Market value[b] (millions of dollars)
Atlantic Richfield	1,808,200	3.89	96.06
AT&T	1,774,200	3.70	91.38
Eastman Kodak	749,400	2.47	61.08
Conoco	1,050,400	2.41	59.48
Phillips Petroleum	1,268,200	2.39	58.97
Proctor & Gamble	788,300	2.25	55.58
General Electric	788,500	2.14	52.83
American Home Products	1,535,000	2.10	51.81
Digital Equipment	546,300	2.07	51.08
Schlumberger	500,300	2.06	50.85

Source: Dorfman, "Kuwait Oil Profits Buy $7 Billion Worth of U.S. Securities."
a. As of April 4, 1981.
b. Applying December 1980 prices to holdings as of April 4, 1981 (this is the method used in the original article).

Santa Fe International Corporation at the end of 1981.[32] Thus KPC now owns a diversified engineering and oil services firm, which at the time of the acquisition also held leases in the United States and the North Sea. Through its Santa Fe subsidiary, KPC also acquired Andover Oil Company for $150 million in 1982, which added to Santa Fe's holdings of U.S. oil and gas reserves.[33]

Even though investments in the United States now dominate the equity portfolio, it was in the British market that Kuwait made its first investment moves. The London-based Kuwait Investment Office (KIO) now manages probably $3 billion worth of British equities and property for the Kuwaiti Ministry of Finance in a financial relationship that dates from 1952 when KIO's predecessor, the Kuwait Investment Board, was formed.[34] The early interest in Britain was natural. When Kuwait's foreign investments began thirty years ago, London was unrivaled as the world's financial center,

32. "KPC Gets Ready to Join the Oil Majors," p. 14.
33. "Oil Firm Purchase Is Set by Santa Fe International Corp.," *Wall Street Journal*, July 26, 1982.
34. In the early years the London office also managed Kuwait's continental and American investments, but responsibility for those investments was returned to officials in the Ministry of Finance in Kuwait when the foreign assets increased following the first oil shock. The Ministry of Finance now uses local banks and other financial agents in the United States and continental Europe to handle investments in those regions. For a description of Kuwait's early investment activities see Khouja and Sadler, *The Economy of Kuwait*, pp. 195–201. KIO apparently still handles much of Kuwait's Japanese equity portfolio.

Kuwait's currency was pegged to the pound sterling, and Kuwait was still a protectorate of the British crown.[35] Although the original motivations have disappeared, Kuwait has continued to find British investments attractive, and it is the only OPEC nation with significant long-term investments in Great Britain.

The first large purchase was the 1974 acquisition of St. Martin's Property Corporation (for £107 million, or about $250 million at that time).[36] St. Martin's had been caught both by the downturn in the real estate market and by a severe liquidity squeeze, which at that time made the purchase appear rather unattractive. It recovered quickly, however, and has served since then as Kuwait's vehicle for London real estate investments. During 1982 KIO announced plans for three more commercial developments. If completed, these projects would increase the value of its British property holdings to over $1 billion.[37]

KIO has also participated in the British stock market, with holdings of perhaps $2 billion by late 1982.[38] These shares are concentrated in the areas of insurance, property, and investment trusts, while investments in British industrial and manufacturing stocks are noticeably absent. This distribution partly reflects the fact that many large U.K. industrial companies have been nationalized.[39] Not only are Kuwait's British holdings concentrated in a very few sectors compared to its American holdings, but KIO has routinely taken larger stakes in British companies; as of 1981 there were fifty-three holdings that exceeded Britain's 5 percent disclosure standard. It has been reported that Kuwait has rarely disinvested in a company.[40]

35. This protectorate began in 1899 and continued until 1961.

36. "How Kuwait Widens Its Portfolio," *Middle East Economic Digest* (February 20, 1981), p. 6.

37. "Kuwait Plans UK Development," *Middle East Economic Digest* (November 26, 1982), p. 42.

38. The value of Kuwaiti investments in British companies that required disclosure had been estimated at $1.5 billion in early 1981, according to "Kuwait Boosts UK Equity Portfolio," *8 Days* (February 28, 1981), p. 37. The London weekly *Investors Chronicle* estimated total equity holdings (both those above the 5 percent disclosure standard and undisclosed investments below that level) of over £1 billion, around $2.35 billion at that time, according to reports in "How Kuwait Widens Its Portfolio," p. 6. The value of the pound has fallen sharply since then.

39. Even Kuwait's investments in financial and property companies may not be entirely British investments because these companies have been more able to place funds overseas since the abolition of exchange controls.

40. "Kuwait Boosts UK Equity Portfolio," pp. 38–39.

Kuwait's West German investments are also substantial, possibly $3 billion by 1982.[41] Although they have been made in relatively few (perhaps thirty) German companies, some of the investments are large. A few represent joint ventures with German companies in third countries.

Kuwait's first large move into the German market took place in 1974 when it paid $440 million for 14.6 percent of the Daimler-Benz automotive firm. This investment aroused some opposition within Germany and led Kuwait to maintain a very low profile over the next several years. But unfavorable publicity did not prevent further large investments. In 1975 Kuwait purchased, for $100 million each, 30 percent shares in the steelmaker Korf Stahl and its American subsidiary, Korf Industries.[42] These investments were not announced for three years.[43] Unidentified Kuwaiti officials described the motivations for the Korf Stahl purchase as a desire "to get into a company with promising technology and good prospects of long-term profitability," but there was no interest "in acquiring a majority stake or in influencing management decisions."[44] The Kuwaiti stake in the American subsidiary, Korf Industries, increased to 51 percent in 1983 as part of a restructuring necessitated by the financial difficulties of the German parent firm.[45]

41. German central bank statistics (see table 2-9) report an increase of DM 7.81 billion ($3.28 billion, using exchange rates at the end of 1982) in OPEC direct investment and portfolio holdings of equity between 1974 and 1982. Kuwaiti investors probably account for the most of these investments, though the shah of Iran made several large investments in 1974, and Qatar, the United Arab Emirates, and private Saudi investors have also purchased German equities. On that basis an estimate of $3 billion for Kuwaiti holdings may at first seem high. There are two reasons for the discrepancy. First, some of the "German" investments actually involve overseas assets, and these of course should not be included in official statistics. Second, official statistics may miss some sizable investments because German reporting requirements are somewhat weaker than U.S. laws. One estimate of German investments reached $4 billion; see "A Sectoral Strategy," *Arab Banking and Finance* (April 1982), p. 51.

42. John D. Law, *Arab Investors: Who They Are, What They Buy, and Where*, vol. 1 (New York: Chase World Information, 1980), pp. 44–45.

43. Technically the investment in Korf Industries should be treated as an American investment, since virtually all its assets are in the United States. The subsidiary, however, was controlled by the German parent firm and thus has traditionally been grouped with German placements in describing Kuwait's foreign investments.

44. Law, *Arab Investors: Who They Are, What They Buy, and Where*, vol. 1, p. 46.

45. Terry Dodsworth, "Korf Industries Sells Two Subsidiaries," *Financial Times*, August 26, 1983; and "Kuwait Takes Majority in Korf U.S.," *Middle East Economic Digest* (September 2, 1983), pp. 29–30.

The next large Kuwaiti investment in conjunction with West German industry occurred in 1980 when 10 percent of Volkswagen do Brasil was purchased for $115 million from its Brazilian shareholders.[46] This was followed by two successive purchases of 10 percent holdings in Metall-gesellschaft at a total cost of $136 million. It was predicted that the engineering firm's business in the Middle East would increase after these transactions and that the design group Lurgi Gesellschaften would show the largest gains.[47]

The largest German investment was KPC's purchase of 24 percent of the Hoechst chemicals group. Acquired over a period of 18 months, this investment had a market value of DM 1.3 billion ($514 million) when it was announced in September 1982.[48] Both sides apparently expected cooperative ventures to arise from the purchase. The chairman of Hoechst's management board remarked that "new emphasis and opportunities might arise for Hoechst from co-operation with Kuwait"[49] and that Kuwait was seeking to combine its petroleum activities with Hoechst's chemical technology and distribution system.[50] One cooperative agreement has since been announced.[51]

Japan is the only other country in which Kuwait is likely to have substantial equity holdings. Kuwait began purchasing Japanese equities in the late 1970s.[52] Very few details are available on OPEC investments in Japan. Nihon Keizai Shimbum conducted a survey in early 1980 indicating that $454 million of equities were directly held by OPEC investors and that Kuwaiti buyers accounted for most of those shares. Total holdings were estimated to be three to five times the size of public holdings.[53] Furthermore, Daiwa Securities estimated that foreign purchases of Japanese equities increased by $4.2 billion in the first nine months of 1980,

46. As in the Korf Industries case, this purchase also included assets outside West Germany but has traditionally been referred to as West German investment.

47. Law, *Arab Investors: Who They Are, What They Buy, and Where*, vol. 1, pp. 46–47; and "How Kuwait Widens Its Portfolio," p. 7.

48. Stewart Fleming, "Hoechst Warns of Dividend Cut and Confirms Kuwaiti Stake," *Financial Times*, October 1, 1982; "Hoechst Says Kuwait Bought 24 Percent of Its Stock," *Wall Street Journal*, October 1, 1982.

49. Fleming, "Hoechst Warns of Dividend Cut and Confirms Kuwaiti Stake."

50. "Hoechst Says Kuwait Bought 24 Percent of Its Stock."

51. See "Energy-Related Direct Investments" later in this chapter.

52. Law, *Arab Investors: Who They Are, What They Buy, and Where*, vol. 1, pp. 48–50.

53. See reports in James Bartholomew, "Tokyo's Secret Petrodollar Connection," *Far Eastern Economic Review* (July 18, 1980), p. 38.

with OPEC investors accounting for half the funds.[54] An estimate of $2 billion to $3 billion for Kuwaiti holdings of Japanese equities at the end of 1982 seems reasonable, given that Kuwait is far more likely than other OPEC investors to buy equities. The Tokyo government has generally looked with favor on these investments and in fact encouraged further flows by raising the ceilings on foreign ownership of Japanese firms in December 1980.[55]

The London-based KIO has handled many of the Japanese investments. The earliest purchases were in resource-related firms, and KIO now has full control over Nippon Kogyo, a mining company that operates in the third world, and Teikoku Sekiyu, an oil company with operations confined largely to Japan. It next moved into the electrical manufacturing sector and by 1982 held 35 million shares of Toshiba Corporation and Mitsubishi Electric Corporation.[56] Substantial purchases of stock in the electronics company Hitachi Limited, in Arabian Oil, and in various pharmaceutical and chemical companies have also been reported over the years.[57]

The Japanese portfolio has been highly diversified, and with the exception of the takeovers of Teikoku Sekiyu and Nippon Kogyo, the holdings have involved small percentages of the outstanding shares. The structure of its portfolio and of Japanese equity markets offers Kuwait the opportunity to trade actively in the market while minimizing the possibility that such trading will noticeably affect the value of the portfolio, although there have been complaints that prices overreact to reports of Arab buying and selling.

Only $3 billion to $4 billion of the Kuwaiti equity portfolio is invested outside these four industrial countries, and it has been widely scattered. For instance, Kuwait has invested as much as $500 million in a number of consortium banks, the largest of which are the Arab Banking Corporation, in which the Kuwaiti capital share is $250 million, and the Gulf Investment Bank, in which the government is directly involved with other Arab states.[58] These pan-Arab consortia aim to become global banks; others are

54. Reported in Stephen Bronte, "Petrodollar Sophistication Grows," *Middle East Economic Digest* Special Report (December 1980), p. 13.

55. OECD, *Financial Market Trends* (November 1981), p. 49.

56. "Heavy Buying on Tokyo Exchange," *Middle East Economic Digest* (October 22, 1982), p. 5.

57. Bartholomew, "Tokyo's Secret Petrodollar Connection," p. 38; Law, *Arab Investors: Who They Are, What They Buy, and Where*, vol. 1, pp. 49–50.

58. These investments are discussed in detail in chapter 9 on Arab banking institutions.

on a much smaller scale, usually designed as a convenient way to channel direct investments or trade finance from Kuwait to the partner.[59] Since early 1983 Kuwait has also bought refining and distribution facilities from Gulf Oil. The facilities, worth several hundred million dollars, are in the Benelux countries, Scandinavia, and Italy.[60] Other Western investments include a Canadian equity portfolio, KIO acquisition of 30 percent of a Canadian copper-molybdenum mine, and property in Marseilles and Paris.[61] There have been investments in South and Southeast Asia, including real estate in Singapore worth $266 million, investments worth perhaps $20 million in Pakistani factories held through the Kuwait Pakistan Investment Company, and a planned Malaysian refinery with a 48 percent Kuwaiti stake valued at approximately $54 million.[62] Finally, Kuwait has also taken part in regional investments, including the Organization of Arab Petroleum Exporting Countries' Arab Petroleum Investment Corporation and various Gulf Cooperation Council enterprises.

Bond Investments

Bonds were a part of Kuwait's investment portfolio long before the first oil shock, and they have continued to be important. They represented approximately $18 billion of mostly medium-term placements at the end of 1982, and included issues from government and corporate borrowers in a variety of currencies.

Kuwait apparently has tended to prefer Eurocurrency markets over domestic markets, but some of the bond portfolio has been invested in domestic market issues of major Western governments. During the 1960s, holdings of British Treasury bonds were a natural consequence of the decision to peg the Kuwaiti dinar to the pound sterling, but the holdings have stayed large even though the dinar is now pegged to an unrevealed basket of currencies in which the dollar seems to predominate. It was

59. Two examples are the Banque Senegalo-Koweitienne and Banco Arabe Español. In many cases the Kuwaiti share is held by institutions such as the Kuwait Foreign Trading, Contracting, and Investment Company in which the government has substantial equity interests.

60. See pp. 114–20 for details.

61. Dorfman, "Kuwait Oil Profits Buy $7 Billion Worth of U.S. Securities"; "KIO Buys into Canadian Mine," *Middle East Economic Digest* (November 5, 1982), p. 38; and "How Kuwait Widens Its Portfolio," p. 8.

62. "How Kuwait Widens Its Portfolio," p. 7.

reported in 1980 that Kuwait held the equivalent of $4 billion in British government bonds, a figure that seems to have varied little since 1974.[63] Kuwait probably holds some U.S. Treasury obligations, and there might also be small holdings of German and Japanese government bonds.

Most of the rest of Kuwait's bond portfolio has been purchased in the Euromarkets, although there have also been some private placements. The announcements of completed bond deals are the major source of information on Eurobonds, but those announcements do not provide information on the ultimate lenders, such as the Kuwaiti government. The government, however, tends to rely on domestic financial institutions as its intermediary in bond transactions. The "Three Ks," the Kuwait Investment Company (KIC), the Kuwait International Investment Company (KIIC), and the Kuwait Foreign Trading, Contracting and Investment Company (KFTCIC), are particularly likely to be involved. If a Kuwaiti institution participates in a Eurobond issue, it is usually the case that the government itself has bought most of that institution's share, although the institution may hold some of the issue on its own books and place some of the bonds with other private investors in the Middle East. Thus one can use the announcements as a source of information on deals the Kuwaiti government ultimately bought into, but not for exact information on the size and distribution of the government's holdings.[64]

Kuwait's Eurobond investments can be conveniently divided into dollar bonds, Kuwaiti dinar (KD) bonds, and all other bonds. The markets other than the Kuwaiti dinar bond market offer nearly the same mix of borrowers and bond maturities, while the interest rates and currency risk depend on the bond's denomination. The KD bond market was designed to offer Kuwaiti lenders an alternative market without foreign currency risk;

63. Law, *Arab Investors: Who They Are, What They Buy, and Where*, vol. 1, p. 41.

64. Occasionally, summary articles have appeared on the bond issues managed by major Arab institutions. The discussion refers only to those deals in which a Kuwaiti financial institution was a lead manager or comanager. See "Bond Issues Managed by Major Arab Institutions in 1975," *Euromoney* (March 1976) Special Section, pp. 32, 35; "A History of Arab Underwriting," *Euromoney* (August 1977), Special Section, pp. 31–41; "Arab Banks as Underwriters," *Institutional Investor—International Edition* (August 1979), pp. 107–10; "The Arab Dealmakers," *Institutional Investor—International Edition* (August 1980), pp. 103–07; "The Arab Dealmakers," *Institutional Investor—International Edition* (August 1981), pp. 95–103; "The Arab Deal Makers," *Institutional Investor—International Edition* (June 1982), pp. 117–28; and H. S. Nashashibi, "Financial Resources for Development," annexes I, II.

unlike the other Eurocurrency markets, placements are made almost entirely within the Middle East and most of these within Kuwait.

Table 6-3 presents data on publicized Eurobond issues that had Kuwaiti managers. The dollar's share of the non-KD part of these transactions has varied from a low of 31.8 percent in 1974 to a high of 92.6 percent in 1982, while the dollar's share of all transactions with Kuwaiti managers was as low as 25.1 percent in 1978 and peaked at 91 percent in 1982.[65] This slightly overstates the dollar's role vis-à-vis the dinar in the Kuwaiti government's portfolio because the government usually takes about half of any KD bond issue but would get much less of any non-KD issue with a global distribution.[66] There is, however, no reason to expect the figures on the dollar's share of non-KD bond holdings to be biased in either direction.

Kuwaiti purchases of non-KD bonds have tended to reflect the market distribution of borrowers. There is a mix of supranational, corporate, and Western public-sector borrowers but very few developing-country borrowers. Most maturities range from five to ten years, and the role of the dollar among non-KD bonds has essentially paralleled market movements (table 6-3). There was an early and clear interest in deutsche mark-denominated bonds, although their role has declined in recent years. Even the interest in Japanese borrowers is not a new phenomenon, although the structure of deals with them has changed somewhat over the years. Kuwait had been participating in dollar-denominated issues for Japanese companies since 1975 and moved rather naturally into yen-denominated issues when they became available in 1980. A number of the recent bond issues by Japanese companies have been dollar-denominated convertible bonds with fairly favorable conversion terms.

The Kuwaiti dinar bond issues represent a rather different sort of bond. The public KD bond issues were an outgrowth of private placements that began in 1968 with a KD 15 million ($42 million) placement for the World Bank. At the end of 1973 the World Bank was still the only entity to have tapped this market, but in 1974 Kuwait decided to make this a public market in which other foreigners could participate. During the first five years the borrowers were almost exclusively national and supranational

65. Most Eurodollar issues do not represent borrowings by American entities. Thus the high variability in Eurodollar issues does not represent a correspondingly high variability in the number of American borrowers.

66. Figures on the role of the Kuwaiti government and its agencies are from Hikmat Sharif Nashashibi and Omar Kassem, "The KD Bond Market: Oslo Joins Finland in a Vote of Confidence," *Euromoney* (January 1979), p. 96.

Table 6-3. *Currency Distribution of Publicized Eurobond Issues with Kuwaiti Managers, 1974–83*
Millions of dollars unless otherwise specified

Distribution	1974	1975	1976	1977	1978	1979	1980	1981	1982	1983[a]
Bond issues with Kuwaiti managers										
Dollar issues	130.0	523.5	395.0	560.0	245.0	510.0	3,027.5	6,716.1	5,925.0	825.0
Kuwaiti dinar issues[b]	0	167.2	212.1	108.2	418.2	383.8	25.9	122.0	111.2	17.2
All other issues[b]	279.3	480.0	185.0	253.5	311.7	194.8	1,518.5	1,743.0	476.2	122.6
All issues	409.3	1,170.1	792.1	921.7	974.9	1,088.6	4,571.9	8,581.1	6,512.4	964.8
Dollar issues as percent of all issues	31.8	44.7	49.9	60.8	25.1	46.8	66.2	78.3	91.0	85.5
Dollar issues as percent of all issues, excluding KD issues	31.8	52.2	68.1	68.8	44.0	72.4	66.6	79.4	92.6	87.1
All Eurobond issues										
Dollar issues as percent of all issues, excluding KD issues	45.2	41.6	64.3	67.0	45.0	66.0	62.4	82.4	83.0	. . .

Sources: For data from January 1974 to May 1977, see the survey on Arab banking in *Euromoney* (August 1977), pp. 32–41; for data from June 1977 to December 1977, see "Market Commentary—International Bond Market," *Euromoney* (August 1977 to February 1978); for data from January 1978 to March 1982, see surveys in *Institutional Investor—International Edition* (August 1979, pp. 107–10; August 1980, pp. 103–07; August 1981, pp. 96–99; June 1982, pp. 117–28); for data from January 1982 to June 1983, see "Market Commentary—International Bond Markets," *Euromoney* (March 1982 to August 1983).
a. January 1983 to June 1983 only.
b. Foreign currency amounts converted into dollars at the average exchange rate for that year.

agencies, which were able to borrow on terms similar to those for top-quality Eurobond borrowers, even though many of the participants in the KD bond market were unable to issue bonds in any other sector of the Eurobond market. From 65 percent to 85 percent of most issues was placed in Kuwait, and around half of any issue was taken by government agencies.[67] Issues by borrowers such as Sudan Airways and Bank Handlowy (Poland's international bank), however, probably were placed almost completely with public institutions. Corporate borrowers avoided the market in the early years despite the favorable interest rates, partly because they feared the foreign exchange risk involved in borrowing dinars and partly because of the perception that only higher-risk entities borrowed there.

The quality of borrowers began improving in 1978 when the favorable interest rate margin brought in several public-sector borrowers from Scandinavia. In 1979 four corporate borrowers entered the market (two French, one American, and one Japanese). In much of 1980 and 1981 the market was closed, largely because Kuwaiti investors were unwilling to forgo the extra interest to be earned on Eurodollar bonds (the margin exceeded 550 basis points in 1981). The 10 percent interest rate ceiling was removed late in 1981, and issues resumed with top quality Western government and corporate borrowers.[68] The market was open for about a year. During that time one issue seemed to have been offered for political rather than commercial reasons: the KD 30 million ($104.5 million) issue for India's Rashtriya Chemicals and Fertilizers in late 1981, most of which was probably placed with the Ministry of Finance.[69] There were not many issues during this period, however, because they were unattractive to Kuwaiti investors (private or government) as long as interest rates on Eurodollar bonds exceeded rates on KD bonds by several hundred basis points. More recently, problems associated with the collapse of the unofficial stock market (Souk al Manakh) caused the government once again to restrict the external use of the Kuwaiti dinar. The public KD bond market reopened in June 1983 with a KD 5 million ($17.3 million) issue for the London-based United Bank of Kuwait. Two public issues for KFTCIC

67. H. S. Nashashibi, "Financial Resources for Development," p. 6; and Nashashibi and Kassem, "The KD Bond Market," p. 96.
68. Ellen Pearlman, "Will Corporations Tap the Kuwaiti Dinar Market?" *Institutional Investor—International Edition* (February 1982), pp. 117–24.
69. "Kuwait Continues Activity in Dollar Issues," *Arab Banking and Finance* (April 1982), p. 4.

came out in November 1983, and one for the Industrial Bank of Kuwait in January 1984.[70] Although there have been only Kuwaiti borrowers in the public market since its recent revival, two private placements for Western borrowers took place in late 1983.[71]

Energy-Related Direct Investments

The part of Kuwait's investment strategy attracting the most attention and controversy in recent years has been its direct investments in the energy industry. These may be more than just another channel for long-term investment of the surplus, but they also fall short of providing the means for Kuwait or OPEC to become dominant in world oil markets.

The Kuwait Petroleum Corporation has been the principal in most of the energy-related direct investments. KPC's current and potential operations can be divided into eight parts: purely domestic operations, especially exploration, production, and marketing; international sales of crude oil; crude oil and product tanker fleets; engineering design and construction; foreign exploration and drilling; foreign refining; petrochemicals operations; and overseas retail operations. Most of the "seven sisters," the largest international oil companies, are involved in all of these areas (with the possible exception of petrochemicals operations), but KPC, like most OPEC national oil companies, had previously operated almost exclusively in the first three fields. Recent purchases and production agreements will take KPC into all eight fields. Thus it is evolving toward becoming an integrated oil company, although Sheikh Ali Khalifah al-Sabah (minister of oil and chairman of KPC) has said that it will not become the eighth sister among international oil companies.[72] The funds for many of these investments were generated during 1980 and 1981, when KPC purchased oil from the government at the official OPEC price, sold it on world markets at a premium, and was allowed to retain the profits. The Kuwaiti National Assembly provided new funds in June 1982 through a law that

70. "KD Bond Market Reopened Despite Deepening Stock Crisis," *Middle East Economic Survey* (June 27, 1983), pp. B1–B2; "KD Bond Market Revives," *Middle East Economic Digest* (November 25, 1983), p. 18; and "IBK Makes Innovative Bond Issue," *Middle East Economic Digest* (January 20, 1984), p. 41.

71. *Middle East Economic Survey* (October 24, 1983), p. B3.

72. From an interview with Petroleum Information International reported in "KPC Stakes Its Claim Worldwide," *8 Days* (January 16, 1982), p. 23.

increased KPC's capital from KD 1 billion to KD 2.5 billion (approximately $8.75 billion).[73]

The foreign exploration and drilling ventures have provoked the greatest concern on the grounds that they could eventually affect control of world oil production. KPC has made four main investments in exploration outside the OPEC and Arab world.[74] One is the International Energy Development Corporation (IEDC), a consortium in which KPC is the majority shareholder. This group has oil exploration programs in seven developing countries and Australia and generally has emphasized the search for smaller fields that, although supposedly unattractive to the major oil companies, would provide a significant share of the energy needs of the countries in which they are located.[75] The joint venture with AZL Resources also focuses almost exclusively on exploration, in this case in the western United States, while the purchase of Andover Oil Company in 1982 provides oil and gas reserves in the middle of the United States.

The largest exploration ventures have been handled through Santa Fe International. That purchase included leases in the North Sea and the western United States, along with a joint ARCO–Santa Fe offshore exploration project near China's Hainan Island.[76] In 1982 Santa Fe also entered into a joint exploration pact with Standard Oil Company (Indiana), and its chairman said that the company was close to a joint-exploration agreement with another major oil company.[77] Such large-scale activities were possible only because KPC had committed $1 billion to Santa Fe's U.S. explo-

73. "Kuwait Lifts Capital of KPC by 150%," *Financial Times*, June 15, 1982.

74. In 1981 the Kuwait Foreign Petroleum Exploration Company (KUFPEC) was created as a wholly-owned subsidiary of KPC. Most of the foreign exploration ventures detailed in this section are officially assigned to KUFPEC; see Mary Frings, "Exploration Net Spread Further," *Financial Times* Survey of Kuwait, February 22, 1984.

75. See John Leroux, "IEDC: An Oil World Pioneer," *8 Days* (February 6, 1982), p. 56; and Richard Johns, "Kuwait Increases Stake in IEDC," *Financial Times*, June 9, 1982.

76. The Mineral Lands Leasing Act of 1920 stipulates that no foreign country can get mineral rights on federally owned lands unless it offers reciprocal rights to U.S. companies. If the U.S. Department of the Interior does not add Kuwait to its list of reciprocal countries, KPC itself might not be able to develop some of the leases that came with the purchase of Santa Fe International Corporation. So far the Reagan administration has ruled only that Kuwaiti investors may not acquire new leases on federally owned lands. See "Kuwaitis Barred From Acquiring Federal Leases," *Wall Street Journal*, March 11, 1983.

77. Steve Mufson and Youssef M. Ibrahim, "Santa Fe International Thrives Since Kuwait Bought It a Year Ago," *Wall Street Journal*, November 29, 1982.

ration budget for the next five years (previous annual budgets included $50 million to $80 million for U.S. activities) and had indicated that a similar amount would be channeled into non-U.S. exploration through Santa Fe and its subsidiaries. Santa Fe International also has considerable drilling technology and experience.

KPC has also been involved in at least five foreign exploration projects in other OPEC and Arab countries. It bought a 50 percent share in the Moroccan oil concessions of Elf Acquitaine in 1981, has been involved in joint studies with Shell Oil on exploration in Ecuador, discovered oil in its Indonesian concession, arranged for seismic surveys and exploratory drilling of offshore tracts for Bahrain, and is the operator of two joint-venture concessions in Tunisia.[78] Yet even if all these projects are very successful, it is unlikely that they will add more than a small fraction to the amount of world oil and gas reserves under Kuwaiti control. In fact, at least three of the projects (IEDC, China, and Ecuador) represent contracts for exploration without any Kuwaiti ownership of the concession. Finally, the Kuwait Investment Office bought a 15 percent stake in Promet, a Malaysian-Singapore oil rig and property group that may provide an entry into other drilling ventures in Southeast Asia.[79]

Kuwait's acquisition of engineering design and construction companies has also been a point of contention, usually on the grounds that such purchases represented an unnecessary or even dangerous transfer of technology. This issue was especially important in the purchase of Santa Fe because its C. F. Braun subsidiary had conducted site preparation studies for a U.S. plutonium production facility. Although this work did not give C. F. Braun access to the weapons technology, it did require that the company design the overall facility to meet the processing plant's needs.[80] This issue was resolved by creating a blind trust for the relevant subsidiaries, which gave KPC Braun's profits but denied it control of management decisions, and by Braun's decision to drop out of such projects.

Kuwait has access to engineering design and construction technology through the takeover of Santa Fe and purchase of a 20 percent share of

78. Central Bank of Kuwait, *Economic Report 1981* (Kuwait: Central Bank of Kuwait, 1982), p. 42; *Petroleum Intelligence Weekly* (December 5, 1983); and Frings, "Exploration Net Spread Further."

79. Wong Sulong, "Kuwait to Buy Stake in Promet," *Financial Times*, December 22, 1982.

80. See *Federal Response to OPEC Country Investments in the United States*, Hearings before a Subcommittee of the House Committee on Government Operations, 97 Cong. 1 sess. (GPO, 1982), pt. 2.

West Germany's Metallgesellschaft. Kuwait decided to use Santa Fe's C. F. Braun subsidiary as an in-house process engineering division according to industry sources and did not wait long to put the newly purchased expertise to use. It canceled the tender for the expansion of KPC's Mina Abdullah refinery and gave this project to Braun only three weeks after the takeover, and it is also expected that Braun will win the contract to design and build a domestic petrochemicals complex for Petrochemicals Industries Company, a KPC subsidiary, if such a complex is ever built. Braun will continue to compete for other contracts, especially in Gulf countries.[81] Kuwait also hopes to improve the engineering know-how of its oil industry through connections with Metallgesellschaft's Lurgi Gesellschaften subsidiary, although it is not clear what form this will take.[82] The primary result of these purchases is that Kuwait will have closer supervision of all phases of the construction of its own petrochemicals complexes, which may improve its competitiveness in world markets but will not have a major effect on its share of world markets.

KPC continues to extend its refining operations, both domestic and foreign. Domestically the expansions of the Ahmadi and Mina Abdullah refineries will raise Kuwait's products capacity to 750,000 barrels a day. This means that it would export almost 70 percent of its oil as refined products.[83] Kuwait has also pursued a number of foreign refining deals. The joint venture with Pacific Resources in Hawaii fell through, but if it had been completed, Kuwait would have owned half of a light-products refinery with a capability of processing 68,000 barrels a day and would also have guaranteed half of its crude oil supply.[84] KPC has also committed itself to purchase small refineries in the Netherlands, Denmark, and Italy (with capacities of 75,000, 83,000, and 75,000 barrels a day, respectively) in conjunction with the purchase of Gulf Oil's retail and distribution facilities in Europe.[85] Another project is the Malacca refinery in Malaysia (owned by two government investment institutions, not KPC), whose

81. "KPC Joins the Seven Sisters," *Middle East Economic Digest* (February 5, 1982), p. 21.

82. "Oil Minister Outlines Strategy for Kuwait's KPC," Supplement to *Middle East Economic Survey* (May 18, 1981), p. 3.

83. "KPC Gets Ready to Join the Oil Majors," p. 14.

84. "KPC Enters Euro-Oil Market," p. 25.

85. Doron P. Levin, "Gulf Oil to Sell Benelux Lines to Kuwait Firm," *Wall Street Journal*, February 2, 1983; Carla Rapoport, "Kuwait to Buy Gulf Oil Assets in Scandinavia," *Financial Times*, March 2, 1983; and Richard Johns, "Kuwaitis Buy Gulf Italy Assets," *Financial Times*, January 12, 1984.

capacity is 150,000 barrels a day.[86] Kuwait, Saudi Arabia, and Bahrain are also planning a Bahrain-based heavy-oil refining unit with daily production of 80,000 barrels of fuel oil.[87] Finally, Kuwait and Saudi Arabia were considering participation in a planned Iraqi-Tunisian refinery with a capacity of 200,000 barrels a day. Kuwait will also be trying to export products from its domestic refineries. The main justification for both the domestic and foreign refining operations has been that refining maximizes Kuwait's return on the less desirable heavy crudes. Oil Minister al-Sabah described it as a "hard-nosed business decision."[88]

The Kuwaiti moves into the petrochemicals industry have been limited so far, with the scale and timing lagging behind those of Saudi Arabia. Even the domestic projects, which would use associated natural gas as feedstock, remain a long way from approval let alone completion. C. F. Braun is handling the feasibility studies for the plants, so the Santa Fe purchase does complement the KPC's plans in this area. The only foreign investments in this area are five Tunisian-Kuwaiti ventures in phosphates and fertilizers, a participation in Gulf Petrochemicals Company (a Saudi-Kuwaiti-Bahraini consortium for the production of methanol and ammonia), and the stake in West Germany's Hoechst.[89]

So far KPC has chosen a very different form of involvement than did the Saudi Arabian Basic Industries Corporation (SABIC). In fact Oil Minister al-Sabah has criticized SABIC's joint ventures on Saudi territory with Western firms as a stumbling block to cooperation between the Gulf countries in product pricing and marketing.[90] The Kuwaitis have tried to keep most of the marketing responsibility in their own hands, as exemplified by various spot and long-term contracts to supply petrochemicals to Japanese firms.[91] But KPC has not been absolutely opposed to marketing and production arrangements with Western companies. In particular, the stake in the West German chemicals group Hoechst AG may eventually lead to a variety of production arrangements in which Hoechst uses basic petrochemicals produced in Kuwait as feedstocks for its plants. One such agreement has been negotiated on ammonia, and arrangements have been dis-

86. "How Kuwait Widens Its Portfolio," p. 7.

87. Central Bank of Kuwait, *Economic Report 1981*, p. 41.

88. "Oil Minister Outlines Strategy for Kuwait's KPC," p. 4.

89. Central Bank of Kuwait, *Economic Report 1981*, p. 43; and *Middle East Economic Digest* (December 16, 1983), p. 101.

90. "Oil Minister Outlines Strategy for Kuwait's KPC," p. 5.

91. *Middle East Economic Digest* (December 16, 1983), p. 14.

cussed for ethylene and styrene.[92] Hoechst and KPC have also signed letters of intent under which Hoechst would sell Kuwait's production of ammonia and fertilizers in third markets.[93] Future agreements might require the resurrection of KPC's plans for domestic petrochemical plants, although on a smaller scale than was previously anticipated.

Overseas retailing of refined products is the last of the areas that KPC has tried to enter, and its current activities are limited. It spent over a year negotiating with Gulf Oil about the purchase of Gulf's European refining and distribution facilities before the first agreement was reached in early 1983. KPC's primary target had been Gulf's terminals and distribution facilities in continental Europe, while Gulf wanted to sell refinery and retail facilities as a package.[94] In the end Kuwait agreed to buy Gulf's refining and marketing operations in the Benelux and Scandinavian countries and in Italy, along with the right to use the Gulf trademark for an undisclosed number of years. Thus KPC has finally entered into foreign retail operations. The market shares of the previous Gulf operations ranged from 3 percent in Italy to 10 percent in Sweden.[95]

Profitability seems to be an important factor in the pattern of KPC's foreign investments. The oil minister has stated that one goal is to "make sure that each single project yields a profit of not less than 20 percent."[96] This leaves some room for interpretation, however, because he has also mentioned the strategic objective of augmenting the oil industry in Kuwait.[97] Furthermore, Kuwait's downstream acquisitions seem to be guided by a desire for such operations independent of other considerations. For example, in connection with the purchase of the Benelux facilities of Gulf Oil, the corporation's finance manager has commented that "we are not looking at the Gulf assets as a possible profit generating connection. The profit aspect has not even been looked at. We wanted to

92. Carla Rapoport, "Hoechst Will Buy Ammonia from Kuwait," *Financial Times*, May 3, 1983.

93. "KPC Strengthens Hoechst Links," *Middle East Economic Digest* (January 20, 1984), p. 41.

94. "Kuwait Readjusts Europe Plans, As Gulf Oil Talks End," *Petroleum Intelligence Weekly* (November 8, 1982), p. 1.

95. Levin, "Gulf Oil to Sell Benelux Lines to Kuwait Firm"; Rapoport, "Kuwait to Buy Gulf Oil Assets in Scandinavia"; and Johns, "Kuwaitis Buy Gulf Italy Assets," p. 17.

96. "Kuwait Sets High Profit Standards for Expanding Abroad," *Petroleum Intelligence Weekly* (September 20, 1982), p. 4.

97. "Oil Minister Outlines Strategy for Kuwait's KPC," p. 3.

go downstream."[98] Still, the profitability criterion would justify domestic petrochemical complexes (because they improve the utilization of associated natural gas), exploration and drilling (especially the U.S. and China ventures, which were then industry favorites), and probably the formation or purchase of an in-house engineering section. It would tend to rule out new construction of foreign refineries and petrochemicals plants because the profitability of the refining and petrochemical industries has been hit hard by the oil shocks and prolonged recession. This means that downstream expansion into international markets should probably be based on refining at home. Profitability might also be enhanced by increasing Kuwait's retailing facilities and experience, though the recent purchase of most of Gulf Oil's European operations should be sufficient for that purpose.

Overall, the investments meet Kuwait's criterion of profitability without implying that the oil market position of Kuwait or OPEC has been strengthened. Thus they should not be of special concern to the West. There could be further foreign direct investments by KPC, especially if the company adds to its exploration concessions or its capabilities for retailing refined products. Further refinery purchases outside the Arab world are likely only if they are part of a package including retail facilities. There also seems little need to purchase additional engineering firms. Now that Kuwait owns C. F. Braun and a share in Lurgi Gesellschaften, the gains from complementarity have probably been exhausted. It is possible, however, that KPC or the Ministry of Finance might make such a direct investment on the grounds of profitability alone, independent of any considerations of complementarity. If KPC were finally to build a domestic petrochemicals plant, it could solve the retailing problem by entering into further marketing and supply agreements with Hoechst or some other petrochemicals group, but new direct investments in this area are probably unnecessary.

An Evaluation of the Kuwaiti Strategy

Kuwait's investment behavior has been conditioned by both the economic and political criteria discussed above, but economic factors have been far more important.

The absence of short-term constraints generated by oil policy or devel-

98. Kathleen Evans, "Enter the Eighth Oil Sister," *Financial Times*, March 17, 1983.

opment needs has had the largest influence on the structure of the port-folio. This absence made it plausible for Kuwait to invest most of its portfolio in long-term instruments, a plausibility that was enhanced by the safety of these instruments and their attractive rates of return. Historically, stocks and bonds have had higher rates of return than short-term instruments such as bank deposits and Treasury certificates. Furthermore, the risk involved is not much higher if the portfolio is a diversified selection of equities and bonds and if they can be held long enough (at least several business cycles, perhaps ten years).

Relative rates of return and safety also influenced the choice of long-term securities within the portfolio. The Kuwaitis have viewed equities as the best way of guaranteeing safe and positive real rates of return because they represent tangible, real assets. This explains the heavy emphasis on equities, the willingness to pursue real estate investments, and an apparent insistence that the appropriate real estate investments involve such income-producing properties as office buildings and resorts. To some extent the emphasis on natural resource and technology-related stocks is another manifestation of the emphasis on tangible assets. The same considerations have focused Kuwait's bond investments on those with maturities of five to seven years. These bonds yield higher returns than short-term claims but are still short-term enough to avoid undue risks to the real value of the security from unanticipated inflation.

Concerns over safety and rate of return have also led to diversification. Kuwait has diversified its equities and bonds to compensate for the different economic risks of the Western economies and has supplemented them with small equity investments in promising third world economies.[99] Considerations of rate of return, safety, and diversification also explain the structure of its equity investments in individual geographic markets. Only the American portfolio is diversified across all sectors, with investments in the industrial, financial, energy, and services sectors, and in property. Most other economies offer a narrower range of attractive opportunities, and Kuwait has restricted its investments accordingly. Thus the main attractions in Japan and West Germany are the industrial firms; in Britain, real estate, insurance, and finance; and in France and Singapore, real estate. In those countries with active stock markets, particularly the United States and Japan, the Kuwaitis have small portfolio holdings of stocks.

99. Political factors may play some role in the third world investments, but many have been in countries such as Singapore and Malaysia that Western lenders also consider promising.

Direct investments have been more common and appropriate in those markets where stock ownership is concentrated, as in Germany, or where trading is very thin.

The distribution of Kuwait's bond portfolio can also be explained by considerations of rate of return, safety, and diversification. Apparently only a small fraction of the portfolio has been invested in such safe but low-yielding bonds as U.S. and British Treasury bonds. In general the higher-yielding Eurobond issues have been preferred. The composition of the Eurobond portfolio seems similar to that of the market portfolio, and by investing in a variety of currencies and in issues from many different borrowers, Kuwait has been able to attain higher yields without too much risk. KD-denominated bonds may also have been part of this quest for safety. However, the supposed attraction of KD bonds, the absence of foreign currency risk, may be irrelevant when so much of domestic consumption and income is priced in foreign currencies.

Complementarity between foreign investments and Kuwait's development plans is the only other economic criterion that seems to have mattered in putting together the portfolio. Complementarity has been a factor in many of the direct investments by Kuwait Petroleum Company, where it was considered a way of more fully using Kuwait's petroleum resources and thereby enhancing the rate of return. Complementarity may also have been a factor in using KD-denominated bonds and participating in various consortium banks. Both decisions were influenced by Kuwait's desire to accelerate its development as a provider of financial services, not just money, and to improve the rate of return on foreign assets.

Management control has not been a separate goal of the Kuwaiti financial strategy. When the government takes over a company, it can, of course, choose its own board of directors, but the previous management is usually retained. Most of the equity investments are too small to get Kuwait any representation on the board of directors, although investments in the 5 percent to 10 percent range (as is common with its investments in British companies) often earn Kuwait one slot on the board of directors.

It is difficult to assign a separate role to concerns about the world economy in Kuwait's investment strategy. Of course Kuwaitis are concerned about the world economy, especially the dollar, and they have contributed to financial stability by not moving rapidly back and forth among countries or currencies. Yet the desire to make money also would rule out such destabilizing behavior. The only "investment" that perhaps can be explained by altruistic concerns for the world economy to the exclusion of other economic criteria is the foreign aid program, which allows Kuwait to express its concerns for particular sectors and regions of the world economy.

Energy investments also are best explained by economic criteria, especially considerations of profitability and complementarity, rather than as an attempt to give Kuwait monopolistic or oligopolistic powers in the energy markets. Kuwait does have exploration rights in a number of countries, but its role in world exploration remains small. Existing antitrust laws in the United States and elsewhere restrict Kuwait's ability to garner and exercise monopolistic powers. Although KPC has expanded its energy operations beyond domestic exploration and production, it has stopped short of becoming the eighth sister.

Foreign policy considerations have played a role in some investments outside the industrialized world. The large loans to Iraq are the most obvious example of an investment dictated by political considerations, in this case Kuwait's concerns for domestic and regional security.[100] Political considerations may also have influenced the issues of Kuwaiti dinar bonds before 1979: regional concerns probably influenced the Arab issues, a desire to promote third world solidarity may have led to the floatation of other developing-country issues, and the wish to show a balance between East and West favored Eastern European issues. The subsidy inherent in these early KD bond issues was rather small. Yet the existence of a subsidy cannot be questioned. These countries were usually unable to borrow in any other medium-term bond markets and had to rely on short-term commercial loans and suppliers' credits.

Kuwait apparently has not been able to extract explicit concessions from these investments, and the amounts involved are small once the Iraqi loans are excluded. When considered with Kuwait's extensive foreign aid program, however, they have probably been large enough to yield some benefits for Kuwait. But these political benefits are generally small and probably cost the West very little.

Kuwaiti Finance Minister Al-Hamad has described the investments as "sound, solid, conservative and constructive . . . attractive for an endowment or respectable institution,"[101] and this characterization is generally true. Overall, the Kuwaiti investment strategy seems to be guided largely by economic factors. The United States has little to fear if Kuwait continues to follow this pattern, a pattern that in this case has existed for thirty years.

100. It appears that these so-called loans are free of interest charges and that neither party expects repayments to be made.
101. Ignatius, "Kuwait's $70 Billion Finance Minister."

CHAPTER SEVEN

Investment Strategies of Other OPEC Members

ALTHOUGH SAUDI ARABIA AND KUWAIT are the only financial powers, the financial market activities of the other eleven OPEC members are also considerable. These countries range from low absorbers such as the United Arab Emirates to high absorbers such as Algeria and Indonesia. Their financial strategies also vary, reflecting different backgrounds and needs; several have actually increased their net foreign debt since the first oil shock.

The same broad classes of economic factors that determine the investments of Saudi Arabia and Kuwait also shape the financial strategies of the other OPEC states, but sometimes in very different ways. The two most important factors are oil policy and development needs. Some of these states have experienced little pressure on either, while others face severe constraints. Rates of return, safety, liquidity, and diversification also play different roles. Except for foreign aid programs, it is unlikely that the actions of these states will be guided by concerns about their economic impact on other parts of the world economy, because no one of them holds foreign assets large enough to have much effect on financial markets.

Political motivations vary significantly from state to state, reflecting diverse locations and historical experiences. Several have threatened or actually made financial moves with political overtones, but none has succeeded in using money as a financial weapon.

The United Arab Emirates and Qatar

The United Arab Emirates is a federation of seven sheikhdoms on the eastern edge of the Arabian peninsula whose nationhood dates back to the British pullout east of Suez in 1971. Oil production in Abu Dhabi, the wealthiest emirate, began in 1967. Two of the other emirates (Dubai and Sharjah) produce oil, but their exports pale in comparison to those of Abu Dhabi.

The United Arab Emirates is in good financial shape, although the status of the individual sheikhdoms varies considerably. Abu Dhabi provides most of the funds for the federal budget and thus for the individual sheikhdoms. At the end of 1982 the United Arab Emirates was the third largest investor among OPEC members, having accumulated $35.5 billion in net foreign assets between 1974 and 1982 (see table 7-1). These holdings included $9.8 billion of deposits by government agencies, corporations, and individuals at European, Japanese, and Canadian banks as of the end of 1982.[1] The government's share of the surplus is hard to estimate because a varying share of the revenues is alloted to budgets of the individual emirs and because a large part is under the control of Abu Dhabi rather than the federal government. Holdings under the control of the federal government or of individual emirates were probably $30 billion at the end of 1982. According to Abdel-Malik al-Hamr, governor of the central bank, there was an excess of oil revenues over budgeted expenditures and general aid contributions of $5 billion in 1980 and up to $3 billion in 1981.[2] These figures, however, may understate the actual surpluses because the budget is often underspent. A reported budget deficit of $1.225 billion for 1982 led to plans for spending cuts in 1983.[3] Nevertheless, the country later reported a current account surplus of Dh 9.5 billion ($2.59 billion) for the first half of 1983.[4]

Until very recently neither oil policy nor development needs seemed to pose significant constraints on the financial strategy of the United Arab Emirates. In particular, a low population and a relatively small territory had always led to a classification among the low absorbers of OPEC. The oil glut has changed that attitude somewhat, and the government has cut back on capital spending and limited the growth of current expenditures.[5]

1. Bank for International Settlements, *Maturity Distribution of International Bank Lending* (December 1983).

2. Barbara Donnelly, "U.A.E.'s Annual Cash Surplus Is Shrinking," *Wall Street Journal*, December 30, 1981.

3. "GCC States Offer Cold Comfort in 1984," *Middle East Economic Digest* (July 15, 1983), p. 17.

4. "Current Account Surplus Falls," *Middle East Economic Digest* (October 21, 1983), p. 60.

5. "GCC States Offer Cold Comfort in 1984," p. 17; and *Financial Times*, March 28, 1983.

Table 7-1. *Cumulative Current Account Surpluses of Eleven OPEC Members, 1974–82*
Billions of dollars

Country	Cumulative current account surplus[a]
Algeria	−10.8
Ecuador	−4.8
Gabon	1.9
Indonesia	−7.4
Iran	31.2
Iraq	20.3
Libya	22.2
Nigeria	−7.4
Qatar	12.7
United Arab Emirates	35.5
Venezuela	4.9

Source: Appendix table A-1.
a. Balance on goods, services, and private and official transfers.

Abu Dhabi's position remains strong, although the need for transfers to the poorer emirates within the federation will impose some limits on its plans. Still, the oil and investment revenues of the United Arab Emirates, accompanied perhaps by some drawings on the principal of its foreign holdings, should provide sufficiently for the country's spending on social services and infrastructure.

Investment policy has a different meaning for Abu Dhabi than for the other emirates. Abu Dhabi itself controls most of the funds. It can to a certain extent consider overseas investments as well as domestic industrialization as an outlet for oil revenues, but the other six emirates are unlikely to build up substantial surpluses. It is probably appropriate for Abu Dhabi to be a net creditor to the rest of the world, given the limited local opportunities for industrialization. However, it has not progressed as far along this road as Kuwait; for example, there is no law mandating that a fixed percentage of oil revenues be set aside as a reserve fund.[6] And the needs of the other emirates make it unlikely that the United Arab Emirates can consider the surpluses to be as permanent as the Kuwaiti surpluses appear.

Control of much of the federal government's foreign assets is vested in the central bank. Its net foreign assets peaked at $3.6 billion at the end of

6. Such a fund has been suggested, however, by Oil Minister Sheikh al-Oteiba.

1982 before declining to $2.8 billion at the end of 1983.[7] These holdings include the country's foreign exchange reserves and loans to the IMF. The country also made $1.15 billion of bilateral development loans between 1974 and 1981 that were largely provided by the Abu Dhabi Fund for Arab Economic Development.[8]

The major instrument of Abu Dhabi's investment policy is the Abu Dhabi Investment Authority (ADIA), which managed an estimated $12 billion at the end of 1981. An official at the authority described it as "essentially a pension fund . . . with investments tending towards minimum market and credit risk."[9] Reportedly ADIA has kept most of its claims in bank deposits and bonds, with a smaller share in equities.[10] In 1978 these equity investments included $900 million of holdings in the United States managed by Morgan Guaranty Trust, part of which involved substantial holdings in airline companies, often 1 percent to 4 percent of the stock outstanding.[11] It has been involved in both of the large Arab-owned consortium banks, Arab Banking Corporation and Gulf International Bank, and has taken shares in other Arab-backed banks. And in June 1984 it made its first large equity investment in a Western company, paying $100 million for 12.5 percent of the "B" shares of Reuters, the British news agency.[12] While ADIA has emphasized safety and liquidity in its individual investment decisions, rates of return seem to have determined the distribution of the portfolio, particularly the government's willingness to switch currencies in pursuit of higher returns. The dollar proportion of the portfolio reportedly declined to 45 percent in the late 1970s.[13] The strategy of Abu Dhabi thus contrasts strongly with that of Saudi Arabia and Kuwait, neither of which allowed large swings in the percentage distribution of their portfolio.

7. IMF, *International Financial Statistics*, vol. 37 (June 1984), p. 452.
8. Organization for Economic Cooperation and Development, *Aid from OPEC Countries* (Paris: OECD, 1983), p. 64.
9. Donnelly, "U.A.E.'s Annual Cash Surplus Is Shrinking."
10. "Abu Dhabi's Expertise," *Arab Banking and Finance* (April 1982), p. 51.
11. "Arabs Fly Away with Airline Stocks," *International Business* (May–June 1979), p. 58; and Nancy L. Ross, "Arabs Buy Stock in 4 Airlines," *Washington Post*, November 23, 1978.
12. A "B" share had only one-quarter the voting power of an "A" share, however, and all the "A" shares remained in the hands of Reuters' newspaper owners or senior staff. See "Abu Dhabi Pulls Off Reuters Coup," *Middle East Economic Digest* (June 15, 1984), p. 39.
13. Graham Benton, "Abu Dhabi's Cash Surplus May Fall to $1 Bn," *8 Days* (January 16, 1982), p. 37.

Two other investment groups are the National Bank of Abu Dhabi (NBAD, 75 percent of which is owned by ADIA) and the Abu Dhabi Investment Corporation (ADIC); the share of ADIC owned by ADIA was recently raised to 90 percent.[14] Both manage funds for Abu Dhabi rather than for the central government. The existence of these institutions reflects Abu Dhabi's decision to become more directly involved in financial markets and perhaps represents preliminary steps toward emulating Kuwait's active and extensive involvement in international finance. NBAD manages the cash balances of the national oil company and the accounts of the government of Abu Dhabi and therefore has a large deposit base for banking activities. It has focused on short-term investments such as trade credits and more recently on floating-rate notes.[15] Thus NBAD's lending activities are well matched to its funding sources. It was a manager or comanager on bond issues worth $1.78 billion in 1981 and $1.8 billion in the first part of 1982.[16] ADIC, high flyer among Abu Dhabi's investment managers, was heavily involved in loan syndications and real estate investments and has run into increasingly difficult problems from illiquid or failed investments, and ADIA now provides most of the directors. Although ADIC has recently resumed participation in syndicated loans, its independence has been sharply curtailed.[17]

In 1982 the government approved the establishment of an international oil investment company, with a capital of Dh 500 million ($136 million) provided equally by ADIA and the Abu Dhabi National Oil Company.[18] It is not yet clear what sort of investments will be made and in which countries the company will be active. The amounts involved are very small, however, and the government has not shown any intention of getting involved in energy-related foreign investments on a scale comparable to that of Kuwait. Rather, it continues to focus on domestic energy invest-

14. "Abu Dhabi Agency Forced to Buy Out Investment Company," *Financial Times*, July 19, 1984.

15. These bonds usually have maturities of between five and ten years, but their interest rate is adjusted every three to six months by adding a small premium to prevailing short-term rates.

16. NBAD itself would only have been responsible for a small fraction of the issue, perhaps 5 percent. For a list of some of the flotations, see Peter Truell, "NBAD Boosts Capital Market Activity," *Middle East Economic Digest* (May 28, 1982), p. 57.

17. "ADIC—A New Role?" *Arab Banking and Finance* (April 1982), p. 55; and *Middle East Economic Digest* (January 13, 1984), p. 41.

18. "Oil Investment Company to Be Set Up," *Middle East Economic Digest* (April 30, 1982), p. 37.

ments, such as modernization of natural gas liquefaction facilities and further development of natural gas fields.[19]

Qatar is a small sheikhdom on the eastern edge of the Arabian peninsula. It ran a cumulative current account surplus between 1974 and 1982 of $12.7 billion (see table 7-1), of which the government share is probably $11 billion. This figure includes net disbursements of $250 million in bilateral development loans between 1974 and 1981.[20] The public and private-sector holdings included $2.34 billion of deposits at European, Japanese, and Canadian banks at the end of 1982.[21]

The main instrument of investment policy is the Qatar Investment Board, a committee headed by the minister of finance, although direct investments are handled separately by the Ministry of Finance. The board decides broad issues, such as which currencies to pursue and whether equities are appropriate, while discretionary portfolio managers in the major financial centers handle day-to-day operations.

Neither oil policy nor development needs would seem to pose major constraints for Qatar's financial policies. The country has scaled back earlier plans for energy-intensive industrialization, and much of the necessary investment in domestic infrastructure has now been completed. Qatar made plans to cut budget expenditures by 20 percent in fiscal year 1983–84 in response to the oil glut, and a number of projects were slowed down or postponed indefinitely.[22] At first the government reported that it would draw on foreign reserves to finance the anticipated 1983–84 budget deficit, but it later reported a small budget surplus for the first nine months of the 1983–84 budget year. It seems likely that Qatar ran a small surplus for the 1983–84 budget year and that, despite original projections, it will run a small surplus again in the 1984–85 budget year.[23] The overall investment policy has been fairly cautious, with an emphasis on safe and liquid but not necessarily short-term investments, including bank deposits, stocks, and medium-term bonds in major countries and currencies. In 1980 the target

19. Lynne Curry, "UAE: ADGAS Loan Reflects Banking Confidence," *Middle East Economic Digest* (August 19, 1983), pp. 20–24.

20. OECD, *Aid from OPEC Countries*, p. 53.

21. BIS, *Maturity Distribution of International Bank Lending* (December 1983).

22. See "Qatar's Planners Reassess Priorities," *Middle East Economic Digest* (April 8, 1983), pp. 30–31.

23. Robin Allen, "Qatar Cuts Down," *Middle East Economic Digest* (November 11, 1983), p. 47; and "Qatar's Budget: 'Better Than Expected,'" *Middle East Economic Digest* (April 13, 1984), p. 31.

share of equities in the portfolios handled by overseas managers was 50 percent; the currency composition can vary considerably.[24]

Qatar also has limited direct investments overseas. In addition to small holdings of commercial real estate,[25] it owns 40 percent of a $300 million hydrocarbon cracking refinery in Dunkirk, France.[26] This joint venture with CDF-Chimie complements a Qatari-based petrochemical venture owned 84 percent by Qatar and 16 percent by CDF-Chimie.[27] Other investments in energy-related industries are also located in Qatar itself. They include a joint-venture fertilizer plant (63 percent owned by Qatar), a joint-venture natural gas liquids (NGL) plant (70 percent Qatari government and 30 percent Shell Gas BV, a subsidiary of Shell Oil), and a second, Qatari-owned NGL plant.[28] The NGL facilities, which use natural gas that had previously been flared, supply Qatar's petrochemical plant. In 1983 Qatar announced plans to export liquefied natural gas from the North Field gas reserves. This project, to be carried out in cooperation with British Petroleum and Compagnie Français des Petroles, will not start exporting until 1992.[29] In 1983 Qatar canceled plans for a second Qatari-based petrochemical plant.[30]

Political concerns do not seem to have influenced the investment decisions of the United Arab Emirates or Qatar. The move out of the dollar in the late 1970s was triggered by the dollar's rapid depreciation, and in fact the shift had taken place before the most commonly cited political factor, the freeze of Iranian assets, occurred. Both countries have committed themselves to the regional investment fund of the Gulf Cooperation Council (GCC), which, given that the GCC itself is a product of regional security concerns, could be construed as a political investment. It is more appropriate, however, to treat the investment fund as an economic decision to rationalize and coordinate the industrialization policies of the various

24. Law, *Arab Investors: Who They Are, What They Buy, and Where*, vol. 1, p. 109.

25. Law, *Arab Investors*, vol. 1, pp. 107–08.

26. *Middle East Economic Survey* (April 4, 1975), p. 6.

27. The Qatari plant was originally owned 80 percent by Qatar, 15 percent by CDF-Chimie, and 5 percent by Gazocean, another French firm. Ragaei El Mallakh, *Qatar: Development of an Oil Economy* (St. Martin's Press, 1979), pp. 85–86.

28. Ibid., pp. 80–85.

29. Ken Whittingham, "Qatar to Spend $4Bn-$6Bn on Project to Export Liquified Gas," *Financial Times*, February 22, 1983; and "North Field LNG Scheme Takes Shape," *Middle East Economic Digest* (April 8, 1983), p. 31.

30. "Qapco Cancels Plant Order," *Middle East Economic Digest* (April 29, 1983), p. 36.

members. Finally, both the United Arab Emirates and Qatar have contributed significant amounts of foreign aid through various development agencies. This aid, though inherently political, is unlikely to have any noticeable impact on Western interests.

Iran

In financial strategies, as in oil and development policy and in politics, there have been two Irans. From 1974 to the end of the shah's reign, oil export revenues consistently exceeded development expenditures, and Iran amassed a current account surplus of $26.3 billion, the third largest among OPEC members (see table 2-4). Its foreign holdings at the end of 1978 did not lag far behind those of Kuwait. Because of its high population and development potential, Iran's absorptive capacity is high, and such large and long-standing surpluses might at first seem unexpected. Expenditures, however, were unable to catch up with expanding revenues from sizable price and production increases. In fact, despite the high absorptive capacity of the Iranian economy in the long run, policy was allowing severe bottlenecks to develop in the agricultural and power sectors, which reduced the usefulness of further spending on industrialization.[31] Oil policy pursued the somewhat contradictory aims of attaining high prices and undercutting Saudi Arabia's influence in world oil markets.

The combination of high oil production and development needs led to an emphasis on safe, liquid, short-term investments. Toward the end of 1979, almost a year after the shah's departure but at a time when no major changes in investment policy had occurred, Iran held $8.04 billion in deposits at non-American banks, $5.72 in deposits at American banks, and $1.27 billion of U.S. government securities.[32] But the shah also made significant longer-term investments overseas. Equity investments included 25 percent shares in Deutsche Babcock, Krupp Huettenwerke, and various Krupp subsidiaries, a 5 percent holding in First Wisconsin Corporation (a U.S. bank-holding company), joint-venture refineries with India and

31. Robert E. Looney, "Absorptive Capacity of the Prerevolutionary Iranian Economy," *Journal of Energy and Development*, vol. 8 (Spring 1983), pp. 319–40.

32. Non-American data are from December 31, 1979, and are reported in BIS, *Maturity Distribution of International Bank Lending* (July 1980). U.S. data are as of November 14, 1979, and are reported in *Federal Response to OPEC Country Investments in the United States*, Hearings before a Subcommittee of the House Committee on Government Operations, 97 Cong. 1 sess. (Government Printing Office, 1981), pt. 1, p. 176.

South Africa, and a 10 percent share in Eurodif, a French-based uranium enrichment consortium. The shah also made 46 loans worth $7 billion during his reign. Those included a further $1 billion loan to Eurodif; $800 million in loans to the United Kingdom, including advance payments on military purchases; and concessional loans to Zaire and the Sudan.[33] Some of these longer-term investments, such as those in Eurodif and foreign refineries, may have complemented Iran's development, but the magnitude of long-term investments was probably inappropriate for a country also committed to a large-scale program of domestic modernization and industrialization.

Iran now has a very different attitude on oil, development, and investments. Many citizens concluded that industrialization was proceeding too quickly and that oil production beyond revenue requirements was squandering Iran's natural resources. Even technocrats in the shah's government reportedly shared this opinion.[34] As a result, oil exports and development expenditures have been reduced, but the revolutionary government still is trying to maintain a large cushion of foreign assets to protect it against disruptions of its oil-exporting facilities. Over the past four years the government has, of course, witnessed one disruption after another: the revolution itself, the hostage situation at the U.S. embassy in Tehran, the war with Iraq, and the current oil glut. The surplus increased from 1978 to 1979 because panic buying by the oil companies spurred price rises sharp enough to offset the fall in exports from 4.45 to 2.41 million barrels a day. During 1980, however, Iran was forced to draw on its foreign assets as exports dropped to 798,000 barrels a day.[35] Its deposits at European, Japanese, and Canadian banks, for example, fell from $8.04 billion at the end of 1979 to $5.59 billion at the end of 1980. In late 1982 aggressive price cutting sent oil exports above 2 million barrels per day and deposits climbed once again, reaching $10.81 billion at the end of 1982, while debts to foreign banks had been whittled down to $2.26 billion.[36]

---

33. Zuhayr Mikdashi, "Oil Prices and OPEC Surpluses: Some Reflections," *International Affairs*, vol. 57 (Summer 1981), p. 422; Tim McGirk, "Lend to Iran or Iraq? You Must Be Serious," *Euromoney* (June 1982), p. 84; and Vahe Petrossian, "Iran Pays Up—And Puts in a Complaint," *Middle East Economic Digest* (August 26, 1983), p. 24.

34. For a discussion of the ideological factors in recent Iranian oil policy see Shaul Bakhash, *The Politics of Oil and Revolution in Iran* (Brookings Institution, 1982), pp. 2–6.

35. Data on oil exports are from OPEC, *Annual Statistical Bulletin 1982*, p. 21.

36. BIS, *Maturity Distribution of International Bank Lending* (July 1980, July 1981, December 1983).

Economic and political factors favor the investment of Iran's surplus in short-term securities. Currently the predominant factor is the uncertainty about revenue and expenditures because of the war with Iraq, but the oil market glut and the reconstruction of the economy will also limit Iran's investment choices after the war ends. So far the country has not converted the long-term investments inherited from the shah into short-term securities, but in many cases this reflects problems in collecting on the loans.[37]

Iran's financial actions will continue to be of interest to the West, especially because it has been willing to threaten sudden movements of its funds. Although the current level of reserves poses no problems for the financial system, Iran's conditions for an end to the Gulf war have included a large-scale transfer of funds from Arab nations to Iran. For example, in May 1983 the Iranian news agency published a government statement that Iran was seeking $90 billion in war reparations.[38] Funds of that magnitude under the control of a revolutionary Iran would at the least require close surveillance by the West, though it seems unlikely that reparations of that scale will be paid.

Iraq

The Iraqi balance of payments has followed a pattern strikingly different from those of other OPEC members over the years. Whereas most OPEC nations saw their balance of payments surpluses decline and then disappear by 1978, Iraqi surpluses were higher in 1977 and 1978 than in 1974 (see appendix table A-1). The surpluses were still large during 1979 and 1980, when they averaged almost $1 billion per month. Only Kuwaiti and Saudi surpluses were higher, and Iraq temporarily was the third largest holder of net foreign assets within OPEC during 1980. However, after the decision to declare war against Iran, the current account balance fell precipitously to a deficit of $9.41 billion in 1982.

Oil production and expenditure needs have been the main constraints on Iraqi financial behavior. The high potential for domestic development made it unlikely that large surpluses would be a permanent phenomenon, but it took some time for development expenditures to catch up with the expanded revenues from successive increases in the volume and price of

37. Petrossian, "Iran Pays Up—And Puts in a Complaint," p. 24.
38. Reported in David B. Ottoway, "Iran Accepts Gulf State Mediation in War with Iraq," *Washington Post*, May 21, 1983.

oil exports. Several other factors may have also helped to boost exports and surpluses from 1977 to 1980. The sudden realization that Iraq's oil reserves were quite large made higher production possible and may even have encouraged it to challenge Saudi and Iranian influence in oil pricing.[39] Alternatively, the high production in 1979 and 1980 may have been intended to build up funds for a war against Iran. But even if there had not been a war, the $130 billion 1981–85 civilian budget would have consumed most of the oil income.[40]

Limited information is available about Iraq's investment strategy. Safe, liquid, short-term claims would have been most appropriate if the expenditures were expected to be used in the near future for development, and Iraq has made such investments. At the end of 1980 it held at least $25.5 billion of bank deposits in Western nations (this excludes any amounts actually held in the United States).[41] The dollar has probably had the largest role, but yen-dominated claims have also been important. Deposits with Japanese banks (mostly in the form of nonresident yen deposits) reached $2.7 billion at the end of September 1980 before falling to ¥130 billion (approximately $500 million) in June 1982; long-term Japanese government bonds were also part of the portfolio.[42] The large role of German firms in Iraq's development plans probably led the Iraqis to hold some reserves in deutsche marks.

It is difficult to describe Iraq's current financial position exactly. Although it tried to maintain its development program despite the war, this policy was eventually suspended. It has drawn heavily on its bank deposits. After reaching $25.5 billion at the end of 1980, deposits with Western banks fell to $15.8 billion at the end of 1981, to $1.21 billion at the end of 1982, and to $837 million as of December 1983 (excluding any

39. Iraq's oil reserves were 59 billion barrels at the end of 1982. The only OPEC members with larger reserves were Saudi Arabia (165.3 billion barrels) and Kuwait (67.2 billion barrels). See OPEC, *Annual Statistical Bulletin 1982*, pp. 33–34.

40. Based on the assumptions that the oil price would average $32 a barrel during these years and that Iraq could maintain its prewar exports of 2.8 million barrels a day, oil revenues would equal $163.5 billion. See Jonathan Crusoe, "War and the Glut Take Their Toll," *Middle East Economic Digest* (March 19, 1982), p. 15.

41. BIS, *Maturity Distribution of International Bank Lending* (July 1981).

42. "Bank Deposits in Japan of 3 Mideast Nations Slump," *Japan Economic Journal*, November 3, 1981, p. 2; "Israel & Iraq Are Stepping Up Withdrawal of Yen Funds to Meet Rising War Expense," *Japan Economic Journal*, July 20, 1982; and "Central Bank Sells Japanese Bonds," *Middle East Economic Digest* (November 26, 1982), p. 30.

funds held in the United States).[43] Iraq reportedly turned to the Arab Gulf states for loans because export revenues were unable to cover both war expenditures and the development program. It is impossible to tell how much these nations have committed to Iraq and how much they have actually disbursed. The highest estimate has been $52.1 billion of commitments through March 1983.[44] Other reports have estimated loans of $23 billion as of February 1982 and $30 billion as of November 1982 or a "maximum $10,000 million" as of March 1982.[45] The Iraqis themselves put the total at less than $20 billion in early 1983 and also said that aid had virtually ceased during the previous year.[46] These loans apparently are interest free, and may be "forgiven" by the Gulf states.[47] Saudi Arabia has assigned up to 70,000 barrels a day in "war relief" oil as additional financial support for Iraq.[48] Western banks and governments have also granted reschedulings and new credits to Iraq. These include a $500 million bank loan in 1983, a $1.6 billion credit from France, a $1.8 billion package from Japan, and $440 million of agricultural credits from the United States.[49] Clearly the surpluses accumulated before the war have largely been exhausted. Furthermore, the oil glut, the costs of the continuing war, and the expenses of the eventual reconstruction make it unlikely that Iraq will become a major holder of foreign assets anytime soon.

Libya

Libya is the only OPEC member outside the Gulf area that has built up large holdings of foreign assets and even in the current oil market situation

43. BIS, *Maturity Distribution of International Bank Lending* (December 1982, December 1983, July 1984).

44. According to David Toufic Mizrahi, $45.6 billion had been disbursed; see "Iraq May be Staring at the Bottom of Its War Chest," *Business Week* (December 6, 1982), p. 58.

45. "War-Torn Iraq Seeks $500 Million Loan," *Financial Times*, November 10, 1982; and Law, *Arab Investors*, vol. 1, p. 102.

46. Shakib Otaqui, "Iraq—Seeking Increased Aid and Credit," *Middle East Economic Digest* (January 14, 1983), p. 7.

47. McGirk, "Lend to Iran or Iran? You Must Be Serious," pp. 81–82.

48. *Petroleum Intelligence Weekly* (August 6, 1984), p. 9.

49 "Euroloan Signing Indicates Confidence," *Middle East Economic Digest* (April 1, 1983), p. 16; "French Banks Agree to Iraqi Refinancing" (August 12, 1983), p. 10; "Japan Agrees to Extend Loan" (August 19, 1983), p. 16; and "U.S. Confirms Further Grain Credit" (March 25, 1983), p. 27.

has managed to avoid making significant drawdowns of its holdings. The country added $22.2 billion to its net holdings of foreign assets between 1974 and 1982 (see table 7-1); at the end of 1973 the net foreign assets of the central bank and commercial banks had totaled only $2.4 billion.

The variation from year to year in Libya's surpluses has largely resulted from its hawkish stand on oil prices, which generates enormous fluctuations in production levels and reserves. Exports ranged from 600,000 to 1.7 million barrels a day during 1982; it has been estimated that 1.07 million barrels a day were required to cover current account expenditures.[50]

Libya's foreign assets are handled by the Libyan Arab Foreign Bank (LAFB) and the National Investment Company. A significant portion of the funds is invested in short-term instruments, which is appropriate given the severe fluctuations in the nation's payments position. For example, Libya held $6.79 billion of deposits at non-American banks at the end of 1980, although this had fallen to $2.67 billion by the end of 1983.[51] LAFB has also been involved in loans, bonds, and equity investments, with a preference for finance, tourism, manufacturing, and real estate investments.[52] Libya has maintained a large exposure in Italy totaling $1.2 billion in 1980, including a $500 million loan to Ente Nazionale Idrocarburi (the Italian national energy company) and a 9.1 percent stake in Fiat, purchased in 1977 for $415 million; the Fiat holding was increased to 13.6 percent in 1982.[53] Libya has also participated extensively in consortium banks, such as the Arab Banking Corporation (Libya's capital share is $250 million) and UBAF (a consortium of Arab and French banks), although more typically it is a minority shareholder in smaller banks whose business is largely restricted to trade financing.[54]

---

50. "Low Output Creates Budget Deficits for Nine OPEC States," *Petroleum Intelligence Weekly* (February 15, 1982), p. 5; and "Bartering an Unfashionable Commodity," *Middle East Economic Digest* (March 19, 1982), pp. 15–16.

51. BIS, *Maturity Distribution of International Bank Lending* (July 1981, July 1984).

52. Law, *Arab Investors*, vol. 1, p. 103. The sources listed in table 6-3 on Kuwaiti investments also include the published loan and bond deals of LAFB.

53. Law, *Arab Investors*, vol. 1, p. 104; and Rupert Cornwell, "Libyan Bank Steps Up Fiat Shareholding," *Financial Times*, September 21, 1982.

54. The Banco Arabe Español, owned by banks from Libya, Kuwait, and Spain, which finances trade between Spain and the Arab world, is a good example.

The Borrowers

In contrast with other OPEC members, Algeria, Indonesia, Nigeria, Venezuela, Ecuador, and Gabon have rarely had the luxury of worrying about how to invest surplus funds. Even though they ran temporary surpluses in the first year or two following the sharp increases in oil prices, their primary concern has been to maintain long-term access to world capital markets. Oil policy and development plans still provide the framework within which financial planning must be conducted. Oil price increases have affected that planning in two important ways: directly, by making more revenues available to the government for development expenditures; and indirectly, by enhancing the ability of these countries to borrow funds for development plans that exceed current revenues.

Even though these countries are net debtors to the rest of the world, they still hold reserves to cover several months of import expenditures in case of unanticipated drops in income. These reserves are particularly important for Algeria and Nigeria in view of their hawkish pricing policies, which can lead to sharp swings in the oil income that provides most government revenues. The reserves are held in safe, liquid, short-term securities, usually Eurocurrency deposits. When these countries do experience temporary surpluses, they can build up reserves or pay off earlier borrowings in advance.

Ecuador and Gabon are OPEC's smallest producers. Gabon has been able to keep oil production fairly close to revenue requirements and should weather the oil market downturn. For Ecuador, however, the effects of the oil market downturn were compounded by slow payments from its Latin American trading partners and by the market's seeming aversion to all Latin American debtors. It had to reschedule $1.2 billion of commercial bank loans falling due between November 1982 and December 1983 and obtained $431 million of new credits. Ecuador also rescheduled $200 million in Western government credits and received a $167 million IMF loan after pledging to undertake austerity measures.[55] Recent policies to encourage foreign exploration and to discourage domestic consumption of

55. "Ecuador Arranges New Debt Agreement," *Financial Times*, October 13 1983; and "Ecuador is Allowed to Delay Payment of $200 Million," *Wall Street Journal*, July 29, 1983.

refined products have strengthened Ecuador's medium-term prospects as an oil exporter.[56]

Algeria, which had a gross foreign debt of $16 billion outstanding in 1982, was the biggest net borrower among OPEC members between 1974 and 1982 (see table 7-1).[57] The first oil price increase had made it possible for the government to borrow heavily from international financial markets to finance an industrialization program during the mid-1970s, while the second oil shock gave Algeria almost three years in which the country did not need to approach the market for new loans (although old loan commitments continued to be drawn upon). Much of this old debt matured during 1982 and 1983, at the time of the oil glut, which prompted Algeria to be more cautious in its development spending. Still, the banks have been happy with Algeria's past payments record and satisfied with its economic prospects, and so far the country has not experienced much difficulty rolling over its loans. Sonatrach, the government petroleum company, was able to increase its Eurodollar loan of early 1983 from $500 million to $700 million because of its favorable record, and a $750 million loan raised jointly for two Algerian banks in late 1983 met with similar success.[58]

Indonesia also had a gross foreign debt of around $16 billion at the end of 1982, including $9.95 billion of commercial bank loans, although it also had deposits at Western banks that amounted to $6.17 billion at the end of 1982.[59] The country's experience as a borrower, however, has not been smooth. Indonesia embarked on an ambitious spending program following the first oil shock, but by 1975 mismanagement of Pertamina (the national oil company) had forced the country to reschedule its foreign debts. The deficits were small in the first few years following the rescheduling but increased sharply in 1978. Because of rapidly expanding hydro-

56. "Ecuador is Staging a Comeback as an Oil Exporter," *Petroleum Intelligence Weekly* (December 12, 1983), p. 9.

57. "Algeria Considers External Borrowing for Project Finance," *Middle East Economic Digest* (October 8, 1982), p. 20.

58. Peter Montagnon, "$700M Loan for Sonatrach," *Financial Times*, June 1, 1983; Montagnon, "Keen Competition to Arrange New Algerian Jumbo," *Financial Times*, October 31, 1983; Francis Ghiles, "Algerian Reappearance Sparks Off Eurocurrency Mandate Battle," *Financial Times*, November 10, 1983; and Montagnon, "Algeria Credit Up to $750M," *Financial Times*, November 24, 1983.

59. Richard Cowper, "Indonesia to Double Foreign Borrowing," *Financial Times*, November 10, 1982; and BIS, *Maturity Distribution of International Bank Lending* (December 1983).

carbon production and higher prices following the second oil shock, Indonesia once again ran current account surpluses in 1979 and 1980, but by 1982 it had been hurt by falling export earnings from oil and other major commodities. A $7.5 billion current account deficit in fiscal year 1982–83 was forecast.[60] Because Indonesia's credit standing is high and its debt service ratio comparatively low, however, it has so far been able to borrow without too much difficulty.[61] Still, the lack of foreign exchange has forced the country to postpone numerous projects to develop heavy industry. The contracts for these projects would have been worth over $10 billion.[62]

Nigeria's financial difficulties have made it one of OPEC's weakest links. It had adopted a 1981–85 development plan predicated on an average oil production level of 2.19 million barrels a day and prices climbing to $55 a barrel by 1985, yet by August 1981 production had fallen to 800,000 barrels a day.[63] Although it finished 1980 with reserves of $10.24 billion, which probably exceeded the outstanding debt, Nigeria's payments position deteriorated rapidly during 1981 and 1982 because of delays in implementing policies compatible with its changed prospects. The country finished 1982 with reserves of $1.61 billion.[64] The situation improved slightly after the first quarter of 1983, as it stayed close to its quota of 1.3 million barrels a day in most of the rest of 1983.[65] The country will continue to experience severe financial pressure for the next several years, however: it faces stiff competition from Libyan and North Sea crudes in the world oil market and has also encountered difficulties raising funds on the international markets because of delays in making payments on its loans. Nigeria has renegotiated some of its trade credits from banks and other sources, but it will probably have to submit to IMF austerity

60. Cowper, "Indonesia to Double Foreign Borrowing."

61. Indonesia was expected to pay 0.75 percent above the London interbank offered rate on its last loan in the 1983–84 budget year. The amount of that loan had originally been set at $500 million but was raised to $600 million and then to $750 million with no change in the pricing. See Chris Sherwell, "Indonesian Credit Increased to $750 M," *Financial Times*, February 29, 1984.

62. See Joseph P. Manguno, "Builders Doubt Indonesia Plans to Halt Projects," *Wall Street Journal*, May 12, 1983; and Richard Cowper, "Indonesia Orders Rephasing of $10bn Projects," *Financial Times*, May 20, 1983.

63. Michael Holman, "Caught in the Battle between Oil Producers and Purchasers," *Financial Times*, November 29, 1982.

64. IMF, *International Financial Statistics, 1983 Yearbook*, p. 391.

65. "OPEC Nears Ceiling as Saudi Output Swings Higher," *Petroleum Intelligence Weekly* (July 18, 1983), p. 1; and "OPEC Oil Output Sliding Back Closer to its Ceiling," *Petroleum Intelligence Weekly* (November 14, 1983), p. 1.

measures to get commercial banks to reschedule other short- and long-term loans.[66] Nigeria's reluctance to devalue its currency and to end domestic subsidies of fuel consumption have so far made it impossible to reach an agreement with the IMF, however, and the country recently announced plans to try to reach a refinancing agreement without IMF approval.[67]

Venezuela also faces considerable financial pressure during the current oil market glut. Its development program was severely pruned during 1982, which reduced output required to balance the current account from 2.4 million to 1.6 million barrels a day.[68] Because it has been considered as a risky Latin American debtor nation like Argentina, Brazil, or Mexico, a perception reinforced by its difficulties in negotiating a rescheduling of debts, Venezuela's access to world credit markets has been hindered. At the end of 1982 it held $13.86 billion of deposits at Western banks, offset by $27.47 billion of loans from those same banks.[69] The election of a new president eased the political problems surrounding rescheduling; in late 1984 banks reached tentative agreement on a rescheduling of $20.75 billion of Venezuelan public-sector debts.[70]

The structure of Venezuela's external assets and liabilities reflects the fact that a number of Venezuelan companies in the public sector were borrowers, while others built up large reserves separate from those of the central bank. Such reserves were placed under the control of the central bank in late 1982.[71] This rationalization has been linked to Venezuela's

66. Steven Mufson, "Nigeria Set to Offer Its Trade Creditors Refinancing Terms on $5.6 Billion Debt," *Wall Street Journal*, March 27, 1984; and Quentin Peel, "Nigeria Opens 'Make or Break' Talks on $3 Bn Loan from IMF," *Financial Times*, February 13, 1984.

67. Quentin Peel, "Nigerian Economy Measures 'Not Enough' to Qualify for New Loan," *Financial Times*, July 12, 1984; and Michael Holman, "Lagos to Seek Trade Debt Refinancing without IMF Accord," *Financial Times*, July 30, 1984.

68. According to data from Texaco reported in "Low Output Creates Budget Deficits for Nine OPEC States," *Petroleum Intelligence Weekly* (February 15, 1982), p. 5; and "Financial Strains on OPEC Starting to Ease, Texaco Says," *Petroleum Intelligence Weekly* (July 19, 1982), p. 5.

69. BIS, *Maturity Distribution of International Bank Lending* (December 1983).

70. Peter Montagnon, "Venezuela Banking Creditors Divided on Debt Package," *Financial Times*, September 1, 1983; James LeMoyne, "New Venezuela Leader Sees Debt as No. 1 Issue," *New York Times*, December 12, 1983; and Doreen Hemlock, "Venezuela Sets Pact with Banks to Realign Debt," *Wall Street Journal*, September 24, 1984.

71. The Venezuelan Investment Fund, which handles the surpluses, and Petroleos de Venezuela, the national oil company, were the other major holders of foreign

policy of lengthening the maturity of its debt and improving its credit standing. The main goal, however, was to enhance its negotiating position with foreign banks, because the cash balances of all Venezuelan public-sector entities can be placed with the banks most responsive to requests for renewing old loans. The country has been willing to use its reserves as a political symbol in the past; it moved over $4 billion dollars of deposits into the U.S. branches of American banks between March 1982 and May 1982 to protest Great Britain's military response to Argentina's invasion of the Falklands.[72] Such moves have exacerbated difficulties in concluding a rescheduling agreement.

---

reserves. The oil company had $6.2 billion in deposits before the central bank took them under its direct control late in 1982. See Tim McGirk, "The Mexican Alarm Has Awakened Venezuela," *Euromoney* (November 1982), p. 128.

72. The funds may have been moved as a precaution against a British freeze, since Venezuela sided strongly with Argentina. The funds stayed in the United States even after the United States sided with Britain. The liabilities of U.S. offices of commercial banks to Venezuela increased from $5.14 billion in March 1982 to $9.44 billion at the end of May 1982 and stayed at that level for the next several months. See Department of the Treasury, *Treasury Bulletin* (September 1982, p. 80, and October 1982, p. 71).

CHAPTER EIGHT

OPEC's Foreign Aid

IN ADDITION to providing investment funds to financial markets, OPEC has become a major source of concessional financing to the developing world. The amounts of aid from OPEC nations have grown considerably since 1973; they are unique among third world countries as net providers of aid. Guided by the various political and strategic needs of the donors, this aid is the one financial channel used by OPEC members to achieve political goals.

Because of its scale and because it is usually provided through noncommercial channels, foreign aid is unlikely to pose any threat to the international financial system. Nevertheless, OPEC nations might use such aid to acquire an influence in the third world that would run counter to Western interests. Whether OPEC's foreign aid poses such a challenge to the West, however, depends on its motivations, magnitude, distribution, and effects.

Motivations

Most OPEC aid is bilateral and designed to advance the interests of the particular donor. Nevertheless, a few common political and strategic concerns have dominated aid decisions, especially because four Arabian peninsula nations (Saudi Arabia, Kuwait, the United Arab Emirates, and Qatar) provided over 85 percent of the funds between 1973 and 1981.

One concern has been to provide financial assistance to the so-called front-line states—Egypt, Jordan, Syria, and the Palestine Liberation Organization—in the Arab-Israeli conflict. This assistance, along with funds provided to the other, poorer Arab states such as the Yemens and Tunisia, signifies a shift of power within the Arab world toward the surplus states. Such financing might run counter to American interest in a stable Middle East. It could, however, also help reduce tension there.

The states with surpluses might also be willing to provide aid to non-Arab countries in exchange for an anti-Israeli stance. If the aid were used to persuade other countries to boycott Israeli goods and thus pressure the country economically, the matter would be extremely serious for the United States; but it might merely be irritating if the aid were used to buy only vocal condemnation.

Strategic considerations, which vary from country to country, have been almost as important as the Arab-Israeli conflict in motivating aid decisions. Saudi Arabia has focused on the need for friendly neighbors on the Arabian peninsula and along the sea lanes by which oil leaves the region. Thus Oman, North Yemen, Somalia, and the Sudan have been among the major recipients of aid from the Saudis and from Kuwait, Qatar, and the United Arab Emirates.[1] The efforts of the Gulf monarchies to support the kingdoms of Morocco and Jordan may help assure their own legitimacy, while Iranian aid to Afghanistan and Pakistan during the shah's regime was probably guided by regional concerns and a desire to outspend the Soviet Union. Nigeria and Venezuela have run regional assistance programs centered on guaranteed oil supplies. Most of these strategic concerns do not conflict with Western policy goals.

Aid has also been used by the OPEC nations as a means of fostering third world solidarity. Solidarity has to a certain extent been defined as a unanimous condemnation of Israel and as a muffling of criticism on the oil price rise, but Algeria and Kuwait have been active in the attempt to construct a united third world position on such issues as technology transfer, trade barriers in the West, the control of multinational corporations, and negotiations on the law of the sea. Although these positions may clash with Western interests in North-South issues, OPEC aid probably has little impact on the basic posture that non-oil developing countries would adopt in these negotiations.

A large amount of Western aid is based on economic considerations. For example, grants and low-interest loans may be tied to the purchase of the donor's food or manufactures. Similarly, OPEC could have provided oil at a below-market price or on concessional financing terms to the third world, although this was hardly necessary during most of the last decade

1. Organization for Economic Cooperation and Development, *Aid from OPEC Countries* (Paris: OECD, 1983), pp. 44, 54, 56, 64, 65.

Table 8-1. *Concessional Assistance from OPEC Members to Developing Countries and Multilateral Agencies, 1973-81*[a]
Net disbursements in millions of dollars unless otherwise specified

Country	1970	1973	1974	1975	1976	1977	1978	1979	1980	1981	Total	Share of all OPEC aid (percent)
											1973-81	
Algeria	...	25	47	41	54	42	41	270	65	65	650	1.1
Iran	4	2	408	593	753	169	240	21	7	-150	2,043	3.5
Iraq	4	11	423	215	231	62	172	847	829	143	2,933	5.0
Kuwait[b]	148	356	631	946	531	1,292	978	964	1,132	1,172	8,002	13.6
Libya	68	215	147	259	94	101	139	105	282	105	1,447	2.5
Nigeria	...	5	15	14	83	50	26	29	42	149	413	0.7
Qatar	...	94	185	338	195	189	98	280	284	175	1,838	3.1
Saudi Arabia	173	1,118	2,153	2,756	3,028	3,086	5,464	4,238	5,942	5,658	33,443	56.8
United Arab Emirates	...	289	510	1,046	1,021	1,052	885	967	906	799	7,475	12.7
Venezuela	1	18	60	21	108	24	87	107	125	67	627	1.1
Total	398	2,133	4,579	6,239	6,098	6,067	8,130	7,828	9,614	8,183	58,871	100.0

Source: Organization for Economic Cooperation and Development, *Aid from OPEC Countries* (Paris: OECD, 1983), pp. 10, 20.

a. Contributions to individual countries, to multilateral institutions largely financed by OPEC members, and to other multilateral institutions such as the World Bank, IDA, the United Nations, and regional development banks.

b. The figures reported here for Kuwaiti aid from 1979 to 1981 include support assistance to confrontation states (Jordan and Syria) under the Baghdad agreement. This change in reporting is not in the main tables of the OECD study but can be found in a note in OECD, *Aid from OPEC Countries*, p. 10.

when oil demand was high. The OPEC nations may have been reluctant to provide such assistance for fear that it would lead to sensitive questions about fairness and equity in oil pricing. Thus the statement of Ibrahim Shihata, then director-general of the OPEC Fund for International Development, that "only OPEC donors stand to gain no financial return from their assistance,"[2] must be carefully weighed against the reasons why OPEC countries have usually chosen to give aid untied to purchases of oil.

The Basic Statistics

Some OPEC nations were giving foreign aid before the oil shocks of the 1970s. Kuwait began distributing such funds in 1962, and in 1970 six OPEC members provided $398 million in assistance (table 8-1), with Saudi Arabia, Kuwait, and Libya responsible for all but $9 million of that. During 1973 ten members provided a total of $2.1 billion in assistance. The assistance increased rapidly to over $6 billion a year from 1975 to 1977. After another big jump in 1978, the amount fell slightly in 1979, largely because of budget deficits in Saudi Arabia, whose aid fell over $1 billion from 1978 to 1979. These cuts were more than reversed in 1980, following the second oil shock, but aid in 1981 dropped to 1978 levels because of the oil glut and the war-related budget problems facing Iran and Iraq.

During these years most of the aid was provided by Saudi Arabia, Kuwait, and the United Arab Emirates. Iran and Iraq once contributed substantial amounts but have now virtually disappeared from the list of donors. Qatar and Libya also extended large amounts of aid. The other six OPEC members have programs that are small or nonexistent.

Although the Western nations as a group are still by far the largest provider of official development assistance, the aid programs of the Arab Gulf nations have been especially impressive in relation to their gross national product. Qatar gave between 2.64 percent and 15.59 percent of its GNP as foreign aid from 1974 to 1981, the United Arab Emirates from 2.88 percent to 11.69 percent, and Saudi Arabia from 4.66 percent to 9.32 percent.[3] Only once during that period has a Western nation given more

2. *The Other Face of OPEC: Financial Assistance to the Third World* (London: Longman Group, 1982), p. 5.

3. OECD, *Aid from OPEC Countries*, p. 21.

than 1 percent of its GNP as foreign aid, while the United States contributed no more than 0.24 percent in any year since 1973.[4]

By now virtually all developing countries except for the so-called newly industrializing countries have received financial assistance from at least one OPEC aid program. As of 1981 at least ninety-eight countries had received bilateral or multilateral assistance.[5] Arab recipients accounted for $29.29 billion or 54 percent of OPEC aid between 1971 and 1981 (table 8-2); the shares of non-Arab Asia and non-Arab Africa were 8.9 percent and 3.1 percent, respectively. The destination of almost one-third of the aid is unspecified, however, mostly because the recipients of a substantial portion of Saudi aid are unknown.[6] The only major difference in the distribution of bilateral and multilateral OPEC aid is the more significant share of the latter received by sub-Saharan African nations.

The geographic concentration of OPEC aid becomes even clearer after examining data on the twenty largest recipients of bilateral aid (table 8-3). India and Sri Lanka are the only non-Islamic countries appearing on this list. The twenty largest recipients accounted for 94 percent of all bilateral aid between 1973 and 1981.[7] The eighteen Muslim nations accounted for 89.3 percent, and the thirteen Arab nations among them received 79 percent of OPEC's bilateral aid. The single largest recipient was Egypt, which received 19.5 percent of OPEC's disbursed bilateral aid. This last figure is all the more remarkable because aid to Egypt virtually ceased after the peace agreement with Israel went into effect in 1979. Egypt received 31.5 percent of all OPEC bilateral aid from 1973 to 1977. Syria and Jordan were the next largest recipients. The total amount going to the three front-line states has been relatively steady: 51.8 percent from 1973 to 1977, 50.9 percent from 1973 to 1981.[8] Thus the early hopes

---

4. The Netherlands gave 1.08 percent of GNP in 1981. See United Nations Conference on Trade and Development, *Handbook of International Trade and Development Statistics: 1981 Supplement* (UN, 1982), p. 331; and OECD, *Aid from OPEC Countries*, p. 15.

5. "Arab Aid Agencies Disburse $16.5 bn by End of 1982," *Middle East Economic Survey* (May 2, 1983), p. B1.

6. OECD, *Aid from OPEC Countries*, p. 56.

7. The same twenty recipients accounted for 92.4 percent of combined bilateral and multilateral aid whose geographic distribution is known that was extended by the OPEC nations. Based on data from table 8-3 and from OECD, *Aid from OPEC Countries*, pp. 160–61.

8. Paul Hallwood and Stuart W. Sinclair, *Oil, Debt and Development: OPEC in the Third World* (London: George Allen and Unwin, 1981), p. 101.

Table 8-2. *Regional Distribution of OPEC Aid, 1971–81*

Region	Bilateral[a]		Multilateral[b]		Total	
	Millions of dollars	Percent	Millions of dollars	Percent	Millions of dollars	Percent
Arab countries[c]	26,612	52.7	2,679	71.5	29,291	54.0
Non-Arab Asia	4,595	9.1	227	6.1	4,822	8.9
Non-Arab Africa	1,060	2.1	634	16.9	1,694	3.1
Other[d]	606	1.2	104	2.7	710	1.3
Unspecified	17,624	34.9	103[e]	2.7	17,727	32.7

Source: OECD, *Aid from OPEC Countries*, pp. 20, 33, 39, 102, 160–61.

a. The dollar figures for bilateral aid were constructed from other data in the OECD study. Table II.1 of that study provided data on total OPEC aid disbursements, while table II.11 provided data on multilateral contributions of OPEC countries to Arab agencies, OPEC agencies, and more broadly based groups (such as the World Bank). The difference was treated as bilateral aid. The dollar figures for regional aid were than determined from the share figures in the OECD study.

b. Arab agencies and OPEC agencies only. No multilateral Arab/OPEC agencies existed before 1974.

c. Algeria, Bahrain, Djibouti, Egypt, Iraq, Jordan, Lebanon, Mauritania, Morocco, North Yemen, Oman, Somalia, South Yemen, Sudan, Syria, Tunisia, United Arab Emirates.

d. Central and South America, Oceania, and Europe.

e. Includes $52 million listed as "unspecified Islamic countries."

that the political isolation of Egypt would increase the flow of OPEC aid to non-Arab countries have been frustrated.

One fortunate by-product of OPEC's focus on Arab and Muslim countries was that a significant share of the aid was channeled to the world's poorest nations. Between 1971 and 1981 OPEC allocated 14.9 percent of its geographically identified bilateral aid to the least developed countries and a further 33.5 percent to other low-income countries. The share going to other low-income countries fell after 1976, but that is largely accounted for by the cutoff of aid to Egypt. Multinational aid has been even more focused on the poorest nations: the least developed countries accounted for 23.8 percent of geographically identified multilateral aid from 1974 to 1981, and other low-income countries received a further 64.3 percent.[9] This latter figure is also swelled by aid to Egypt; the Gulf Organization for the Development of Egypt (GODE) alone provided $1.73 billion (table 8-5). Syria and Jordan, which also received substantial assistance, are classified as middle-income countries.

The provision of aid through multilateral institutions is to some extent equivalent to easier terms because the lack of a single donor makes it more difficult to impose political and economic conditions on it. Multilateral institutions also provide a means of broadening the geographic distribution of the aid. Their role as a channel for OPEC aid, however, has been much smaller than was once anticipated. They were first used in 1973 (table

9. OECD, *Aid from OPEC Countries*, pp. 17, 32, 33, 102.

Table 8-3. *Twenty Largest Recipients of Bilateral OPEC Aid, 1973–81*

Recipient	Amount (millions of dollars)	Share of bilateral aid[a] (percent)	Cumulative share of bilateral aid[a] (percent)	GNP per capita in 1980 (dollars)
Egypt	6,112.8	19.5	19.5	550
Syrian Arab Republic	5,975.5	19.0	38.5	1,480
Jordan	3,894.5	12.4	50.9	1,500
Pakistan	2,083.8	6.6	57.5	310
Yemen Arab Republic[b]	1,439.2	4.6	62.1	430
Morocco	1,389.6	4.4	66.5	830
India	1,337.2	4.3	70.8	230
Sudan	1,239.2	3.9	74.7	360
Oman	1,172.6	3.7	78.4	4,840
Lebanon	937.7	3.0	81.4	1,070[c]
Somalia	712.8	2.3	83.7	260
Bahrain	668.0	2.1	85.8	8,200
Mauritania	618.6	2.0	87.8	400
Turkey	476.7	1.5	89.3	1,390
Bangladesh	410.3	1.3	90.6	130
Democratic Yemen[d]	399.1	1.3	91.9	420
Tunisia	274.8	0.9	92.7	1,260
Afghanistan	141.5	0.5	93.2	170[e]
Sri Lanka	128.0	0.4	93.6	270
Senegal	120.9	0.4	94.0	420
Twenty countries	29,532.8	. . .	. . .	. . .
Bilateral OPEC aid[a]	31,424.0	. . .	. . .	. . .

Source: For aid data from 1973 to 1976 see United Nations Conference on Trade and Development, *Handbook of International Trade and Development Statistics, 1979* (New York: UN, 1979), pp. 420–23; for aid data from 1977 to 1981 see OECD, *Aid from OPEC Countries*, pp. 148–49; for per capita GNP data see World Bank, *World Bank Atlas*, various issues.
a. Includes all bilateral flows identified by region.
b. North Yemen.
c. 1975 per capita GNP.
d. South Yemen.
e. 1979 per capita GNP.

8-4) and were most prominent in 1976. In 1977, net disbursements were $1.1 billion, largely accounted for by GODE. From 1979 to 1981 OPEC-financed multilaterals made net disbursements of $972 million while OPEC members made $1.06 billion of net disbursements to UN agencies, development banks, the World Bank, and the IMF.[10] OPEC's retreat from using its own multilateral agencies reflects the changing pattern of its

10. Ibid., pp. 96, 154–56.

Table 8-4. *Channels for OPEC Aid, 1973–81*
Millions of dollars unless otherwise specified

Year	Bilateral	Multilateral	Bilateral (percent of total)
Commitments			
1973	2,532	52	98.0
1974	5,153	796	86.6
1975	7,850	555	93.4
1976	5,242	3,537	59.7
1977	6,248	1,712	78.5
1978	10,696	770	93.3
1979	5,929	512	92.1
1980	8,715	1,177	88.1
1981	7,498	2,706	73.5
Net disbursements			
1979	6,490	851	88.4
1980	8,171	957	89.5
1981	6,822	875	88.6

Source: OECD, *Aid from OPEC Countries*, pp. 147, 149, 154–56.

surpluses. In the early 1980s the oil glut and the Iran-Iraq war increased the budget pressures; the Gulf Arab states have become almost the sole provider of funds to OPEC's multilateral institutions. Under such circumstances they are unlikely to channel very much of their funds to such institutions and thereby dilute the political returns from the aid. Multilateral aid to Arab states will probably be least affected by this trend, while the OPEC Fund's goal of disbursing substantial amounts of aid worldwide may go unfulfilled. The impact on the contributions to non-OPEC multilaterals, such as the World Bank, will fall somewhere in between.

Mechanisms for Disbursing OPEC Aid

A variety of means have been used to channel OPEC aid to the developing countries. The most common method, in light of the magnitudes involved, has been to provide general balance of payments support through lump sum transfers handled by finance ministries. This sort of aid often results from decisions at the highest government levels and usually reflects explicit political concerns. Most bilateral assistance to the frontline states is handled in this way. Such loans are hard for the donors to control once disbursed, but they circumvent this difficulty by providing the funds for only several months or a year at a time. The donors are therefore in a position to review regularly the conditions of the loan and the political performance of the borrower.

Another common method is to provide project aid and technical assistance through national aid agencies. The oldest bilateral agency is the Kuwait Fund for Arab Economic Development (KFAED), which was established in 1961 only a few months after Kuwait's independence. KFAED has served as a model for other aid agencies, especially for the Abu Dhabi Fund for Arab Economic Development (ADFAED). KFAED and the Saudi Development Fund (SDF) have been the major bilateral OPEC aid agencies. SDF provided 19.8 percent and KFAED 18.1 percent of net concessional assistance from bilateral and multilateral OPEC institutions between 1974 and 1981 (table 8-5).[11] The Iraqi Fund for External Development (IFED) was also an important source of concessional funding until the war with Iran.

Despite their titles, the aid from all four funds is now available to Arab and non-Arab countries alike. Except for IFED they focus on project aid, especially for infrastructure, water, health, and food projects. The technical expertise of these funds has increased over the years, and they tend to evaluate projects on criteria comparable to World Bank standards. They often engage in cofinancing projects with one another, with the World Bank, or with other multilateral institutions, which helps speed the disbursement of funds and reduces the number of technical staff required. There are, however, some differences in the orientation and management of these agencies. The Iraqi Fund, for example, has been more involved in oil import financing than the others. IFED also serves more as an operational agency of the Iraqi government, whereas the other three agencies function somewhat independently. The share of the national agencies in total aid also varies considerably from country to country. Less than 17 percent of aid has gone through the national agencies in Saudi Arabia or the United Arab Emirates in any year, while KFAED's share of Kuwaiti aid exceeded 30 percent from 1979 to 1981.[12]

11. KFAED has been making disbursements since 1962, however; its net disbursements are $1.43 billion and thus slightly larger than those of SFD. See OECD, *Aid from OPEC Countries*, p. 46.

12. The figures for Saudi Arabia and the United Arab Emirates include all loans and grants administered by the funds. The figures for Kuwait exclude the substantial Kuwaiti aid to the front-line states. The role of KFAED in total Kuwaiti aid is much lower once these other flows are taken into account. See ibid., pp. 26, 72–74.

Table 8-5. *Concessional Aid from National and Regional OPEC Aid Agencies, 1974–81*

		Disbursements		
Agency	Commitments (millions of dollars)	Amount (millions of dollars)	Percent of commitments	Percent of all agencies' disbursements
Abu Dhabi Fund for Arab Economic Development	590	311	52.7	4.4
Arab Bank for Economic Development in Africa[a]	487	368	75.6	5.2
Arab Fund for Economic and Social Development	1,121	649	57.9	9.3
Gulf Organization for the Development of Egypt[b]	1,811	1,725	95.3	24.6
Iraqi Fund for External Development[c]	1,748	337	19.3	4.8
Islamic Development Bank	223	74	33.2	1.1
Kuwait Fund for Arab Economic Development	2,793	1,269	45.4	18.1
OPEC Fund for International Development	1,291	733	56.8	10.5
Saudi Fund for Development	3,224	1,386	43.0	19.8
Others[d]	161	160	99.4	2.3
Total	13,449	7,012	52.2	100.0

Source: OECD, *Aid from OPEC Countries*, pp. 46, 59, 67, 74, 95, 96.
a. Includes the Special Arab Aid Fund for Africa, which merged with the Arab Bank for Economic Development in Africa in 1976.
b. No longer operational.
c. Only covers operations through October 1980.
d. The OAPEC Special Account, Islamic Solidarity Fund, and Arab Fund for Technical Assistance to African and Arab Countries. The OAPEC Special Account was not renewed after 1976.

Aid has also been channeled through multilateral institutions over the years. The first such agency was the Arab Fund for Economic and Social Development (AFESD), which was founded in 1968 but did not begin operating until 1973. Originally designed to extend aid only within the Arab world, its charter was later expanded to include all developing nations. AFESD emphasizes project loans. The Islamic Development Bank (IDB), another major source of financing, restricts operations to Islamic nations. Not all IDB financing is concessional, since its charter includes provisions for equity participations and trade financing. The Arab Bank for Economic Development in Africa (BADEA) restricts its operations to Africa. Founded in 1973 in response to African complaints about the oil price hikes, in 1977 it absorbed another multilateral, the Special

Arab Aid Fund for Africa. BADEA concentrates on project lending and technical assistance grants. So far its volume of commitments and speed of disbursement do not appear to have satisfied the complaints from the sub-Saharan countries.

The OPEC Fund has been the largest source of global multilateral aid from OPEC nations. It dispenses project, program, and balance of payments loans and grants for technical assistance projects. It has also functioned to some extent as OPEC's representative in the North-South debate by administering OPEC aid to the UN Development Program, the International Fund for Agricultural Development, and the Common Fund. The OPEC Fund has covered the widest range of countries of any OPEC aid institution; by April 1983 it had approved 328 loans to eighty-two countries.[13]

Previously, the Gulf Organization for the Development of Egypt (GODE) was also an important dispenser of aid. Saudi Arabia, Kuwait, Qatar, and the United Arab Emirates funded this agency, which provided $1.725 billion in aid to Egypt from 1976 to 1978 (table 8-5). Although GODE ceased to operate after the peace treaty between Israel and Egypt went into effect, it remains by far the largest net disburser of concessional funds among OPEC's multilateral financial agencies.

In general, such multilateral agencies provide OPEC aid on the easiest political terms, in the sense that the multiplicity of donors and their conflicting interests make it harder to dictate the political behavior of recipients. The absence of clear political gains when the chain from donor to ultimate recipient is long seems to make donor countries reluctant to use such channels, which may explain why disbursements from multilateral OPEC agencies accounted for only 6.5 percent of the aid distributed by OPEC from 1974 to 1981.[14]

Finally, it is worth noting the variations in the performance of disbursements from these funds. On this measure BADEA has done the best of funds still in existence, with disbursements equal to 75.6 percent of commitments between 1974 and 1981 (table 8-5). The Iraqi Fund, on the other hand, had disbursements equal to only 19.3 percent of commitments. Most of OPEC's other bilateral and multilateral aid agencies have performance measures near 50 percent.

13. Ibrahim F. I. Shihata and Antonio R. Parra, "The Establishment and Evolution of the OPEC Fund," in Ibrahim F. I. Shihata and others, *The OPEC Fund for International Development: The Formative Years* (St. Martin's Press, 1983), p. 38.

14. Based on data in tables 8-1 and 8-5.

OPEC Aid and Higher Oil Prices

One of the political problems confronting the OPEC nations has been the effects of higher oil prices on developing countries. The OPEC nations have steadfastly insisted that the price shocks impose no obligation, logical, legal, or moral, on OPEC to provide aid to make up for the impact of higher oil prices. The non-oil developing countries themselves have not taken a united stand on this issue, but individual countries and regions of the developing world have complained of insufficient aid from OPEC.

The OPEC nations have put forth several reasons why aid should not be tied to the increase in oil bills. One such is affordability: oil bills increased most for middle-income countries, especially the newly industrializing countries, which should have been able to afford the oil relatively easily. OPEC nations claim to orient their aid to the world's poorest countries, independent of their oil bills. Second, OPEC is unwilling to tie its aid to the oil price increases because it in no way concedes that current oil prices are unfairly high. Because the fairness of a price is difficult, if not impossible, to judge, this section will compare oil bills and OPEC aid without defining fair prices. Third, OPEC has argued that the developing countries should focus their efforts on raising all commodity prices received by the third world rather than on attempting to lower the price of oil. Finally, the Gulf Arabs have been especially leery of granting states—except the front-line states—assistance not tied to specific projects for fear that the money will be wasted.[15]

While it is true that some developing nations have received OPEC aid in excess of their oil import bills, it is difficult to argue that this was because of OPEC's special concerns for the developing world. Paul Hallwood and Stuart Sinclair made detailed calculations of the incremental oil bills of third world nations after the first oil shock under various assumptions. They found that aid to Africa had indeed exceeded additional outlays on petroleum products between 1974 and 1977 when the extra cost was assumed to be $8 per barrel. There was, however, no single year in which

15. For example, Oil Minister Ahmed Zaki Yamani once responded to a question on aid to the third world by commenting that Saudi Arabia was "trying to help Africa, and we had to send a team to visit these countries to see if there are some projects to be financed. They didn't have any. All they want is that X amount of dollars should be sent to them and they dispose of it. And usually the way they dispose of it is not the right way." Question and answer session reported in "Oil and Money in the Eighties," supplement to the *Middle East Economic Survey* (October 5, 1981), p. 7.

this was true if Egypt was excluded from the calculations. Even at an extra cost of $6 per barrel only Egypt, Somalia, and the Sudan were net gainers. The only Asian oil importers who gained more from OPEC aid than they lost from their incremental oil expenditures were Afghanistan, Bangladesh, and Pakistan; India suffered a large loss.[16]

It is unlikely that net benefits have increased since 1977. While OPEC aid has expanded considerably, oil import bills have also doubled because of the 1979 oil shock. In addition, the pattern of OPEC aid has not changed very much, except that Jordan and Syria now receive the aid money that once went to Egypt. Thus only a very few countries have gained more from OPEC aid than they paid out in incremental oil bills, and many of those (Egypt, Somalia, the Sudan, Pakistan) were of special strategic interest to major OPEC donors.

The OPEC nations have been sensitive to attempts to tie oil price increases and aid. Nigeria's suggestion in February 1975 that crude oil be sold to African states at reduced prices was rejected because it was contrary to OPEC rules.[17] Various other schemes have also been proposed, one of which would allow non-oil developing countries to pay half the oil price in hard currencies and the rest in local currencies. The local-currency portion would then be deposited in the national development bank (or a similar institution) as a long-term loan.[18] While OPEC nations as a group have not accepted any of these proposals, several individual countries have recently developed forms of "tied" aid. Iraq allowed part of the oil price to take the form of concessional long-term credit, though these arrangements are unimportant now because of its low production. Venezu-

16. Hallwood and Sinclair, *Oil, Debt and Development*, pp. 110–28. Arabian light crude cost $2.07 a barrel in February 1959 before the major oil companies cut the posted price to $1.80 a barrel; this price lasted into the early 1970s. If the price of $2.07 a barrel had been indexed to industrial country export prices, oil would have cost $3.36 a barrel at the end of 1973; if indexed to primary commodities, the price would have been $3.66 a barrel. The price of Arabian light market crude was $11.65 a barrel in January 1974. Thus the figure of $8 per barrel for the incremental cost of oil is a useful standard.

17. Ibid., p. 95.

18. Under this scheme the value of the loan would be indexed to hard currencies such as the dollar or to a composite currency such as the Special Drawing Right of the International Monetary Fund and would pay market interest rates, so the concessional element of the loan is rather small. See Michael Lyall, "Arab Aid to Black Africa: Myth Versus Reality," in Dunstan M. Wai, ed., *Interdependence in a World of Unequals: African-Arab-OECD Economic Cooperation for Development* (Westview Press, 1982), pp. 191–92.

ela joined with Mexico, a non-OPEC oil exporter, to guarantee quantities of oil to nine Central American and Caribbean nations while allowing for partially deferred payments on soft terms.[19] The four African members of OPEC have also guaranteed supplies at official OPEC prices.[20] Although such arrangements are less attractive to the third world than the reduced prices suggested by Nigeria in 1975, they do improve the terms for those countries while satisfying OPEC's traditional desire to avoid explicit two-tier pricing schemes.

Finally, OPEC has tried to defuse the oil price issue by shifting the grounds of the debate. In particular, it has asserted that low prices for non-oil commodities, not high prices for oil, are the problem. To reinforce this argument, the OPEC Fund has coordinated OPEC's strategy toward the International Fund for Agricultural Development and the Common Fund.[21] The Common Fund, designed to finance export-related commodities schemes in the developing world, has been promoted as one part of the so-called new international economic order. Participants in the Common Fund negotiations agreed that there should eventually be $400 million to finance buffer stocks (the first window) and $350 million to promote research and development on improving the marketing conditions for raw materials (the second window). Each member of the Common Fund was to subscribe $1 million plus an additional contribution based on the country's size and wealth.[22] OPEC nations pledged $100 million to the Common Fund, to be handled by the OPEC Fund for International Development.[23] This included an offer to pay the initial $1 million subscription fee for any of the low-income developing countries. As of October 1981 the OPEC Fund had contributed $46.4 million to the second window and had

19. Venezuela suspended one part of this facility following the OPEC decision to lower the price of crude oil in March 1983; see Jose de Cordoba, "Venezuela Suspends Some Loans to Caribbean," *Washington Post*, March 17, 1983. It was expected that Venezuela and Mexico would toughen the terms of the agreement when it came up for renewal in August 1983 by decreasing the amount that can be deferred and the period over which the deferrals are repaid; see Kim Fuad, "Venezuela and Mexico to Tighten Oil and Loan Terms," *Financial Times*, April 26, 1983.

20. Shihata, *The Other Face of OPEC*, p. 14.

21. See Shihata and Parra, "The Establishment and Evolution of the OPEC Fund," p. 32.

22. For details on the Common Fund see Shihata, *The Other Face of OPEC*, pp. 90–92.

23. Shihata and Parra, "The Establishment and Evolution of the OPEC Fund," p. 32.

also paid the subscriptions for thirty-five developing countries, which amounted to another $37.16 million.[24]

The debate on tying OPEC aid to the higher oil bills of the third world seems to have died out by the end of 1982. This happened despite the decrease in OPEC aid after 1980, a decrease due in part to the rapid decline in OPEC surpluses. Two things probably explain the disappearance of this issue. First, OPEC did increase aid substantially following the second oil shock (see table 8-1). Even if it did not cover their increased oil bills, the aid helped quiet the grumblings of many third world countries. Second, some of the complaints in 1979 might have been made in anticipation of continuous real increases in the price of oil during the 1980s. But both the real and nominal price have fallen substantially over the last two years, especially if the various differentials, premiums, and discounts are included in the calculations. This has shifted the attention of the third world from oil prices to the volumes and prices of their own commodity export trade, which is conducted almost entirely with the West. Thus although aid helped to reduce the friction between OPEC and the third world on oil prices, contemporaneous developments in the oil market and in other commodity markets also diminished the immediacy of the issue.

The Political Consequences of OPEC Aid

While there is no question that political considerations have shaped the OPEC aid process, it should not be assumed that surpluses have given these states a monopoly on regional political influence. Furthermore, when their political efforts have met with success, it has not necessarily been because "petrodollars" sealed the pact. In fact, the presence of the surpluses has occasionally raised the ante for political cooperation.

The Arabian peninsula states' aid to front-line states is the clearest case of politically motivated OPEC aid. Following the June 1967 Arab-Israeli war, Egypt received about $200 million per year in aid from Saudi Arabia under the Khartoum agreement. Commitments from the Arab oil-exporting countries to Egypt increased markedly after the October 1973 war to a level of $4 billion a year in aid and debt-service relief.[25] Actual disbursements were lower but still considerable, with almost $6 billion of bilateral

---

24. Shihata, *The Other Face of OPEC*, p. 112.
25. Hallwood and Sinclair, *Oil, Debt and Development*, p. 104.

disbursements to Egypt from all OPEC countries between 1973 and 1978 and a further $1.725 billion disbursed by GODE.[26] The Gulf states also financed the Arab Organization for Industrialization, a $1 billion program based in Egypt to improve Egyptian and Arab arms manufacturing capability. Syria and Jordan also received assistance as front-line states.

Egypt's sudden movement toward compromise with Israel—President Sadat's visit to Jerusalem took place in November 1977 and the peace treaty between Egypt and Israel was signed in March 1979—led to an almost complete withdrawal of financial support from Arab donors. Bilateral aid from all OPEC nations to Egypt (largely Arab aid) fell from $745 million in 1977 to $166 million in 1979 to $4.8 million in 1980, while multilateral aid fell from $861 million in 1977 to $42 million in 1979 to $7.9 million in 1980.[27] A number of other political actions were also taken after the actual signing of the peace treaty. The Arab Organization for Industrialization was closed because, according to Prince Sultan Bin Abdel-Aziz, Saudi defense minister, Egypt's actions were "in conflict with the reasons and objectives of setting up the Arab arms industries' organization."[28] Nineteen of the twenty-one members of the Arab League severed diplomatic relations with Egypt, the headquarters of the Arab League was moved from Cairo to Tunis, and Algeria and Libya tried unsuccessfully during the 1979 summit to have Egypt expelled from the Organization of African Unity (OAU).

These actions were not sufficient to deter Egypt from concluding the peace treaty or to persuade her to renege on it, but in the presence of a weaker leader or less favorable economic circumstances (the price of Egypt's oil exports more than tripled from 1978 to 1980) these actions and threats might have been sufficient to weaken Egyptian resolve. A large part of the funds that would probably have gone to Egypt during 1979 and 1980 were shifted to Jordan and Syria instead. This may well have signaled to Jordan that the costs of a separate peace treaty with Israel were likely to be unacceptably high and thereby removed one possible route to a Middle East peace. It is ironic, however, that the actions against Egypt were directed not by the Arab Gulf states, which were the main suppliers of funds to Egypt, but by Algeria, Libya, and Syria. That the Gulf states

26. Based on tables 8-1 and 8-5 and data in OECD, *Aid from OPEC Countries*, p. 148.

27. Ibid., pp. 148, 160.

28. See Robin Allen and Alan Mackie, "Arab Sanctions Begin to Bite on Egypt," *Middle East Economic Digest* (May 18, 1979), p. 3.

eventually succumbed to these pressures from the other Arab states indicates that, contrary to some predictions, the surpluses have not shifted the balance of power within the Arab world completely to the large oil producers.

The limits on the political use of oil wealth have also been exposed in the Gulf states' pursuit of regional security interests. The Saudis seem to have taken the lead in these efforts, and they have met with several successes. Somalia reportedly received $400 million to compensate for the expulsion of Soviet advisers,[29] and aid to Oman has strengthened a neighbor that controls strategic oil routes.[30] Generous payments to the central government and to several of the northern tribes have given the Saudis a stronger position in North Yemen and have led to a reduction in the number of Soviet advisers and in that nation's reliance on the Soviet Union. Yet there have also been failures. Saudi Arabia promised $125 million in aid to South Yemen, along with guaranteed crude oil supplies for the refinery in Aden, but this was not enough once Saudi Arabia's political demands became clear.[31] The Saudis then scaled back their aid program. Around the same time the Algerians reportedly turned down an offer of Saudi aid that was conditioned on the withdrawal of Algerian support for the Polisario Front in the western Saraha.[32] Similarly, Mauritania made a separate peace with the Polisario guerrillas despite a slowdown in the disbursement of Kuwaiti aid.[33] And in the crucial case of Egypt discussed earlier, the surpluses were neither large enough to prevent a peace with Israel nor useful in moderating the demands of the hard-liners within the Arab League.

A third example of the role of aid in support of foreign policy goals is in the area of Arab-African cooperation. Africa's relations with the Arab world, appropriately described as an "ambiguous but politically charged minuet,"[34] have centered on three issues since 1970. The primary objective

29. "Together Against the Red Peril," *The Middle East* (May 1978), p. 24.

30. The aid to Oman may also have been intended to lessen the influence of the shah of Iran, who had provided considerable military assistance to the sultan of Oman in the war against the Dhofari rebels.

31. The Saudi goals reportedly included South Yemeni support of Saudi security needs in the Red Sea area, support of Egypt's initiative to Israel, and an end to South Yemeni support of radical movements in the Arab world. See "Together Against the Red Peril," p. 23.

32. Ibid., p. 24.

33. Hallwood and Sinclair, *Oil, Debt and Development*, p. 105.

34. Ernest J. Wilson III, "Africa, the Energy Crisis, and the Triangular Relationship," in Wai, *Interdependence in a World of Unequals*, p. 125.

of the African Arab nations was the further isolation of Israel. The original goal of black African nations was to break all OPEC ties with South Africa (and with Rhodesia in earlier years), but another goal, concessional financing for oil import bills and development projects, soon became equally important.

The first steps toward political solidarity came at the time of the 1973 Arab-Israeli war. Many sub-Saharan states broke off diplomatic relations with Israel before the 1973 war or immediately afterward, while the Arab states agreed during the Arab summit conference of November 1973 to cut off oil supplies to South Africa, Rhodesia, and Portugal.[35] The political solidarity between Africans and Arabs that seemed destined to emerge was never quite realized, however, because the oil shocks generated a third issue in which Arab gains appeared to be at Africa's expense. Before the end of 1973 the OAU convened an extraordinary meeting and requested reduced oil prices and direct government-to-government sales, but OPEC rejected the requests as too complex. The Algiers meeting of the Arab nations did lead to an offer of aid and technical assistance, but such aid was not tied to oil payments.[36] The economic costs and benefits of African-Arab solidarity became more evident during the next few years. Africa's disappointment continued to increase until the complaints were quieted with pledges of $1.45 billion in aid at the first African-Arab summit meeting in Cairo in March 1977.[37] The complaints of the African nations resumed with the second oil price shock and came to a head at the OAU summit meeting in 1979. At that meeting the director of BADEA assured the Africans that 82.5 percent of the previously promised funds had been allocated by June 1979.[38] While that action avoided an open break during the summit, tensions have continued simmering. The aid disbursements, which totaled $1.69 billion between 1971 and 1981 (see table 8-2), still have not satisfied sub-Saharan Africa. OPEC agencies stepped up the level of new commitments to $548.5 million in 1981 (although not all of this assistance was on concessional terms), but this

35. See Robert Anton Mertz and Pamela MacDonald Mertz, *Arab Aid to Sub-Saharan Africa* (Munich and Mainz: Kaiser-Gruenewald, 1983), pp. 31–47.

36. Ibid., pp. 32–33.

37. Lyall, "Arab Aid to Black Africa," p. 186.

38. BADEA's calculations, however, included all bilateral and multilateral commitments OPEC had ever made to non-Arab Africa, including commitments made before the Cairo summit. New commitments during the interval between the two meetings were considerably lower. Lyall estimates $51 million in new commitments, although this seems to understate the amounts involved. See "Arab Aid to Black Africa," pp. 186, 193–94.

was not enough to patch up relations with all the African nations.[39] Zaire, which had long felt it had not received aid commensurate with its size or needs, resumed diplomatic relations with Israel in May 1982. All thirteen members of OPEC resolved in June 1982 to break off economic and diplomatic relations with any country that restored diplomatic relations with Israel. Nonetheless, Liberia decided in August 1983 to resume its ties with Israel.[40]

The recent friction is evidence of the differences between Arab and African views of solidarity. The Arabs believe that Africa traded downgrading ties with Israel for the cessation of Arab commercial ties with South Africa, while the Africans expected considerably more from the Arabs on some sort of ability-to-pay criteria. Earlier hopes for an African-Arab economic community foundered because the Arab surplus states could not provide a significant market for Africa's output (mineral, agricultural, or manufacturing) and were unwilling to provide the quantities of aid that these countries desired. Furthermore, some African nations undoubtedly feared an expansion of Arab political influence at the expense of non-Muslim Africa. The disappearance of the surpluses has already caused the Arab states to reevaluate their aid programs, and disbursements to non-Arab Africa fell sharply in the first half of 1983.[41] This could lead to a further erosion of African-Arab political solidarity unless falling oil prices remove some of the other pressures on the relationship.

On an additional note, during the UN Conference on Trade and Development in 1979, several Latin American nations, led by Costa Rica, formed the Organization of Petroleum Importing Countries and lobbied for concessional oil prices. This dispute quickly disappeared after the OPEC Fund made loans to several of the poorer Latin American nations (Haiti, Bolivia, and Honduras). Although this action provides another example of OPEC's use of aid to improve political relations with the rest of the third world, it also emphasizes that the surpluses themselves generated new political problems for the OPEC nations.

These four sets of issues encompass most of the situations in which OPEC aid could be used for political purposes. They show that the OPEC

39. "Political Tensions Cloud Arab-African Cooperation," *Middle East Economic Digest* (June 4, 1982), pp. 24–27.
40. "States Restoring Relations with Israel Face Loss of Arab and OPEC Oil," *Middle East Economic Survey* (September 5, 1983), p. B1.
41. "Arab Aid Commitments Fall Sharply in 1983," *Middle East Economic Digest* (November 18, 1983), p. 48.

nations have clearly and frequently attempted to use aid for political purposes and that in a number of situations aid probably helped ensure success. The failures, however, expose the limitations of aid as a political tool. When the interests of the donor and recipient are widely separated, aid will not work, or at the least, the OPEC nations have been unwilling to supply the necessary quantity of funds. Furthermore, the OPEC nations only have the funds available because of the oil price increases, yet the size of the surpluses has increased the third world's expectations of what OPEC can pay, while the source of the surpluses has raised third world estimates of what OPEC owes them.

Finally, it is difficult to judge the indirect impact of OPEC aid on Western interests. Increased aid has, at the least, complicated the peace process in the Middle East. Promises of aid prompted non-Arab third world nations to join in attempts to isolate Israel diplomatically and helped isolate Egypt after Camp David. The security interests of Western nations and Gulf Arab countries can also often coincide, however, which has contributed to a situation in which Arab aid flows sometimes support Western security interests in the region (excluding regional concerns related to the Arab-Israeli dispute). Therefore, while the West cannot ignore the political impact of OPEC aid, it should not automatically assume that all of it will have significant and negative impacts on Western interests.

CHAPTER NINE

Arab Banks and International Financial Markets

THE EXISTENCE of balance of payments surpluses inevitably involved the OPEC states in the world financial system. Concurrently the international role of commercial banking institutions owned by Arab members of OPEC has expanded. Although the Arab banks are unlikely ever to become the dominant influence in international financial markets, a number have matured into institutions important in international finance. They have also attracted attention as another possible channel for recycling OPEC surpluses. This makes it worthwhile to analyze these institutions, their role in the recycling process, and their likely impact on world financial markets.

This chapter will discuss Arab banks in general and banks from the Gulf surplus states, Libya, and Bahrain in particular. Banks from non-Arab OPEC nations will not be discussed because their countries are more often borrowers than providers of funds in international financial markets. Bahrain is included because it is an important regional financial center and because several banks owned by Arab surplus states are headquartered there, even though Bahrain itself is not a member of OPEC.

The History and Development of Arab Banks

Banking in the Arab countries has developed in three distinct stages that can be characterized by the ownership structure of institutions established during those periods. The first stage, which lasted until the first oil shock, began with many countries relying on the Middle Eastern branches of British-owned banks for their banking services. A few Arab-owned banks were established in the region before 1950; after that there was a sharp increase. Expanded opportunities for trade and development following local oil discoveries helped prompt the founding of such institutions as the National Bank of Kuwait, the National Commercial Bank of Saudi Arabia, and the National Bank of Abu Dhabi. During this period, too, Beirut emerged as an important regional financial center, especially for the international placement of private funds. Many of the banks set up during this period are sizable, but they were not very active in international markets until the early 1980s because of the attractive returns available on domestic business. Banks from Kuwait have been the most conspicuous exception to this rule.

The second stage began about 1973 and continued until approximately 1979. Arab institutions grew rapidly, new international markets opened in Bahrain and the United Arab Emirates, and Kuwait increased the access of foreign borrowers to the local Kuwaiti dinar bond market. Furthermore, Arab banks established during the first phase of growth participated in a number of internationally oriented ventures with Western banks. Designed to combine Western financial know-how with the capital available to the Arab countries, these joint ventures grew rapidly in the mid-1970s. Typical examples are the Union de Banques Arabes et Francaises (UBAF) and the Banque Arabe et International d'Investissement (BAII), both of which are based in Paris and owned by a large number of bank shareholders. There are three other major consortium banks from the second period. The Arab Latin American Bank is a consortium of Arab and Latin banks specializing in business with Latin America. The Gulf International Bank (GIB) is based in Bahrain and is owned entirely by the governments of Saudi Arabia, Kuwait, Iraq, the United Arab Emirates, Bahrain, Oman, and Qatar. Finally, the Saudi International Bank (SIB), based in London, is half owned by the Saudi Arabian Monetary Agency and half by a group of international banks led by Morgan Guaranty Trust. While a number of such consortium banks formed during the 1970s, these five have been the most involved in international markets. The wide dispersion of ownership has led to some problems for these banks, both on questions of overall business strategy and on individual loans, but such problems have been common to all consortium banks.

The third stage of Arab banking began with the second oil shock. As the oil-producing countries began once again to accumulate large surpluses, their governments grew more interested in investments in the banking industry. This time, however, new investments were focused on wholly Arab-owned banks. Two institutions have benefited most so far. The capital base of GIB was increased from $105 million to $265 million in 1980, allowing it to expand international operations. Also in 1980 the Arab Banking Corporation, a consortium owned by Libya, Kuwait, and the United Arab Emirates, was created. Based in Bahrain, this bank started with an authorized capital of $1 billion. Kuwait has also expressed the intention to set up its own $1 billion institution, although nothing definite has yet resulted from those plans.

Several other important changes have taken place during the third stage. First, some of the larger institutions from the major surplus countries have increased their international orientation. This seems particularly true for privately owned institutions from Saudi Arabia and Kuwait, such as the National Commercial Bank and the National Bank of Kuwait. Second, the Saudis have completed the "Saudi-isation" of foreign-owned bank branches in their country and as a result now own 60 percent to 70 percent of these banks. This change of ownership was accompanied by substantial capital increases for most of them. Some of the banks might also eventually move into the Euromarkets if Saudi development slows down. Finally, a number of Islamic banks have been established that operate in accord with the Islamic prohibition on payment of interest. There is no restriction on the distribution of profits, however, so an Islamic bank functions somewhat like a mutual fund, distributing to depositors a share of the profits derived from its investments. Islamic institutions have not yet had a major impact on international finance, although institutions such as Dar al Maal al Islami and the Al Rajhi Company for Islamic Investments are specifically oriented to international transactions.

It is appropriate to conclude this brief historical review with a few facts that help to put the role of Arab banks in proper perspective. First, although there are a large number of Arab banks, many are new and most are small compared to major Western banks. Only 31 Arab banks ranked among the world's top 500 as of December 31, 1982. Rafidain Bank of Iraq, the largest Arab bank, ranked ninety-ninth on that list. The world's largest bank, Citicorp, had assets of $120.68 billion as of the same date, an amount greater than the total assets of the twelve largest Arab banks.[1] Finally, only a few Arab banks now play major roles in international financial markets. That group includes the larger consortium banks established in the second and third phases and a few of the older and larger institutions based in Saudi Arabia, Kuwait, or the United Arab Emirates.

1. "The Top 500," *The Banker* (June 1983), pp. 152–242.

It also includes one bank from a deficit country (the Arab Bank of Jordan) and the Libyan Arab Foreign Bank. Thus the probable list of internationally active Arab banks includes only 2 of the 5 largest Arab banks, 6 of the top 10, and 13 of the top 30.

Arab Investments in Banking: The Motivations

Accumulated current account surpluses have inevitably drawn the surplus states into the world financial system. It was not inevitable, however, that those countries would acquire their own commercial banks. In fact the countries continue to participate in the international financial system as direct providers of funds to ultimate borrowers, largely through purchases of bonds and equities, and as sources of bank deposits to financial intermediaries that in turn provide the funds to the ultimate borrowers. Recently, however, some governments have become involved in internationally active financial institutions to a limited extent, as have the private sectors in several of the surplus states.

The discovery of oil in the Arab nations initially led to the foundation of banks designed to assist local development. All the Arab countries encouraged this sort of domestic financial institution. Kuwait, however, was the first to start moving into international finance. The "Three Ks," the Kuwait Foreign Trading, Contracting and Investment Company (KFTCIC), the Kuwait Investment Company (KIC), and the Kuwait International Investment Company (KIIC), began managing foreign bond issues in the late 1960s and were important participants in the Eurobond and Kuwaiti dinar bond markets in the 1970s. This activity was encouraged by the Kuwaiti Ministry of Finance, which used the Three Ks as intermediaries in a large share of its bond purchases.[2] Moreover, Kuwait has been represented in many of the consortium banks, either through shares held by one of the Kuwaiti institutions or through direct government participation, and has taken a lead in forming the two government-owned consortia, GIB and ABC. While the United Arab Emirates has also been involved in forming international banks, including GIB and ABC, the roles of Saudi Arabia, Libya, and Qatar have been much more circumscribed.

2. More than 80 percent of KFTCIC and 50 percent of KIC are owned by the government; KIIC is entirely in private hands.

The differing attitudes of these five countries toward banking reflect their overall investment policies. Because neither Kuwait nor the United Arab Emirates has felt constrained by the nature of its oil and development policy, liquidity of investments is not a pressing concern. Investments in banking are thus appropriate if they satisfy rate of return, diversification, and safety criteria. Both countries expect equity investments to earn higher rates of return than bonds or bank deposits and are willing to bear the extra risk. They have premised their banking investments on the assumptions that for structural reasons the cumulative surpluses will be drawn on very little and that banking offers attractive opportunities for national development. Thus Abdlatif Yousef al-Hamad, then the Kuwaiti minister of finance and planning, wrote that the Gulf states are "bound to look at the banking system not only as a sector servicing the rest of the economy, but also as a principal branch of the national economy in its own right. Diversification—which is a constant theme in these countries' development thinking and development policy—particularly includes diversification into the world of finance and, given the constraints on local markets, into that of international finance."[3]

While basic economic criteria have prompted Kuwait and the United Arab Emirates to form internationally oriented banking institutions, the same criteria explain why Saudi Arabia, despite its much larger surplus, has been significantly less involved in such ventures. International banks are a very illiquid investment. Because of their oil and development policies, the Saudis cannot rely on large, permanent surpluses, so they have adjusted their investment strategy accordingly. Saudi Arabia's investments in GIB and SIB are small compared to the bank investments of Kuwait and Abu Dhabi and are likely to remain so. Libya and Qatar, on the other hand, would be somewhat interested in bank investments, but their smaller surpluses limit their ability to invest.

Two other factors have interested some Arab countries in banking investments. One is that banking represents a natural extension of a historical involvement in trade. Officials from Kuwait and the Emirates seem most inclined to make this argument. The second is the belief of some Arabs that they are already fully exposed to the risks of international banking once they deposit money at a Western bank, so they might as well set up their own banks and enjoy a greater return on their money. One part

3. "Prospects for Arab International Banking in the 1980s," *The Arab Banker* (July 1982), p. 34.

of this argument, usually connected to arguments for increased investments in the developing countries, was stated by Hazem El-Beblawi of the Industrial Bank of Kuwait: "Regardless of what they do with their surplus funds, OPEC surplus countries will anyway be left with developing countries as the ultimate debtors of their surplus."[4] The argument is not legally accurate because deposits with a Western bank are the obligation of that bank and not of any country to which it subsequently lends the funds, but it has probably supplemented the other economic factors guiding surplus states toward the banking industry.

One country, Bahrain, is motivated by a rather different set of factors. Bahrain is not a member of OPEC nor will it ever be a major net supplier of funds to international markets, since its oil reserves are small and will soon be exhausted. It has, however, tried to become an international financial center and serves as a base to a number of Arab financial institutions.

Bahrain went into business as an international financial center in 1975 when the Bahraini Monetary Agency began offering limited licenses to international banks to conduct offshore business from offices located in Bahrain. Because offshore banking units (OBUs) cannot operate in the local currency, they have a limited impact on the conduct of Bahrain's monetary policy. At the same time they help the local economy through the new employment opportunities and licensing fees they generate. The banks, meanwhile, counted on three benefits: a booking center with low tax rates; a base for conducting business with regional markets, especially with Saudi Arabia and Kuwait, in which countries they were not allowed to establish branches; and another office that might attract deposits from the Gulf surplus states. The experiment has been successful, although Bahrain has not lured a significant share of government deposits away from other financial centers.

Some of the privately owned Arab banks will also gradually expand into overseas business. This movement, which also can be phrased in terms of risk and return, imitates on a smaller scale the past movements of American, British, German, and Japanese banks into international lending. The recent slowdown in the domestic economies and limited opportunities for domestic development and investments will increase the attractiveness of

---

4. "The Predicament of the Arab Gulf Oil States: Individual Gains and Collective Losses," in Malcolm H. Kerr and El Sayed Yassin, eds., *Rich and Poor States in the Middle East: Egypt and the New Arab Order* (Boulder, Colorado: Westview Press, 1982), p. 217.

international markets. At the same time, local banks have become acquainted with a number of international borrowers (companies and countries) because of those borrowers' direct or indirect participation in development projects throughout the Middle East.

Finally, the structure of international markets has affected the type of international financial activities into which the Arab banks have entered. Their lack of previous experience and activities in the international arena, combined with a certain shortage of manpower, has channeled the major share of their international activity into syndicated lending. This is especially convenient for newer banks, which are flush with funds they would like to place quickly but are without a list of long-standing clients.

Arab Banks and International Markets

The boom in Arab banks' international activity occurred after the second oil shock as the newest consortium banks were joined by the old-line domestic banks in a search for foreign outlets for their funds. The ideal measure of this activity would compare the total international activities of Arab banks with that of all banks. Unfortunately such statistics are unavailable, and the analysis must be limited to syndicated lending. This leads inevitably to an overstatement of the role of Arab banks, because they have focused their international activities on the syndicated Euro-credit market. In addition the available statistics on syndications must be interpreted carefully. Thus it is worthwhile to look briefly at what syndicated lending is and what the statistics can actually measure.

Syndicated lending is a fairly recent development in international banking, dating perhaps from the mid-1960s. A number of banks join together to provide a loan to a country or company in an attempt to reduce the costs and legal difficulties involved in arranging such financing. These loans have one or several lead managers, who then sell down the loan to other banks. The largest loans will usually have one tier of lead managers and a second tier of comanagers. The comanagers are responsible for selling down smaller shares of the loan than a lead manager, while each lead manager may be responsible not only for its own share of the loan but also for coordinating the activities of a subset of the comanagers. When there are multiple lead managers and comanagers, the responsibilities are often divided along geographic lines. For example, one or several American banks might be lead managers in charge of all the American bank participants.

There are at least three standards for measuring a bank's activity in the syndicated credits market. The preferred measure would calculate the actual amount of loans the bank held on its own books. This sort of detail is not available. A second would look at the total face value of the deals in which a bank was involved. For example, a bank that was involved as a lead manager in a deal for $100 million, even if it only provided $5 million in funds, would receive credit for $100 million in lead managements. This second measure, while imperfect, is readily available. One example of such a measure calculates that Arab-led syndications accounted for 44.7 percent of syndicated lending during the first four months of 1981.[5] This figure takes the total face value of all deals with at least one Arab bank as lead manager and divides that quantity by the total value of all syndicated credits during that period.

A third measure often available comes closer to assessing the share of Arab banks in the syndicated credits market. This measure assigns a sole lead manager the full value of the loan, while joint lead managers are credited with the amount divided by the number of lead managers. This measure still overstates the role of lead managers because it does not correct for the extent to which they sell down the loan. It can, however, provide a fairly accurate measure of the role of Arab banks in the syndicated Eurocredit market because Arab lead managers are often brought into a deal specifically for the purpose of selling shares to other Arab banks.

Having defined the meaning of the various statistics on market share, it is now possible to examine the available data. Table 9-1 shows that Arab banks accounted for $41.5 billion of lead managements from 1976 to 1983, and over 68 percent of this business was arranged between 1981 and 1983.[6] The top ten Arab banks handled $27.3 billion, or almost 66 percent, of the total.

Gulf International Bank, a pan-Arab consortium, leads the list of Arab banks with $5.2 billion in lead managements. The Al UBAF group, an Arab-French consortium, is next, but its activity has fallen sharply in recent years. The Arab Banking Corporation ranked third, even though it

5. See Morgan Guaranty Trust data reprinted in Omar Kassem, "The Arab Role in Financial Intermediation," in Peter Field and Alan Moore, eds., *Arab Financial Markets* (London: Euromoney Publications, 1981), p. 28.

6. Although Arab institutions were significantly involved in Eurobond issues before 1976, their involvement in Euroloans was very small. Even the figures for 1976 and 1977 involve only eleven banks, each participating in one to twelve loans. See Peter Field, "Arab Banks in the International Markets," in Field and Moore, *Arab Financial Markets*, pp. 34–35.

Table 9-1. *Arab Banks' Lead Management of Syndicated Loans, 1976–83* [a]

Millions of dollars

Banks	1976–77	1978	1979	1980	1981	1982	1983	1976–83
All Arab banks	2,700.41	3,190.90	2,716.11	4,573.81	10,939.43	10,348.89	6,985.42	41,454.97
Top ten Arab banks	1,958.90	2,127.57	1,809.64	3,110.56	7,881.57	6,783.71	3,615.84	27,287.79
Gulf International Bank	30.00	272.80	344.16	742.30	1,468.64	1,409.51	952.11	5,219.52
Al UBAF Group	1,425.90	687.83	452.80	523.56	633.71	364.60	428.96	4,547.36
Arab Banking Corporation	...	...	...	386.79	1,731.24	1,316.49	652.70	4,087.22
Banque Arabe et Internationale d'Investissement	403.00	674.31	176.50	174.86	396.98	305.84	305.36	2,436.85
Kuwait Foreign Trading, Contracting and Investment Company	100.00	117.37	78.75	120.00	847.51	597.25	374.16	2,235.04
Arab Bank	...	25.89	288.30	89.97	1,161.25	403.19	181.00	2,149.60
National Commercial Bank (Saudi Arabia)	...	163.30	200.80	212.95	438.27	916.80	201.21	2,133.33
National Bank of Kuwait	...	57.55	185.00	310.83	397.03	439.49	325.14	1,755.04
Saudi International Bank	...	0.00	15.83	363.03	460.59	470.15	104.91	1,414.51
Arab African International Bank[b]	...	128.52	67.50	186.27	316.35	560.39	90.29	1,349.31

Sources: Peter Field, "Arab Banks in the International Markets," in Peter Field and Alan Moore, eds., *Arab Financial Markets* (London: Euromoney Publications, 1981), pp. 34–35; "Arab Euromarket Activity Drops to $10.3 Bn in 1982," *Middle East Economic Survey* (January 10, 1983), p. B2; and *Middle East Economic Survey* (January 30, 1984), p. B3.

a. Sole lead managers are credited with the full amount of the loan, joint lead managers with the amount of the loan divided by the number of lead managers.

b. Including Al Bahrain Arab African Bank.

did not come into existence until 1980. ABC and GIB have been running neck and neck for the last two years and are likely to assert their preeminent role among Arab banks in the future. The fourth bank, BAII, another Arab-French consortium, has, like UBAF, seen its role decline in recent years.

The next four banks are ones that existed long before the oil shocks. They are among the leading banks in their countries and have considerable capital and business connections to exploit as they try to move into international lending. The list of the top ten Arab banks is rounded out by the presence of two consortium banks. Of these, the Saudi International Bank appears still to have considerable potential for further moves into international markets.

The Arab banks have been active in lending to both Arab and non-Arab borrowers, as tables 9-2 and 9-3 show. They were responsible for $12.08 billion of lead managements from 1976 through the first quarter of 1981; $5.56 billion, or 46.1 percent, of this money went to borrowers from fourteen Arab nations and the other $6.52 billion to borrowers from fifty other nations. This distribution, which scarcely matches the overall pattern of Euromarket activity (in which industrial country and Latin American borrowers predominate), demonstrates the tendency of Arab banks to focus on somewhat more familiar regional borrowers in their early years. Public and private entities from the United Arab Emirates accounted for $10.1 billion, or 8.4 percent of the total, while other sizable shares went to borrowers from Morocco, Spain, Algeria, Saudi Arabia, and Italy. Interestingly enough, although both Mexico and Brazil have been the world's biggest developing-country borrowers, they ranked only fifth and seventh among the developing countries to which Arab banks lent between 1976 and the first quarter of 1981.

Two other factors help explain this distribution. At least in the beginning the Arab banks tended to favor those Arab developing countries whose economic and political stability the surplus states would be likely to support in times of crisis. Morocco is probably the best example of this tendency. Its debt burden is already one of the highest in the developing world, a matter that has led to some concern at Western banks.[7] Some of the borrowing by individual emirates of the United Arab Emirates, such as

7. Morocco entered into rescheduling negotiations with banks in the summer of 1983. As of July 1984 no agreement had been signed. See "Morocco to Reschedule Debt," *Financial Times*, August 25, 1983; and Francis Ghiles, "Morocco Believes It Holds the Winning Hand," *Financial Times*, July 25, 1984.

Table 9-2. *Euroloans to Arab Borrowers Lead Managed by Arab Banks,*
January 1976–March 1981

Location of Borrower	Number of loans	Amount (millions of dollars)
United Arab Emirates	50	1,013.07
Morocco	19	956.67
Algeria	26	720.43
Saudi Arabia	30	640.30
Qatar	6	460.00
Bahrain	17	434.30
Jordan	16	393.56
Kuwait	19	291.24
Iraq	2	181.50
Oman	3	150.00
Egypt	10	149.75
Lebanon	6	91.85
Tunisia	3	51.25
North Yemen	3	31.00
Total	210	5,564.92

Source: Hikmat Sharif Nashashibi, "Developing Arab Capital Markets," *Arab Banker*, vol. 2 (July 1982), p. 49.

Sharjah and Ras-al-Khaimah, is also probably done on the assumption that richer members (such as Abu Dhabi) would be willing to bail them out of any difficulties. There also is a view that Arab borrowers, whether from surplus or deficit states, are the natural client base for Arab banks and are worthy of special attention. Thus in 1978, when Arab banks were first getting the attention of outsiders, Abdullah Mazrui of the National Bank of Abu Dhabi said, "We're aiming to achieve a recycling of petrodollars through the Arab countries. Instead of funds going through foreign institutions—say in Europe—and then back to an Arab country, we like to be involved directly in the funding."[8]

There seems to have been some change in the lending patterns of Arab banks since 1980. Lending to Latin America became important from 1980 to 1982, accounting for approximately 20 percent of all syndicated lending by Arab banks, and Asian borrowers accounted for another 16 percent (table 9-4). These figures far exceed the comparable numbers for 1978 and

8. Peter Field, "How the Gulf Banks Cut the Rates for Their Borrowers," *Euromoney* Gulf Banking Survey (August 1978), p. 9.

Table 9-3. *Euroloans to Non-Arab Borrowers Lead Managed by Arab Banks, January 1976–March 1981*

Location of Borrower	Number of loans	Amount (millions of dollars)
Spain	23	952.15
Italy	41	623.96
South Korea	12	384.17
France	11	360.20
Brazil	17	337.14
West Germany	6	327.00
Argentina	6	267.51
China	15	250.04
Hungary	3	250.00
East Germany	7	243.83
Greece	9	231.70
Mexico	4	207.61
Philippines	14	201.01
United States	3	174.17
Nigeria	7	159.91
Other[a]	97	1,544.68
Total	275	6,515.08

Source: Nashashibi, "Developing Arab Capital Markets," p. 49.
a. Includes thirty-five countries with borrowings ranging from $1.10 million to $138.10 million.

1979. Arab borrowers continued to account for the largest share of Arab bank lending, but that share fell somewhat after 1979.[9]

Other statistics provide some perspective on the role of Arab banks in syndicated lending. They accounted for only 4.2 percent of all syndicated lending from 1980 to 1982 (see table 9-5), ranking behind North American, French, British, and Japanese banks as a source of new funds. The only regions in which they provided more than 10 percent of new funds were the African market (17.85 percent) and the OPEC market (13.38 percent).[10] These were also the only regions where they ranked higher than the fifth largest provider of syndicated loans. Arab banks were the third

9. Figures for 1983 have been strongly influenced by the reschedulings in Latin America. Arab bank exposures there were relatively small, and the banks have rarely been managers or comanagers of the reschedulings and new loans. They have, however, been expected to contribute to those credits.

10. "Syndicated Lending—Out for the Count," *Euromoney* (February 1983), p. 38.

Table 9-4. *Regional Distribution of Syndicated Lending by Arab Banks, 1978–83*
Billions of dollars

Year	Arab countries	Western Europe	Eastern Europe[a]	Latin America	Asia	Sub-Saharan Africa	Other	Total[b]
1978	1.68	0.15	0.17	0.20	0.09	...	0.03	2.32
1979	1.38	0.56	0.17	0.19	0.19	...	...	2.49
1980	0.91	0.78	0.33	0.76	0.63	0.17	...	3.58
1981	3.01	1.96	0.68	1.94	1.24	0.24	0.04	9.10
1982	4.28	1.50	0.36	1.77	1.63	0.12	0.14	9.80
1983	3.58	1.53	0.13	0.06	1.49	0.07	0.13	6.99
1978–83[b]	14.85	6.47	1.84	4.93	5.26	0.59	0.34	34.28

Source: *Middle East Economic Survey* (January 30, 1984), p. B2.
a. Including the Soviet Union.
b. Figures may not add because of rounding.

Table 9-5. *Distribution of Syndicated Lending, 1980–82*

Region	All banks (millions of dollars)	Arab banks		
		Amount (millions of dollars)	Percent of Arab bank lending	Percent of all syndicated loans to the region
Latin America	102,729	5,480	30.75	5.33
Eastern Europe	12,684	880	4.94	6.94
OPEC	41,489	5,552	31.15	13.38
Far East	52,847	1,261	7.08	2.39
Non-oil developing Africa	5,009	894	5.02	17.85
Western Europe	93,628	3,685	20.68	3.94
North America	115,776	68	0.38	0.06
Total	424,162	17,820	100.00	4.20

Source: "Syndicated Lending—Out for the Count," *Euromoney* (February 1983), p. 38.

largest source for Africa (trailing French and British banks) and for OPEC (trailing U.S. and British banks).

Thus statistics point out four particularly interesting facets of the international activity of Arab banks. First, that activity has grown rapidly since the middle 1970s. Second, the ten banks that are dominant, accounting for almost 66 percent of Arab syndicated bank lending from 1976 to 1983, are split approximately equally between large consortium banks founded in the 1970s and the larger, older, formerly domestically oriented banks. Third, the portfolios of the Arab banks are more strongly directed toward Arab borrowers and less toward borrowers from Latin America than are the portfolios of Western banks. Finally, while the share of syndicated lending provided by Arab banks is significant, it is also usually small, and in only two regions (OPEC and other Africa) have Arab banks in recent years even ranked so high as the third largest source of syndicated loans.

Potential Concerns

The growing involvement of Arab banks in international finance has led to concerns for Western nations that can roughly be categorized as competitive, supervisory, and political.

The entrance into international banking of a new set of competitors was bound to have some effects on profits, especially in those businesses on which the new banks concentrated—syndicated Eurocredits and Arab borrowers. Apparently they did drive down the spreads paid by Arab borrowers; the effects were especially noticeable in 1978 when a number of the banks first broke into this market. The Abu Dhabi Investment Company, for example, arranged a $100 million, eight-year credit in 1978 for Morocco at a spread of 0.875 percentage points above the London interbank offered rate (LIBOR), which slashed 0.25 percentage points from the previous spread obtained by Morocco.[11] Similarly, a $100 million, ten-year credit was put together for Qatar's steelworks in 1978 by ADIC, GIB, Qatar National Bank, and Chase Manhattan, which marked the first time an Arab borrower received a spread of less than 0.75 percentage points over LIBOR.[12] Moreover, the benefits of competition were not limited entirely to Arab borrowers. One of Chrysler's financial subsidiaries raised $100 million in 1978 from Arab banks, even though the original plan was to raise only $50 million to $75 million.[13] In general, however, the measurable effects of competition on loan terms were restricted to Arab borrowers.

The potential supervisory problems stem from the lack of a complete supervisory and regulatory framework in many Arab nations. Although it is unlikely, problems for Arab banks might spread to the international financial system. The major problem is the absence of clear lender-of-last-resort procedures for some Arab banks. The consortium banks in particular do not have a sole authority that could back them up. It is unlikely that Bahrain, a relatively poor country, could support the banks with headquarters, branches, or subsidiaries there if they ran into liquidity problems. Fortunately, the biggest Arab banks are owned by the major surplus countries, so there is no question that the funds are available for them. Furthermore, their activities so far have not been especially risky. There have, however, been several problems in the past with Arab banks. One such incident occurred in 1977 when the Currency Board of the United Arab Emirates (forerunner of the Central Bank) ceased to act as a lender of last resort at the same time that credit was being tightened. This led to the closing of two banks (one from the Emirate of Ajman, the other from

---

11. Field, "How the Gulf Banks Cut the Rates for Their Borrowers," p. 2.

12. Qatar paid a margin of 0.625 percentage points for the early years and 0.75 percentage points in the final years; see Field, "How the Gulf Banks Cut the Rates for Their Borrowers," p. 2.

13. Ibid., p. 6.

Bangladesh).[14] A second instance involved the activities of the Abu Dhabi Investment Company (actually an investment bank, not a commercial bank). ADIC had earlier been a major Arab participant in the syndicated loan market, but by 1981, losses (apparently from its property portfolio) had made it insolvent.[15] The National Bank of Abu Dhabi, itself owned by the government of Abu Dhabi, took control of ADIC's operations, and eventually the Abu Dhabi Investment Authority bought all outstanding private-sector holdings in ADIC.[16] Finally, the recent crash of the Souk al Manakh, an unofficial stock market in Kuwait, although it does not appear to have been a threat to the continued operations of Kuwaiti banks, has threatened large losses. The crash could have led to serious liquidity problems for Kuwaiti banks if the Kuwaiti government had not quickly stepped in to limit losses facing companies and individual investors.

The use of Arab bank lending to help attain Arab foreign policy goals is also of potential concern to the Western nations. Of course, the Western nations themselves have not completely abstained from trying to guide their own banks' lending practices.[17] Still, it is appropriate to discuss the nature and magnitude of the interaction between Arab bank lending and the foreign policy interests of the Arab governments.

There are certain natural limits on the extent to which Arab banks can be used as instruments of foreign policy. The number of internationally active Arab banks is small and their resources are not particularly large in comparison to those of the governments of the surplus states. In addition, because some of the larger Arab banks are consortia owned by several governments, any political guidance in lending decisions for these banks is predicated on a unity of foreign policy goals among the shareholders that seldom occurs.

Still, there have been several clear cases where foreign policy concerns have determined lending patterns. The break between Egypt and the other Arab nations that resulted from its conclusion of the peace treaty with

14. Alan Moore and Hugh Carroll, "Banking in the United Arab Emirates," in Peter Field and Alan Moore, eds., *Arab Financial Markets* (London: Euromoney Publications, 1981), p. 112.

15. Cited in "The Economist Financial Report" of December 10, 1981, in *How Central Banks Manage Their Reserves* (New York: Group of Thirty, 1982), p. 6.

16. "Abu Dhabi Agency Forced to Buy Out Investment Company," *Financial Times*, July 19, 1984.

17. See, for example, J. Andrew Spindler, *The Politics of International Credit: Private Finance and Foreign Policy in Germany and Japan* (Brookings Institution, 1984).

Israel also led to withdrawal of a $300 million syndicated loan in the spring of 1979. The Union de Banques Arabes et Françaises (UBAF) had been one of the Arab lead managers of the issue along with the Arab African International Bank (AAIB) and the European Arab Bank (EAB). Citibank tried to rescue part of the deal despite the Arab bank pullout but was unsuccessful. The behavior of Arab banks considerably irritated Egypt. Not only did Egyptian institutions hold a share in all three banks, but Egypt was the largest shareholder in AAIB (42.5 percent) and AAIB's headquarters were in Cairo. Because the second round of oil price increases rescued Egypt from immediate financial difficulties, the efficacy of such pressure tactics went untested. The political damage was later repaired when four Arab banks (UBAF, AAIB, EAB, and United Gulf) joined in a $200 million stand-by credit lead managed by Chase Manhattan in 1982.[18]

The Arab-Israeli dispute has also affected bank behavior in two other incidents. In March 1982 a number of Arab banks withdrew from an $800 million loan to Gulf State Utilities (a U.S. borrower) because Israel's Bank Leumi was also providing funds. The Arab Banking Corporation did decide to stay in the loan, however, and provided $12 million.[19] In the summer of 1982 Arab banks also decided to withdraw their applications for membership in the Society for Worldwide Interbank Financial Telecommunications payments system after Israeli banks became members.[20] These two cases have led more to inconveniences for other banks than to any significant changes in global lending patterns.

Even when the discussion is limited to banking decisions without connections to the Arab-Israeli dispute, in some cases Arab governments have clearly involved themselves in the credit allocation process of their banks. Kuwait seems to have been especially active in directing its banks toward certain borrowers. The use of the Kuwaiti dinar bond market to lend Ministry of Finance funds to developing country borrowers has already been mentioned.[21] The Three Ks were the main channels used in that market. They have also been used in arranging several loans.

Deals with Yugoslavia have been particularly interesting. The Three Ks

18. Richard Johns, "Arab Banks Lend Again to Cairo," *Financial Times*, April 30, 1982.

19. Irving Trust Company (of the United States) led the loan, in which 109 banks participated. See *Middle East Economic Digest* (January 14, 1983), p. 3.

20. Paul Lewis, "Arab Bank Boycott of Data Links," *New York Times*, February 17, 1983.

21. See chapter 6.

have been involved in three loans there worth $750 million since 1980. The first, in September 1980, was an all-Arab bank issue, lead managed by KFTCIC and comanaged by ABC, GIB, Libyan Arab Foreign Bank, and Industrial Bank of Kuwait. This loan was contracted at market terms then prevailing for Yugoslavia: $250 million for eight years, with three years of grace and a spread of 1.125 percentage points above LIBOR.[22] However, KFTCIC reportedly took a $134 million share, an amount that exceeded its paid-in capital as of December 1980.[23] The second loan was an exclusive affair of the Three Ks: concluded in June 1981, it provided $250 million for seven years at 1.125 percentage points above LIBOR. The third tranche of the commitment was completed in April 1982. At that time Yugoslavia was finding it nearly impossible to raise new money from Western banks. While Deutsche Bank of West Germany was trying to syndicate a DM 200 million ($82 million) seven-year loan with a 1.5 percentage point margin over LIBOR, no other loans from Western sources were in the works. Yet the Three Ks arranged a loan for another $250 million over ten years, with a reported spread over LIBOR of 1.125 percentage points.[24]

The most plausible explanation for these loans has been that the government had promised $750 million to Yugoslavia, and that the government provided the share that the banks were unwilling or unable to provide.[25] The subsidy involved is difficult to measure, but it should be noted that a large share of Yugoslavia's new bank funds came from Kuwait in 1981 and 1982. Loans outstanding from Western banks to Yugoslavia, on the other hand, declined from $10.4 billion at the end of 1980 to $9.8 billion at the end of 1982.[26] It was reported late in 1982 that Kuwait had promised Yugoslavia another $1 billion.[27] The foreign policy motivations are somewhat vague. Yugoslavia was a founder of the nonaligned movement with

22. Donal Curtin, "Yugoslavia's Fund-Raising Marathon," *Euromoney* (November 1980), p. 17.

23. "The Whiff of Politics That Hangs Over Arab Banks," *Euromoney* (July 1981), p. 57. The authorized and paid-in capital of KFTCIC was KD 30 million (about $115 million) at the end of 1980. See Nemeh E. Sabbagh, "The Kuwaiti Banking Sector," in Field and Moore, *Arab Financial Markets*, p. 64.

24. *Middle East Economic Survey* (April 26, 1982), p. I.

25. Ibid.

26. See Bank for International Settlements, *Maturity Distribution of International Bank Lending* (July 1981 and July 1983). The loan decline, which was measured in dollars, may partly have been due to depreciation of the deutsche mark.

27. "Yugoslavia Promised $1,000 Million," *Middle East Economic Digest* (November 26, 1982), pp. 41–42.

which Kuwait identifies, and support for Yugoslavia fits well with the Kuwaiti desire to deal with both East and West. It is also worth noting that these loans to Yugoslavia can scarcely be characterized as contrary to American interests.[28]

Two other borrowers have benefited from the Kuwaiti government's interest. In 1980 China received a $300 million loan for five years at 0.50 percentage points above LIBOR, which led one Kuwaiti banker to comment, "We did it because of the Ministry of Finance, but the terms weren't very attractive." The Kuwaiti government may also have been involved in April 1981 with the Banco Nacional do Desenvolvimento Economico, a Brazilian borrower that raised $260 million in an all-Arab deal in which KFTCIC's share was reportedly at least $130 million.[29]

From this review of the major cases of Arab government direction in banking decisions it would appear that the Arab-Israeli dispute is the main issue likely to inspire actions that contradict Western interests and that even there the major effect has been to make Arab banks unwilling or unable to participate in deals that also have Israeli participation. The withdrawal of Arab banks from the loan to Egypt in 1979 was probably a very special case, which fortunately had no lasting effects on Western interests. There will probably continue to be cases in which Arab governments guide their institutions to particular borrowers because it is a very convenient way of making loans at close to market terms to these borrowers. Kuwait is especially likely to continue using this mechanism. The long-term nature of the Kuwaiti surplus makes it feasible to get involved in loans with a seven- to ten-year maturity, while the use of Kuwaiti banks in arranging such loans satisfies the criteria of complementarity between government investments and Kuwait's economic role as a financial center. Bank intermediation has also proven useful in simultaneously reconciling the government's desire for economic profits and for third world solidarity.

Debt Reschedulings for Developing Countries

Not until 1981 did Arab banks become involved in the syndication of loans for non-Arab developing countries on a significant scale (table 9-4),

28. In fact, about the same time that the third tranche of the Kuwaiti loan was being arranged, the U.S. State Department held a closed-door briefing on Eastern Europe for bankers in which the main message was that the government of Yugoslavia deserved more favorable treatment. See Frederick Kempe, "U.S. Hopes Banks Treat Yugoslavia Unlike Poland," *Wall Street Journal*, April 23, 1982.

29. "The Whiff of Politics That Hangs Over Arab Banks," p. 57.

so they have far less money at stake in those countries than do American, Japanese, or European banks. Still, the succession of reschedulings in 1982 provided a rude awakening to the risks of operating in the syndicated loan market and at a minimum has led Arab banks to reevaluate the nature of their international activities.

Except for the Kuwaiti loans to Yugoslavia, Arab banks had very little exposure in Eastern Europe, so the Polish and Romanian negotiations had little effect on them. The banks, however, had become active in Latin America after the second oil shock. Because of the Falklands war and domestic economic mismanagement, Argentina was the first to delay payments. Arab banks reportedly had approximately $900 million outstanding to Argentina at the time.[30] Although in general Argentina's difficulties did not cause Arab banks to withdraw from Latin American markets, they did change their style of lending in an attempt to protect themselves. For instance, Arab banks had been lead managers of $1.28 billion in loans to Mexico between July 1979 and August 1982, almost all of which had been arranged since April 1981.[31] Before February 1982 the banks had not made loans to Mexico with a maturity of less than seven years, but they participated in loans with maturities of nine months and three years in May 1982 and a loan with a nine-month maturity in August 1982 just before the crisis. These loans were secured, one designed as an oil rig leasing facility, the second collateralized by oil exports. Arab banks were hardly alone in the movement toward short-term, secured loans. Even in those just mentioned they accounted for only 15 percent of the amount raised.[32] Mexico's problems also led Arab banks, like their Western counterparts, to focus attention on Venezuela and Brazil, the other two Latin American countries with large borrowings.

Arab bank lending to Brazil was of approximately the same magnitude as lending to Mexico. Twenty-one Arab banks had lead managed $1.38 billion in loans between 1977 and 1982, including $653.2 million in 1981 and $422.5 million in 1982.[33] But although Arab banks increased their new lending to Mexico from 1981 to 1982, they substantially decreased lend-

30. "UK Freeze of Argentine Assets Alerts Arab Bankers," *Arab Banking and Finance* (April 1982), p. 68.

31. In this estimate each lead manager is assigned an equal share of the loan; see *Middle East Economic Survey* (August 23, 1982), pp. I–III.

32. This calculation is based on the assumption that each manager or comanager provided an equal share of the loan. The data are from *Middle East Economic Survey* (August 23, 1982), p. II.

33. These figures include $74.2 million of deals still in progress at the end of 1982. See *Middle East Economic Survey* (December 27, 1982), p. B1.

ing to Brazil. The slowdown occurred mostly after the Mexican shock, although ABC and SIB both remained involved (as lead manager and comanager, respectively) in loans to Brazilian borrowers.[34]

Some Arab banks have been very active in Latin America. ABC has lead managed $634.18 million in Brazil, $542.88 million in Mexico, and $250 million to $300 million in Argentina. GIB, Arlabank, and SIB followed, with management participations ranging from $230 million to $440 million.[35] These figures probably overstate the actual amount of loans on the larger banks' books. Other estimates, based on the $5 billion Mexican loan of early 1983, which added 7 percent to the existing exposure of international banks, are that ABC has $410 million outstanding in Mexico and GIB has $257 million.[36]

Arab banks have clearly become a significant source of funds for Latin America. Yet their lower stake in the region has made them less willing to follow automatically the lead of major Western banks during reschedulings. For example, they cut their interbank credit lines to Brazil 32 percent in early 1983—less than did many European banks but still a considerable amount.[37] With the exception of ABC and GIB, most were reluctant to participate in the new $6.5 billion credit to Brazil that was signed in January 1984, though only a few actually held out.[38] Their continued willingness to lend will help to resolve the financing problems of Latin American borrowers.

The Future of Arab Banking

Many Arab banks are still seeking to expand their international assets, and the crucial question for them centers upon what markets to enter. Syndicated lending to governments and other major foreign borrowers

34. *Middle East Economic Digest* (December 3, 1982), pp. 3, 6.

35. "UK Freeze of Argentine Assets Alerts Arab Bankers," p. 68; *Middle East Economic Survey* (August 23, 1982), p. II; and *Middle East Economic Survey* (December 27, 1982), p. B1.

36. Peter Field, "Adjusting to the End of the Boom," *Euromoney* (May 1983), p. 154.

37. "GIB Manager Defends Arab Banks' Strategy," *Middle East Economic Survey* (June 20, 1983), p. B1.

38. Andrew Whitley and Peter Montagnon, "Brazil Steps Up Efforts to Reach Loan Target," *Financial Times*, December 5, 1983; and *Middle East Economic Digest* (February 3, 1984), pp. 3, 5.

allowed them to place large amounts of funds while they were building up their business, but the evidence from the first quarter of 1983 seems to foreshadow a smaller role over the next few years than in the banner years of 1981 and 1982. Based on lead management positions, Arab banks handled only 3.9 percent of Euroloans in the first quarter of 1983, compared to 6.3 percent and 10.9 percent in the same periods in 1981 and 1982. Although they participated in 7.8 percent of syndicated loans in 1983, after taking part in 8.2 percent and 7.0 percent in 1981 and 1982,[39] the 1983 loans were for $6.99 billion while those in 1981 and 1982 exceeded $9 billion (see table 9-4).

The slowdown in syndications engendered by the debt problems of the developing nations has led Arab banks (and Western banks) to explore other areas of the banking business, especially trade finance and investment banking. Because both will require the formation of customer relationships and the acquisition of trained staff, they must be long-term developments. The large domestic banks with extensive customer bases probably have the most promising opportunities in trade finance. It is less clear that either domestic or consortium banks will be able to move very far into investment banking. Their local placing power is curtailed because private investors account for perhaps only 15 percent of the net foreign assets held in the region, while government investors already have a number of institutions arranging their placements. Still, some attractive opportunities are available. For example, Abdullah A. Saudi, president of the Arab Banking Corporation, indicated that the markets for floating rate notes and floating rate certificates of deposit were a likely target. These financial instruments mesh well with the short-term funding sources of Arab banks and at the same time usually represent claims on top-quality borrowers.[40]

The other main alternatives for Arab lenders are loans to Latin American, Asian, or Middle Eastern borrowers. The banks have already slowed the growth of Latin American lending. Their exposure to that region will continue to grow, however, because they have been pressured to extend new funds in reschedulings. This is especially true for the banks with the

39. "March Lending Leads Euromarket Recovery," *Middle East Economic Survey* (April 11, 1983), pp. B1–B4; and *Middle East Economic Survey* (January 30, 1984), p. B3.

40. "ABC's Exposure Will Stay International Despite Market Problems," *Middle East Economic Survey* (November 15, 1982), p. B3. Floating rate notes are usually arranged for Western governments, while floating rate certificates of deposit are issued by the leading Western banks.

greatest current involvement (ABC, GIB, SIB, and Arlabank). The increase in margins following the reschedulings will help to retain their interest.

Asian lending has been highly touted by some Arab bankers for a number of years, but in reality they have been slow to move into the region. The margins on syndicated credits for Asian borrowers have been as narrow as those for top-rated Western borrowers, which has reduced much of their attraction, while the property market requires considerable experience and is also risky for a bank with short-term funding. As a result, investments in Asia have focused on syndicated loans to corporate and public-sector borrowers from countries such as South Korea, Taiwan, and the Philippines. In other words, loans have been concentrated on those borrowers that have already established commercial ties with the Middle East.

Regional Middle Eastern lending will also expand, but some problems will have to be overcome. Information on local corporate and private borrowers is virtually nonexistent, and the Kuwaiti stock market crash has demonstrated that controls on the use of loans are imperfect. Still, the banks have long considered Arab borrowers their natural customer base, and the drop in oil revenues for these borrowers should increase other lending opportunities. Algeria, Iraq, Jordan, Oman, Qatar, and Tunisia have all raised loans since January 1983 or are in the process of raising new loans; Arab banks have taken a major share.[41] Furthermore, under terms set by the Saudi government, its joint ventures must arrange private bank loans to finance the final 10 percent of construction costs. A number of these ventures began to tap the credit markets in 1984, thus creating new local customers for Arab banks.[42]

Arab banks still have a long way to develop, but in a short time they have clearly achieved many of the capabilities of the more established banks. They have not displaced and will not displace Western banks. They are, however, attaining the status of partners with the Western banks, even though their activities will continue to be on a smaller scale.

41. See "Arab Banks Raise Eurodollar Loan," *Middle East Economic Digest* (January 7, 1983), p. 22; "Euroloan Signing Indicates Confidence," *Middle East Economic Digest* (April 1, 1983), p. 16; "Oman Puts Its Case," *Middle East Economic Survey* (June 13, 1983), pp. B3–B5; Margaret Hughes, "Tunisians Award Mandate for $120M Loan Deal," *Financial Times*, November 4, 1983; Peter Montagnon, "Algeria Credit Up to $750M," *Financial Times*, November 24, 1983; and "Fine Margin on Credit for Qatar Petroleum," *Financial Times*, February 2, 1984.

42. "Loan to Saudis Well Received," *Financial Times*, June 12, 1984; and *Middle East Economic Digest* (June 22, 1984), p. 24.

CHAPTER TEN

OPEC's Foreign Investments: Past, Present, and Future

OVER THE PAST DECADE, economic factors have dominated political factors in investment strategies, a situation likely to continue for the rest of the 1980s. Foreign aid, for which political concerns almost by definition must be a factor, has been and will continue to be the main exception. In the past, Iran has been willing to make financial threats for political reasons, but the small size of Iranian holdings and the demonstrated willingness of the United States to counter such threats should minimize the risks of politically motivated investment decisions in the future.

For all thirteen countries, oil and development policies set the bounds within which financial strategies operate. The tightness of these bounds, however, varies considerably. In the first one or two years after a sharp oil price increase, for example, all the OPEC nations tend to run surpluses. These surpluses disappear rapidly, however, in most of the countries. Only Libya and the Arabian peninsula producers have run large surpluses over most of the past decade, which has led to their classification as low absorbers. Yet even among these five nations the limits that oil and development policy impose on financial strategy are varied. Furthermore, all the countries now face tighter constraints on their financial actions.

Given the oil glut and their development needs, Venezuela, Ecuador, Algeria, Gabon, Nigeria, and Indonesia will continue to have very little scope in their investment and borrowing strategies. In fact, financial planners in these nations will be preoccupied during the 1980s with maintaining their country's creditworthiness. The management of their reserves, which are exceeded by borrowings, will be guided mostly by considerations of safety and liquidity.

Iran and Iraq, which are now operating with international assets slightly in excess of liabilities, depending on the extent to which Arab aid to Iraq is

185

written off, could once again become significant net creditors to the international financial system. That is unlikely to occur during the next few years, however, because of the sizable burdens that the oil glut and war have imposed on these two countries. For these reasons Iranian and Iraqi financial strategies are likely to emphasize safety and liquidity during the rest of the 1980s.

Libya's large foreign investment holdings will continue to give it some leeway in adjusting oil production and development decisions. Because of its tendency to be a hawk in oil pricing, Libya's oil production and revenues may be as variable as they have been in the past, forcing it to continue emphasizing safe and liquid investments. At the same time, Libya seems likely to continue to make direct investments (equities and property) in the Mediterranean region and will maintain its current level of involvement in consortium banks.

Because Saudi Arabia, Kuwait, the United Arab Emirates, and Qatar controlled 85 percent of OPEC's net foreign assets at the end of 1982, their decisions will in large measure determine the course of OPEC investments in the 1980s. At the same time they face a different set of constraints and opportunities than do other OPEC nations.

Despite huge accumulated surpluses, Saudi Arabia may well experience the greatest pressures in the next few years. The Saudis are more subject to oil market conditions than other OPEC producers because not only are they the swing supplier of oil within OPEC but also the residual supplier for world energy markets. At the same time they also experience substantial pressures on spending because of their development needs and their important role in regional politics. They have recently shown the ability to cut spending quickly in response to oil market conditions, but it is less sure that such restrictions on spending can be sustained. Annual revenues are currently $65 billion, largely reflecting anticipated investment income of $13 billion and exports of 5 million barrels a day at $29 a barrel. Because expenditures are about $80 billion ($75 billion of budgeted expenditures yearly, and perhaps a further $5 billion outside the budget), Saudi Arabia must draw on reserves at an annual rate of $15 billion. In fact, the current real levels of oil prices and expenditures would require producing 6.5 million to 7.0 million barrels a day to balance the budget, a level that could be reached only with a resurgence of the oil market. Although Saudi Arabia is allowed up to 5 million barrels a day in OPEC's current arrangements, any permanent increases in OPEC production above 17.5 million barrels a day would have to be shared between it and other members. For all these reasons, the Saudi investment strategy over the next few years is more likely to be concerned with the optimal drawdown of previously accumulated reserves.

Their past investment strategy has placed the Saudis in a good position to weather the current oil market downturn. They have always emphasized the safety and liquidity of a potential investment first, and only then considered rates of return and diversification. This emphasis led to heavy investment in Western government securities and bank deposits, which can easily be drawn on. Furthermore, Saudi holdings in corporate bonds have rarely had maturities of more than seven years, so a large share of these can also be liquidated over the next several years by simply not reinvesting interest or principal repayments. Thus Saudi Arabia would seem to be well positioned to ride out a short- or medium-term glut in the oil market if prices do not fall further. Should the glut prove longer and deeper than is currently anticipated, however, the Saudis will be forced to reduce spending further to ensure that their reserves last through the downturn.

The $29 a barrel marker price for OPEC crude oil has recently come under considerable downward pressure. Even if, as some studies have predicted,[1] there is a recovery in oil markets toward the end of the 1980s that could restore Saudi Arabia's annual current account surpluses, there is no reason to expect a major shift in Saudi investment strategies. First, they might need to rebuild the reserves depleted in the mid-1980s. Second, they would still be subject to large fluctuations in revenues because of their continued role as a swing producer. Finally, the surpluses could well be small if spending were to recover simultaneously. The Saudis would therefore still need to focus first on the safety and liquidity of their investments, then on diversification and rates of return. There is unlikely to be any strong pressure to move into equities or long-term bonds unless the real value of the surplus were to recover to 1982 levels and oil market prospects to brighten significantly. Major investments in new, internationally oriented financial institutions are unlikely, although additional domestically oriented banks may be chartered. Despite the decline in the surplus, the Saudis might make new investments in the petrochemicals industry— most likely joint ventures with Western partners that would use basic

1. See, for example, International Energy Agency, *World Energy Outlook* (Paris: OECD/IEA, 1982), especially pp. 461–62; and Bijan Mossavar-Rahmani and Fereidun Fesharaki, *OPEC and the World Oil Outlook*, Special Report 140 (London: The Economist Intelligence Unit Limited, February 1983), especially pp. 12, 16, 17.

petrochemicals produced in the Jubail and Yanbu complexes as raw materials. Such agreements would not boost the Saudi role in petrochemicals markets much beyond the currently planned share of 4 percent to 5 percent. Instead, they are more likely to reflect Saudi Arabia's weak position in a glutted market.

Among OPEC members, Kuwait is best placed to ride out the current glut. Its financial planners have enjoyed a great deal of flexibility because of the wide margin between revenues and development needs, a pattern that will continue almost unchanged. A significant fraction of apparent budget deficits over the next few years will represent legally mandated additions to reserves, that is, transfers of accumulated reserves from an off-budget account to an on-budget account. The rest of the deficit should easily be covered by investment income, which is not treated as revenue in the Kuwaiti government's budget projections. Thus it is likely that Kuwait's foreign assets will continue to grow throughout the mid-1980s. Such a situation is unlikely to constrain the nation's financial actions. As a precautionary measure the Kuwaitis may gradually increase their holdings of safe, liquid assets from the current levels. At the same time, further direct investments in the energy and financial industries would not be surprising. These industries will continue to appeal strongly because such equity investments are believed to yield higher rates of return and to provide a hedge against inflation and because the energy and financial sectors are seen as complementary to Kuwait's oil resources. Thus the Kuwaiti investment strategy for the rest of the 1980s is likely to follow a well-established path.

Qatar and the United Arab Emirates will probably be able to conduct their financial policies without major constraints from oil market conditions or development policy needs. Their situation is not as favorable as Kuwait's, however, because they may run small current account deficits the next few years and will have to draw on accumulated reserves. Thus these countries are also likely to continue their emphasis on safe, liquid investments while being willing to pursue increased rates of return through active trading of equities and switching of currencies. Finally, the United Arab Emirates and Qatar may eventually follow a Kuwaiti-style investment strategy with an emphasis on direct investments in the energy and financial sectors, but only if an oil market recovery should once again produce sizable current account surpluses.

The current oil market glut has largely removed earlier fears that ever-increasing foreign investments by OPEC members would pose a serious threat to the West. Nevertheless the investment strategies of individual member nations will continue to be of interest in the 1980s because of the size of the accumulated holdings and the interactions between investment strategies and oil policy decisions.

Constructing Estimates of OPEC Current Account Balances

THE CURRENT ACCOUNT SURPLUSES accumulated after 1974 constituted most of the net foreign asset holdings by private and public sectors in the OPEC nations as of the end of 1982. Thus estimates of those surpluses are crucial to the discussions on investments and investment policy presented in chapters 3, 5, 6, and 7. This appendix describes the construction of those estimates.

The preferred source of data was the IMF's *Balance of Payments Year-book* (*BOP*). The data for 1982 were not available for many countries, however, and several no longer report or never have reported that data to the IMF. The next best source was data on current account balances reported by the OPEC Secretariat in the *Annual Statistical Bulletin, 1982* (*ASB*). Those figures were based largely on data from the IMF's *International Financial Statistics* (*IFS*). The OPEC estimates were calculated on a slightly different basis, for they excluded official transfers. In most cases where data were missing from *BOP*, the OPEC data served as a basis for the estimates of table A-1. In two cases, however, other adjustments had to be made.

Adjustments

For Algeria, Ecuador, Indonesia, and Libya there were no 1982 data in *BOP*. The 1982 data in *ASB* were adjusted by the 1981 value for official transfers from *BOP*. Saudi Arabian data for 1982 were also absent from *BOP*. In this case the 1982 data in *ASB* were adjusted by the 1980 value for official transfers from *BOP*. The 1980 value was chosen over the 1981 value because a sharp cutback in Saudi aid seemed likely in response to

Table A-1. *Current Account Balances of the OPEC Nations, 1974-82*[a]
Millions of dollars

Country	1974	1975	1976	1977	1978	1979	1980	1981	1982
Algeria	176	−1,661	−886	−2,323	−3,538	−1,631	249	85	−1,210
Ecuador	38	−220	−7	−341	−701	−625	−642	−1,002	−1,320
Gabon	166	−9	−49	6	74	248	384	400	680
Indonesia	598	−1,109	−910	−47	−1,422	975	2,859	−737	−7,562
Iran	12,267	4,707	4,717	5,081	−462	7,115	−1,316	−5,130	4,263
Iraq	2,619	2,705	2,495	2,990	3,813	10,968	12,335	−8,233	−9,409
Kuwait	8,273	5,927	6,929	4,558	6,130	14,036	15,272	13,702	5,786
Libya	2,670	392	2,844	2,762	1,499	4,022	8,240	−2,977	2,717
Nigeria	4,897	42	−357	−1,009	−3,764	1,669	4,269	−5,850	−7,324
Qatar	1,570	976	1,021	365	689	1,610	2,886	2,699	864
Saudi Arabia	23,025	14,386	14,360	11,991	−2,212	11,167	41,399	45,127	881
United Arab Emirates	3,504	2,271	2,588	1,917	1,373	3,962	9,432	7,671	2,815
Venezuela	5,810	2,171	254	−3,179	−5,735	350	4,728	4,000	−3,456

Sources: See pp. 191–193 for sources.

a. Balance on goods, services, and private and official transfers.

changed oil market conditions. Such a cutback also occurred in 1979.[1] Kuwaiti data for 1974 are unavailable in any edition of *BOP*. In this case the 1974 data in *ASB* were adjusted by the 1975 value for official transfers from *BOP*.

Data from *BOP* for Gabon, Nigeria, and Venezuela covered all years from 1974 to 1982, so no adjustments were needed. No data are available for Qatar and the United Arab Emirates in *BOP*. The data in *ASB* on current account balances before official transfers were adjusted downward by the amount of bilateral grants and multilateral contributions reported for these two countries by the Organization of Economic Cooperation and Development's *Aid from OPEC Countries*.

Finally, data on the current account balances of Iran and Iraq are available in *BOP* only from 1974 to 1977. Trade data are available in *IFS*, however, from 1974 to 1982. The *BOP* data were used for 1974 to 1977, and estimates constructed for later years. First the difference between the trade balance in later years and the trade balance in 1977 was calculated. This difference was then added to the 1977 figure for the current account balance from *BOP* to yield estimates for the current account balance after 1977. The trade balance was defined as the difference between export revenues and the *IFS* estimate of import expenditures, which is itself based on the IMF's *Direction of Trade Statistics* data. Thus the estimates for Iran and Iraq are approximate at best.

Bibliography of Data Sources for Appendix

International Monetary Fund. *Balance of Payments Statistics Yearbook*. Vol. 33, part 1: 1982. Washington, D.C.: IMF, 1982.

———. *Balance of Payments Statistics Yearbook*. Vol. 34, part 1: 1983. Washington, D.C.: IMF, 1983.

———. *International Financial Statistics Yearbook*. Vol. 36:1983. Washington, D.C.: IMF, 1983.

Organization of Petroleum Exporting Countries. *Annual Statistical Bulletin, 1982*.

Organization for Economic Cooperation and Development. *Aid from OPEC Countries*. Paris: OECD, 1983.

---

1. This is discussed in chapter 8.

Index

195